HISPANIC MEDIA, USA

A Narrative Guide to Print and Electronic Hispanic News Media in the United States

By Ana Veciana-Suarez

With a Foreword by Felix Gutierrez

This Guide was made possible by funding from

Chevron

Coors

the media institute

Washington, D.C.

Table of Contents

Please note the following changes:

Page 3
(and throughout the book)

<u>Diario</u> <u>las</u> <u>Americas</u> should read:
<u>Diario</u> <u>Las</u> <u>Americas</u>

Page 5
(bottom)

Hispanic American Corporation should read:
Hispanic American Broadcasting Corporation

Page 14
(bottom)

The sentence "Medical services, immigration advice, and insurance were the most advertised products" should read: "Medical services, legal advice, and insurance were the most advertised products."

<u>NOTE</u>: <u>La</u> <u>Opinion</u> carries no immigration-related advertising, and this has been its policy for over 20 years. We regret the mistake and any misconceptions it may have caused.

Page 208
(middle)

Listing for WCIU-TV should read:
WCIU-TV (Channel 26)
141 W. Jackson Blvd.
Chicago, IL 60604
312/663-0260

Page 220
(bottom)

Zip code for station XEMO-AM should read: 92011

Foreword

> The Spanish-language press is on the decline...it is
> probable that in 15 years the Spanish-language press
> will virtually have died out.
>
> -- John H. Burma,
> Spanish-Speaking Groups
> in the United States, 1954

Like many projections made confidently in the 1950s, John Burma's predicted death of the Spanish-language press did not occur. In 1970, 16 years after the prediction, Editor & Publisher reported Spanish-language newspapers were a healthy and growing part of the nation's media system. In 1986, 16 years after that report, Spanish-language print and broadcast media, along with their English-language counterparts, experienced another banner year and continued to grow at a rate confounding those who earlier foresaw their death.

The mid-1980s have been boom years in the commercial development of Latino media in the United States. They have seen the following:

* In radio, at least 15 new Spanish-language radio stations opened in 1986, capping a growth from 67 full-time Spanish-language radio stations in 1975 to 170 in 1986. Record prices were paid for Spanish-language radio stations in Los Angeles ($40 million for an AM-FM combination) and New York ($20 million for an AM station).

* In print, Spanish and English newspapers and magazines continued to open and expand and led to the organization of the National Association of Hispanic Publications (NAHP), which represented 42 periodicals with an estimated circulation of 1.34 million in 1986.

* In television, competing Spanish-language channels and program networks developed in key markets across the country, and Spanish International Communications Corporation (SICC) stations and related stations were sold to Hallmark Cards, Inc. for about $300 million.

The upswing in Spanish-language media, growth in English-language Latino media, and the buying of Hispanic media by non-Hispanic companies were keyed to three trends in the 1980s; each is destined to become more important as the United States moves into the 21st Century. These are:

* A U.S. Latino population growing and projected to continue growing at a higher rate than the U.S. population overall.

* The increased importance of target marketing and of advertising strategies geared to reaching segments within the mass audience by corporations.

* A growing competition for audience segments as increased print and broadcast media outlets, additional media alternatives resulting from new technologies, and refined audience measurement techniques make it nearly impossible for any one medium to claim to reach all groups in the potential mass audience.

These trends have helped trigger an infusion of corporate advertising dollars into Latino media and, as these outlets became more profitable, a growth in the number of media the advertisers could support.

Advertisers spent nearly $400 million to reach the U.S. Hispanic market's estimated 16.9 million consumers with an aggregate household income of $113 billion in 1986, Hispanic Business magazine reported. This figure represented a 19-percent increase from 1985's estimated $333.5 million and more than doubled the estimated $166 million spent by advertisers in 1982. Advertising increases averaging $58 million per year, from 1982 through 1986, helped make Latino media a lucrative sector of the communications industry.

The advertisers trying to reach Latino consumers have not been limited to the traditional purveyors of ethnic foods or products. In fact, the top 15 Hispanic market advertisers on Hispanic Business' roster includes only one company whose product line is Hispanic-oriented, Goya Foods. Heading the list are such mainstream U.S. companies as Procter & Gamble, Philip Morris, Anheuser-Busch, McDonalds, and Adolph Coors.

This corporate advertising commitment to Latinos and the media they use, coupled with the increased entry into the Latino media field by non-Hispanic companies, recognizes the continuing economic importance of these media and the consumers they reach. Along with the growth has come a need to understand the new array of Latino print and broadcast media; who owns them, what their histories are, how they run their news and business operations, and how they relate to their communities and clients.

Once characterized as extensions of Latin American media into the United States or merely Spanish-language translations of their English-language counterparts, Latino media in the United States are forging new identities based on their own news philosophies, business principles, and the newly competitive marketplace in which they find themselves. With more diversity within Latino media than at any time in this nation's history, it is nearly impossible to generalize about them except to say that their audiences are primarily Latino.

By taking a microscopic look at these media nationally and in key markets, journalist Ana Veciana-Suarez fills an important void in our knowledge. In preparing this book she reviewed the growth in Hispanic media, talked with scholars and professionals and, most importantly, visited print and broadcast media across the United States and national news organizations serving them. Her book not only describes the growth of these media, but takes a first-hand look at how they operate. The rich diversity in these media is reflected on these pages, which provide a solid foundation on which scholars, professionals, and community leaders can make informed judgments regarding the media serving Latinos in the United States.

The organization of the book allows readers to make assessments of the same medium, such as Spanish-language radio, in several markets and also competing media in the same city. Given the dependence of some media on wire service news reports, the book also allows readers to assess the use of Spanish-language wire service news operations. Finally, in looking at new models, the book also looks at the relatively new phenomenon of commercial English-language print media for Latinos.

While no book can claim to be comprehensive without running the risk of being obsolete upon publication, this manuscript provides the broadest look at Latino media yet available. And, by building on information gained through personal visits to these media, it gives readers an unprecedented insider's look at how these media operate.

As Hispanic media in the United States continue to grow and redefine their role, larger questions will be posed and, hopefully, addressed. Beyond the intent of this book, these issues are nonetheless raised by the trends in Latino media that are described on these pages. They include:

* The need for more coverage of issues relating to the lives of Latinos in the United States;

* The long-range commitment to the Latino audience of the growing number of non-Hispanic owners of Latino media;

* The use of Spanish/English/Bilingual formats in media as language use in Latino communities becomes more complex;

* Differences in concepts of advocacy and objectivity between Latino and general-audience news media; and

* The social responsibility of Latino media to their largely low-income audiences as they operate and grow by selling their audiences as a consumer market to be tapped by advertisers.

Armed with an insider's look at Latino media, readers of this book will be better able to form their own responses to these and other issues. They will also be able to appreciate the growth and diversity of these media, the growing importance of Latino media in the communications system of the United States, and the important roles these media play in the lives of those who use them.

Latino media have been a part of the United States since the first English/Spanish bilingual newspaper, <u>El Misisipi</u>, was founded in New Orleans in 1808. Now, nearly 180 years later, they continue to grow and expand. Despite the premature predictions of their death, they promise to be part of the United States for a long time. Knowledgeable observers of the American scene can no longer afford to ignore them.

-- Felix Gutierrez
School of Journalism
University of Southern California
January 1987

Introduction

To the United States they have come, from the south and from the west, from the Caribbean islands and the Andean highlands. U.S. Hispanics have arrived in this country they call Norte America in search of a better life and for the sake of freedom. With them they have brought a vast wealth of tradition and a rich, colorful history.

The Latin roots of the United States can be traced further back than the Pilgrims and the Mayflower, Jamestown and Captain John Smith. St. Augustine, Florida, the oldest city in the United States, was founded in 1565 by a Spaniard, although explorer Juan Ponce de Leon had visited the area as early as 1513. The first European settlements from Texas west to the Pacific Ocean were established by Spain. And for years, the Pacific Northwest and the Louisiana Territory were under Spanish rule.

In the centuries that followed, the Hispanic influence has been both subtle and cumulative. The flow of people and ideas between Latin America and its northern neighbor has been like a river with two strong and vibrant currents going in opposite directions. Mostly, however, the flow of people has been to the north.

In 1980 U.S. Hispanics numbered 14.6 million, or 6.4 percent of the U.S. population. By March 1985, the Census Bureau reported that Hispanics had grown by 2.3 million, to 16.9 million people, or 7.2 percent. The growth was nearly 15 percent in a little over five years. In comparison, the national population increased 3.3 percent.

Strategy Research Corporation's U.S. Hispanic Market 1987 estimated the number of Hispanics at 18,877,100 -- or 7.5 percent of the total U.S. population. And some Hispanic leaders say the numbers are greater if one includes undocumented aliens. At this rate of increase, it is estimated that Hispanics will form the largest minority in the United States by 1990, with 30 million people.

1

The youth of this segment of the population is one of its main characteristics. The median age is 23.6 and more than one-fourth of U.S. Hispanics are children under 12, according to Strategy Research Corporation. (Compare those figures to a median age of 31.3 for the white non-Hispanic population.) This means many Hispanics still have their child-bearing years ahead of them.

The higher birth rate among Hispanics as well as the steady influx of both legal and illegal immigrants have been the determining factors in the sizable increase of the population.

From 1951 to 1984, Hispanics accounted for more than 30 percent of the immigration into this country, making them the largest group of immigrants. Mexicans, as expected, formed the largest immigrant population in those 33 years -- almost 1.7 million, or 13.2 percent of all immigrants. In the same time period, 589,737 Cubans came to the United States, 4.7 percent of the total number of immigrants. Only Germany and the United Kingdom sent over more immigrants than Cuba.

Mexicans are, by far, the nation's largest share of Hispanics with 10.9 million, or 57.6 percent, according to Strategy Research Corporation. Puerto Ricans number 2.7 million, and Cubans 1.1 million; the rest are from other Caribbean islands and Latin American countries.

Hispanics are concentrated in a few key states. According to the 1984 U.S. Hispanic Almanac, 86 percent lived in metropolitan areas. Sixty-three percent lived in the top 10 media markets. Mexican-Americans preferred California, Texas, and other Southwestern states. They have also traditionally flocked to the Chicago area. Puerto Ricans, on the other hand, have concentrated in New York, Chicago, and the Northeast. Some have also gone to Florida. Cubans have concentrated in Miami and the New York-New Jersey area. Central and South Americans have scattered, but generally prefer the urban areas where sizable Latin colonies already exist.

Two states alone -- California and Texas -- are home to more than one-half of the U.S. Hispanic population. Thirty-two percent live in California and 22 percent in Texas, according to Strategy Research Corporation. The top 10 U.S. Hispanic markets (in order) are: Los Angeles, New York, Miami, San Antonio, San Francisco, Chicago, Houston, McAllen/Brownsville, El Paso, and Albuquerque. Los Angeles, with more than 3.6 million Hispanics, is the largest, while New York, with 2.5 million, comes in second.

According to Strategy Research Corporation, the U.S. Hispanic median family income in 1985 was $22,900 -- well below the U.S. median income of $32,800. Cubans tended to earn the most ($27,500), while Puerto Ricans earned the least ($15,000). Most were employed as operators, laborers, technicians, salespersons, and in the service industries.

U.S. Hispanics are a polyglot group with different beliefs and customs. There is as much or more diversity in Hispanic communities as there is among English-speaking counterparts. Some U.S. Hispanics left their countries for political reasons -- the Cubans and Central Americans and Mexicans between 1910 and 1920. Most, however, came for economic reasons.

Despite these differences, the language has served as a common denominator among the many nationalities. In interviews conducted by Strategy Research, which does many studies for Spanish-language media clients, at least 90 percent of Hispanics surveyed said the first language they learned to speak was Spanish. The same study concluded that more than two-thirds of the population preferred to speak Spanish at home and 18 percent spoke both languages.

The question of language use is of vital importance, for many media executives interviewed for this book said audiences either tuned in or read their products because of the audience's dependency on the mother tongue.

"We take great pride in the Spanish we print," said Horacio Aguirre, publisher of Diario las Americas in Miami. "Our readers who know the language can truly enjoy it and read some of the best writers in their own language."

While most media aimed at Hispanics is produced in Spanish, there is a sizable amount printed in English. Usually the product takes the magazine format -- slick, colorful, and geared to the upwardly mobile, assimilated Hispanic. For this group, English is a fact of business life. It is the language of transactions, the language of the melting pot.

"What kids learn in school is English. What they learn to read is English. Eventually what they feel most comfortable in is English," said Daniel Lopez, who publishes two English-language monthly magazines. "In the business world, the people who are making it must be fluent in English. And those are the type of people we target."

Lopez and other executives of English-language Hispanic media believe that the days of Spanish-dependent Hispanics are numbered. Assimilation is inevitable -- third- and fourth-generation Latins will likely continue some old and dear traditions while they turn to the English language for reading and self-expression. They point to past immigrant groups to prove their case.

Among the Spanish-language media, on the other hand, executives are optimistic about the future. A constant stream of immigrants from Latin America guarantees them a market. And, they add, unlike past ethnic groups who have been lost in the U.S. population with only their last names to demonstrate their ethnicity, Hispanics cling to the language much more strongly. As a matter of fact, the primary market of Spanish-language media is composed of Hispanics who speak only Spanish and cannot get news through the mainstream media.

Strategy Research Corporation reported in its 1987 study that more than 78 percent of Hispanics can write Spanish well or very well. Cubans ranked highest, with 98 percent claiming proficiency in spoken Spanish. Puerto Ricans said they had the least proficiency, with 26 percent responding that their Spanish skills were no better than "fair." At the same time, skills in English are best among Hispanics in the Central and Southwestern United States. Overall, Spanish-language proficiency is almost three times greater than English-language proficiency.

This is clearly one reason why there is such a ready market for Hispanic news media in the United States.

Spanish-language television was viewed by more than two-thirds of all Hispanics interviewed by Strategy Research for its U.S. Hispanic Market 1984 study. Almost one-half listened to Spanish-language radio stations while 21.5 percent read Spanish-language newspapers. Hispanics in Texas and the Southwest had the lowest levels of viewership, listenership, and readership, probably because they tend to be more assimilated.

Hispanics spent, on the average, about two-and-one-half hours watching television, and one hour and 15 minutes listening to radio every day. They spent 54 minutes per day reading newspapers, according to Strategy Research.

Spanish-language media -- whether print or broadcast -- is concentrated in the areas of its audience: the large metropoli and the smaller towns with significant Hispanic populations. However, because of television's reach, particularly through cable, Spanish-language broadcasting is pervasive.

There are five major daily Hispanic newspapers in the United States, all of them in the top three U.S. Latin markets of Los Angeles, New York, and Miami. But there are also hundreds of weeklies and monthlies, all quite successful in the Southwest and the Northeast, in Chicago and Miami, and in Middle America. Circulation, with some rare exceptions, is not audited. But numbers of copies range from 92,000 for the Sunday El Miami Herald to the hundreds or thousands for the smaller weeklies.

Though print media may vary according to region, all share certain characteristics. They:

* Provide Latin American news in much greater detail than their English-language counterparts. Many media executives believe that readers choose them because the Anglo newspapers do not provide readers with news from their homelands.

* Contain extensive coverage of the local Latin community. While much of the barrios news is relegated to the inside pages of English newspapers, if that, it gets considerably better play in Spanish newspapers.

* Carry editorials that promote and defend Hispanic issues -- immigration, bilingual education, housing, etc.

Spanish-language radio is more popular than newspapers, particularly among women. Most U.S. Spanish stations are AMs, although there are several FMs in the larger markets. Like newspapers, stations are found in markets with a high Hispanic concentration, but large numbers don't necessarily mean more stations. New York, for example, has four Spanish-language stations compared to Miami's seven stations. And in Chicago, with more than 740,000 Hispanics, Spanish-language radio is only a recent phenomenon.

By far the most popular station format is musical programming. Only Miami has more news/talk-show stations than music stations. The music played, however, varies according to the audience. Generally, California and Texas stations prefer nortenas and rancheras. Miami and the Northeast, catering to their Puerto Rican, Cuban, and Caribbean listeners, play salsa. Many also try to appeal to a broad cross-section, playing international hits from Latin America. Of course, the amount of specialization is in direct proportion to the number of stations. In other words, the more stations, the more segmentation.

Newscasts are usually limited to morning and afternoon drive slots, with headline news broadcast on the hour or half hour during the rest of the day. Depending on the philosophy of the station, its news staff will emphasize either Latin American news or local news. Most have correspondents in Latin America to provide up-to-date information. And all have a strong sense of community responsibility, sponsoring concerts and fundraisers, and airing telethons and public-service programs.

Spanish television, like radio, is geared to entertainment. The bulk of its programming is devoted to spicy novelas (soap operas) imported from Latin America. Variety shows are also popular. Dubbing of American programs into Spanish is infrequent. Instead, the emphasis is on programs produced by Spanish-speaking countries, not only because of the familiar language but also because such programs more accurately reflect the cultural values and social mores of Hispanics. This, combined with involvement in the community, results in strong loyalty from the audience.

Univision -- formerly the SIN television network -- was the first Spanish-language network in the United States, with more than 405 affiliates in both the large and small Hispanic markets. But by late 1986, the stage was being set for a challenge from a new network.

Telemundo, the new network, began its first national broadcast in January 1987. Owned by Reliance Capital Group LP, the network has interest or owns stations in major Hispanic markets: WNJU-TV Channel 47 in New York, KVEA-TV Channel 52 in Los Angeles, WSCV-TV Channel 51 in Miami, and WKAQ-TV Channel 2 in San Juan, Puerto Rico. In addition, its broadcasts will be seen on stations in Chicago, Brownsville, Hartford, and two cable systems in Houston and San Antonio.

The entry of Telemundo into the Spanish-language broadcast market came at a particularly difficult time for Univision. Univision's most important group of affiliates -- the Spanish International Communications Corporation (SICC) stations -- were sold to Hallmark and First Chicago Venture. The purchase was challenged by several groups, including Hispanics and rival investors. Moreover, it precipitated an extensive restructuring that culminated in the mass resignation of more than 15 staff members in Univision's news division.

These former Univision employees formed Hispanic American Corporation, the Miami-based news agency that produces the national news show for Telemundo.

Univision's restructuring, however, also resulted in the expansion of its news division. Its new ventures included the nation's first weekend Spanish-language news show and the first late-night national Spanish-language news show. Additional news bureaus were established in San Antonio and Los Angeles.

Univision's expansion, the sale of the SICC stations, and Telemundo's creation are clear indications that there is a great interest among investors in the Spanish-language media market. And certainly increased competition will mean not only a choice for U.S. Hispanics but an improved product.

At the same time, the uncertainty and changes made it particularly difficult to obtain information for this book from either the then-SIN or SICC officials. Despite repeated calls to their offices in New York and San Antonio, I was not able to conduct personal interviews with executives from the companies in the summer and early fall of 1986.

The information in the Univision and SICC section of the book were obtained through some correspndence with Rosita Peru, who headed SIN's programming, and the assistant general manager of the SICC station in San Antonio.

Other information here, with rare exceptions, was gained through extensive personal interviews with owners, general managers, and program directors of the Hispanic media profiled. Research took me to New York, California, Texas, and Florida, to television studios and radio stations and newspaper offices. The variety among the products was astounding. The overwhelming majority of media people were eager to provide information, and anxious that their stories -- the tribulations and successes, the perils and promises -- be told to an English-speaking audience. They were especially enthused with the idea that advertisers and public-relations firms would be among the readers because many felt they had been ignored for too long.

The narrative part of this book is not intended to be inclusive of all Spanish-language media. Because of space limitations, I was forced to limit the number of Spanish-language media outlets profiled. Choices were made even more difficult because of changes in the media markets. But all outlets that responded to our written questionnaire were included in the directory section.

For the newspaper section of the narrative, I chose the five major Spanish-language dailies -- La Opinion, Noticias del Mundo, El Diario/La Prensa, Diario las Americas, and El Miami Herald, for obvious reasons: All have substantial circulations and monetary backing. All except Noticias have existed for more than a decade, proof of longevity and a strong readership base.

Because Texas has no major Spanish-language dailies, I profiled some of the weeklies. Again, the Texas newspaper section does not include many publications that have been in existence for more than a few years. I limited myself to writing about the papers in Dallas, Houston, and San Antonio. Some of these are new; others have been around for a while.

In televison, the choices were a bit more clear cut. I profiled, as best I could without personal interviews, the two dominant forces in Hispanic broadcasting, Univision and SICC. In most of the major markets, the Univision/SICC tandem overwhelms the competition. In some cities, however, it is a much tighter race. The two largest Hispanic markets in the United States -- Los Angeles and New York -- are also home to some of the more hotly contested broadcasting races. Both cities have excellent examples of full-time Spanish-language stations providing counter-programming. In Los Angeles, I profiled KVEA and in New York, WNJU. Both stations are now part of Telemundo.

The proliferation of Spanish-language radio stations made the culling more difficult. It appeared best to do it by city, selecting large cities with sizable Hispanic populations. Thus, I profiled most stations in Los Angeles, New York, Chicago, Miami, Houston, Dallas, and San Antonio.

Finally, I was also limited to sampling English-language Hispanic media. I included news and business magazines because those had demonstrated either staying power or a national audience. Among them was Vista, a newcomer that celebrated its first anniversary during the writing of this book.

Its editor, Harry Caicedo, expressed the optimism of his colleagues succintly: "Most Hispanics have developed a pride in their heritage and an interest in their culture. That's going to mean good business for us."

I. Spanish-Language Newspapers

The newspaper is a medium of habit. Immigrants who had, morning after morning, read a diario in their homelands, will continue to do so in the new country. If their informational needs are met in Spanish, so much the better. For most readers, the newspaper remains their primary source of information.

While a common language unites all readers of the Spanish-language press in the United States, their tastes for news differ. Hispanics tend to be more homogeneous in Los Angeles, Miami, and Texas, with one particular country of origin dominating. New York, on the other hand, is much more heterogeneous, making it difficult for news executives to determine what news to emphasize.

Readers of weeklies in Texas and dailies in California -- La Opinion and Noticias del Mundo -- are predominantly of Mexican origin. Not surprisingly, these papers play up news from Mexico. By the same token, Diario las Americas and El Herald, both in Miami, place a great deal of emphasis on news from Cuba, Nicaragua, and, to a lesser degree, Latin America. This should come as no surprise, for the overwhelming majority of the audience is from Cuba. In New York, Spanish newspapers try to carry a little of everything to meet the needs of their readers. As a matter of fact, El Diario/La Prensa is looking at the growing South American population as its future readership base. And in Miami, Los Angeles, and Texas, where the Central American population is steadily growing, newspapers are providing more and more news from those countries in an effort to attract new readers.

All Spanish-language newspapers rely heavily on the wires for their news. While some have a small staff of reporters, most must depend on Associated Press (AP); United Press International (UPI); EFE, Spain's news wire; and Notimex, Mexico's news wire, for national and international news. In some cases, some must rely on the wires even for local news. Press releases are also published verbatim in many newspapers because of the shortage of staff. Executives agree that this is not an ideal situation, but is necessary to keep overhead down. They prefer to use their resources wisely -- in the coverage of the barrios.

Big or small, daily or weekly, Spanish-language newspapers offer regular sections much like their English-language counterparts. They carry sports, editorials, features, and national and local news. Some, such as La Opinion, have weekly magazines. Others have standard weekly sections. Diario las Americas, for example, has a weekly page on financial and economic news. On Thursdays, it carries a food section, and on Sundays it devotes an entire section to women's news.

In addition to the standard fare, all papers have, at one time or another, published special supplements to commemorate patriotic events. Such supplements are a way of obtaining advertising revenue while building reader loyalty. The papers all carry social news regularly. Much like the suburban weeklies of the English-language community, these papers do not shy away from publishing the graduation portrait or the banquet picture. They do not mind running short articles about the neighbor who has excelled in college or the local garden club's annual bazaar. Such is their life-blood.

"Some of these items might never be published or they would be at the bottom of the heap," said Jose Cardinale, national editor-in-chief of Noticias del Mundo. "We publish them because it is important to the communities."

Publication of special supplements and community items is an example of the papers' commitment to the communities they serve. Hispanic publications often serve as a forum for Hispanic issues -- and not only on the editorial pages. Management at La Aurora, a weekly in Dallas, chose the motto "Educar es Redimir" (To Educate is To Redeem) because it saw the newspaper's function as educator and facilitator. El Diario/La Prensa in New York, owned by Gannett, has as its slogan "El Campeon del Hispano" (Champion of the Hispanics). Readers are encouraged to call in their problems.

"We have worked hard at that reputation," said Carlos Ramirez, El Diario/La Prensa president and publisher. "Anybody who has a problem with, say, a landlord, will call the paper for help."

Newspaper readers are, on the whole, better educated than the U.S. Hispanic market at large. According to readership studies conducted by the newspapers, more are college educated and have more disposable income. Diario las Americas readers, for instance, earn almost 21 percent more than the Miami Hispanic market. Almost 30 percent had some college education compared to almost 25 percent of Miami Hispanics. The same is true for other newspaper readers, such as those of Noticias del Mundo in New York -- 47 percent had attended college or done some post-high-school work.

They are, of course, attracted to the papers by news about their homelands and their local communities. But many enjoy the editorial pages that are full of columns and editorials sympathetic to their causes and plight.

Editorials are strongly pro-Hispanic, although Hispanic candidates don't always win the papers' endorsements. Many editorials concentrate on international and national issues that are of interest to the Hispanic population -- U.S. policy in Central America or Fidel Castro's exporting of communism, for instance -- without ignoring controversies in their backyard.

Most of the newspapers in this section -- with the exception of the newer publications such as Noticias del Mundo and La Aurora -- were turning a profit in 1986. All owners envisioned a promising future, based on the growing Hispanic population and the steady influx of refugees from Latin America.

The advertising that appears in the papers is overwhelmingly local, although there are several national accounts, including air lines, soft drinks, the U.S. government, and large department-store chains. Smaller ads tend to be for Hispanic-owned businesses. Anglo-owned businesses in Hispanic neighborhoods make up another sizable segment. Like the news stories in the paper, advertisements are tailored to the audience. Readers can find a wealth of immigration lawyers, trade schools, bodegas, clinics, and tours to Latin America advertised in these pages. Most ads run only in Spanish, with the translations usually done by the paper itself. Some newspapers, however, will run ads in English or in both languages.

Although advertising revenue is healthy, circulation is not what it could be. Most publications are not audited and none have the market saturation executives would like, which is true of the English-language press as well. In Los Angeles with 3.6 million Hispanics, for example, Noticias' circulation is 30,000 and La Opinion's 70,000. Pass-along rates are much higher among Hispanics, but these newspapers still do not reach a considerable portion of their markets. This, of course, may improve, as U.S. Hispanics grow older, set down new roots, and establish media habits.

Two Spanish-language dailies -- La Opinion and Diario las Americas -- are still owned by the founding families. The three others -- El Diario/La Prensa, El Miami Herald and Noticias del Mundo -- are owned by Anglo corporations. This could be viewed as an unfortunate trend: the loss of press ownership power by U.S. Hispanics. At the same time, it could signal a growing interest among Anglo investors in the Spanish-language media's potential for profit. The weeklies, monthlies, and specialized media, however, are still largely owned and operated by Hispanics.

Certainly money and careers can be had in this medium. Jose Lozano, publisher of La Opinion, the oldest Spanish-language newspaper in the United States, likes to tell this story:

> "In 1948, when my father graduated from Notre Dame, he thought that he was going to have to look for another job in 10 years. He didn't think the newspaper was going to make it past that. And here we are, stronger than ever. I certainly don't expect to be looking for a job in 10 years."

11

DAILIES

La Opinion

Ignacio E. Lozano Sr. began his newspaper career in the United States in 1913. The Mexican native founded La Prensa of San Antonio, a daily for his compatriots who sought news from the homeland in their native language. Though La Prensa was widely successful, by the early 1920s Lozano realized that greener pastures were farther west, in the growing Hispanic population of Los Angeles.

And so he founded La Opinion on September 16, 1926. It was no coincidence that the first issue came out on Mexican Independence Day, for Lozano envisioned a newspaper that would provide his people with information about their new country as well as keep them abreast of events in Mexico. There were two other Spanish-language dailies, but Lozano thought there was room for all to grow.

"His philosophy was that this would be more than just a newspaper," said Jose Lozano, his grandson and current publisher of the paper. "He wanted it to be the voice of the Mexican people."

In 1950, Ignacio Lozano realized his lifelong dream when La Opinion moved into its own plant in Los Angeles. His son, Ignacio Jr., assumed the duties of publisher not long after that, when Lozano died in September 1953. The younger Lozano then began the paper's gradual transformation into a general-audience publication that would appeal to all Hispanics in the Los Angeles area, not just Mexican-Americans.

"The Mexicans aren't the only Hispanics. There is also a large Central American community and it's growing. We could not ignore that," said Jose Lozano, who is responsible for the day-to-day operations of the paper.

In 1976 as La Opinion celebrated its golden anniversary, Ignacio Lozano Jr. was named U.S. Ambassador to El Salvador by President Gerald Ford. The elder Lozano left son Jose and daughter Leticia as co-publishers. The paper's circulation was 22,000 and it had been flat for some time. When the elder Lozano returned nine months later, circulation was growing.

It is now about 70,000 weekdays and Sundays, audited by the Audit Bureau of Circulation (ABC). The newspaper is published seven days per week on broadsheet. La Opinion employs 238 people; there are 42 editorial employees, including five local reporters.

Of the 70,000-copy press run, only 10 percent is home delivered. The rest are sold at newsstands and coin ranks. Home delivery figures are low, Lozano explained, for several reasons: the transience of the population, the Latin American habit of buying the paper on the streets, and an early home-edition deadline that keeps night baseball scores out of the paper. Several hundred copies are also distributed in cities in and out of California, including Phoenix and Las Vegas. The paper sells for 25 cents.

The newspaper has been successful, Lozano said, because La Opinion fills the need for information of a public that either cannot read the Los

Angeles English-language papers or does not identify with them. The newspaper's coverage of the local Hispanic community and Latin America in general attracts both recent immigrants and second-generation professionals who read other papers but get Latin news from La Opinion.

"We're more a champion of the people," Lozano said. "Why? It goes back to their cultural identity. We are the most easily accessible forum and we're in their language. They write letters. They phone us. We may not be able to help them directly, but we will send a reporter to check it out or we tell them where they can get help."

In 1985, La Opinion commissioned Scarborough Research Corporation of New York to do a study of its market. It portrayed the La Opinion reader, as Lozano put it: "Not monolingual but with a predominant preference for Spanish. Very few readers cross over to the Los Angeles Times or Herald, as they do with English-language television. They are what we call Spanish-language consumers. More than half are first-generation immigrants who prefer Spanish, but there are second- and third-generation Latinos interested in conserving their cultural identity."

According to the study, almost 86 percent of La Opinion's weekday audience uses both Spanish and English at home. Fourteen percent use only Spanish. Most readers -- 75 percent -- are Mexican, with Salvadorans making up the second-largest readership group with 11 percent.

About 58 percent of La Opinion weekday readers are men, though women take a slight lead on Sundays. Both male and female readers tend to be young -- about 73 percent of the weekday readers are between 18 and 44. Small families were decidedly in the minority: Almost 46 percent lived in households with five or more members.

Almost 14 percent have attended at least some college, but the majority (59 percent) have not completed high school. Thirty-two percent of the households had an income of $25,000 or more while almost 50 percent earned $20,000 or more.

Advertising

Most of the advertising that appears in La Opinion, about 90 percent, is bought by local merchants and companies selling retail goods, medical services, food, and other items. Jose Lozano said the newspaper is looking for more national advertisers. After hiring a new ad director with a strong national-advertisement background, La Opinion is aiming to increase its national advertisers by 15 percent. All ads appear in Spanish.

"In the last few years, we have been getting more national advertisers," Lozano said. "There is more awareness of the population. There is an impression by some that we are a 10- to 12-page weekly that comes out when we can get the money together. And that's just not so. In Los Angeles alone we have been telling agencies that $7-8 billion is being spent by Hispanic consumers."

The size of ads appearing in the paper vary widely, as do the type of services and companies. In the June 3, 1986 edition, for example, entertainment events commanded the larger ads. A theater chain had a full page ad, a restaurant advertised its dinner show with a quarter-page announcement, and a variety of smaller ads for movies, dances, and fairs were sprinkled through the last pages of the first section. Medical services, immigration advice, and insurance were the most advertised products. Seven pages were devoted to classifieds.

The monthly magazine ads were aimed more at a female audience: travel, hair salon, fabric shops, and clinics.

News Coverage

La Opinion's regular daily sections include news, sports, and entertainment. The first section blends national, international, and local news with the latter being emphasized extensively. "Local takes up more room because it has more direct impact on the reader. Nobody covers the Hispanic community of Los Angeles like we do," Lozano said.

Many times the front page is strictly international news, primarily from Latin America. But in some cases, a local news story -- and not necessarily one about a Hispanic issue -- will lead the page. In the June 10, 1986 edition, for example, the resignation of the superintendent of Los Angeles' public schools received slightly less play than a wire story on a critical report about NASA. That same day, a local story about Hispanic and Asian groups protesting a U.S. English Only resolution also made it on the front page, along with the civil commotion in South Africa, Soviet arms sales to Nicaragua, the purchase of UPI, and the forced landing of a U.S. plane in Peru.

On June 23, 1986, La Opinion led with a wire story of guerrilla attacks in Lima. Of the seven front page stories, six dealt with Hispanic issues, including those with datelines from Washington. The elections in Chihuahua in Northern Mexico were also played prominently on the front page of the Sunday edition of July 6, 1986.

"This is the type of news that is not local but is of great interest to our readers," Lozano said.

Aside from a heavy dose of Latin American news, "our coverage of national news is as good as any," he said. Pages 2 and 3 of the news section are devoted to local news with a sprinkling of national news having a strong Hispanic angle. Community news, which would probably not appear in other papers, predominates. In the June 23, 1986 edition, for instance, the lead story on Page 3 was the inauguration of a president of a local Mexican-American organization. Page 2 had a story about the visit of students and teachers to the Los Angeles Times. Likewise in the July 3, 1986 paper, page 2 and 3 contained stories about immigrant students attending the Fourth of July celebration in New York, Los Angeles' donation of an ambulance to El Salvador, a city-council story, and a warning from police about Fourth of July celebrations. A weekly round-up of Los Angeles

14

community news appears regularly but not daily on Page 2, titled "Panoramas Angelinos" or Los Angeles Panorama.

La Opinion also runs a round-up of local news in a column titled "Notas Cortas" or Short Notes. These briefs are mostly news and police items.

The newspaper also has daily pages on Latin America (in addition to the extensive coverage on the front page), an international page, a page for state news, and another for national news.

The daily "Panorama" feature section is full of news, pictures, and notes about the music, theater, and artistic worlds, both Latin and Anglo.

Once a week, La Opinion devotes the Panorama section to women's issues. In an August 24, 1986 edition, for instance, Panorama had a story about a feminist group in Brazil, an extensive story about Argentine mothers whose children have disappeared in political purges, and a profile of an art exhibit sponsored by a local women's organization.

By far the most-read and most-popular part of the paper is the sports section. "We cover baseball, soccer, and boxing extensively because that's what our readers want," Lozano said. And that's what they get. During the 1986 World Cup in Mexico, soccer dominated the paper's sports coverage. Layouts were splashy with a generous dose of pictures of soccer heroes. In the June 22 edition, the first five pages of the eight-page section were devoted exclusively to the World Cup. There were stories about the matches and about the tearful defeat of the Mexican team, the Argentine-English rivalry on and off the field, and the French celebration in Paris.

At other times, it is the local teams and the Latin American athletes who occupy the front page of the section. In the July 6 edition, a Dodgers' shutout against the Pittsburgh Pirates led the section, followed by a Toronto Blue Jays' victory over the California Angels. There were also wire stories on Cuba as champion of the Central American Games, a Wimbledon victory, and a Panamanian boxer's championship bout in the Philippines.

La Opinion also carries a monthly real-estate section and Sunday magazines. It produces special supplements on traditional Hispanic celebrations. On Sundays, readers get a TV guide complete with stories about Spanish-language programming and profiles of Hispanic actors, writers, and producers. The guide comes with color and black and white comics, including such traditional favorites as Peanuts, Tarzan, The Flintstones, Dennis the Menace, and Garfield. In addition, the guide has a Sunday magazine insert titled "La Comunidad" (The Community), with feature stories and commentaries on such topics as Mexican novelists, theater productions, and profiles of artists and writers.

The Sunday monthly magazine deals with both Hispanic and general-interest issues -- from how to deal with stress to fashion by Hispanic designers.

La Opinion uses AP and UPI in both Spanish and English, EFE, several syndicated feature services, and a city wire service. More than 20 percent of the copy that appears in the paper is locally produced, written, and edited by La Opinion staff, Lozano said.

Editorial Policy

La Opinion's management believes strongly in taking stands on socially sensitive issues, be they Hispanic oriented or not. "Everything impacts on Hispanics when you think of it, not just what is traditionally thought of as Hispanic issues. When it comes to social justice, we try to stand up for the right of the little guys, but we also believe in fiscal responsibility in spending of public funds. Those could be viewed as being diametrically opposed to each other," Lozano said.

There are two editorial writers -- the editorial editor and the executive editor. Decisions are made by a four-member editorial board comprised of those two writers and Ignacio and Jose Lozano. The editorials appear only in Spanish.

The paper also endorses candidates at all levels of government and usually endorses the Hispanic candidate. "If everything else is equal, we go for the Hispanic," Lozano said. "But we don't endorse somebody just because he or she is Hispanic. We vote for the person who will do the job."

Editorial topics vary, from international to local. On June 23, 1986, the editorial board wrote about Mexico's troubled economy. Two weeks before that, it suggested that a critical report on NASA be used to help improve the agency. In an editorial on July 6, 1986, the paper congratulated the local School Board for its approval of a pilot program to teach Anglo children Spanish at the elementary-school level.

The columns that appear on the editorial page are just as varied. In the June 3, 1986 edition, for example, one column talked about Mexican-U.S. relations, another about Syria and a third about Peru. Likewise, on July 6, 1986, there were columns about George Bush, Fidel Castro, SALT II, and Mexican author Octavio Paz. The writers were syndicated through Editors Press Service, Hispanic Link, FIRMAS (an EFE feature syndicate), Agencia Latinoamericana (ALA), and United Feature Syndicate. Others were guest columnists of the paper.

The Business of News

Lozano, who called the paper's finances "very healthy," said the family is counting on reaching the 150,000 circulation mark by 1988. There are also plans to move to larger facilities outside of downtown Los Angeles to accommodate a growing paper and its production equipment.

Noticias del Mundo

The first issue of Noticias del Mundo was published in 1980 in New York. The brainchild of News World Communications Inc., a Unification Church International subsidiary that owns the Washington Times, Noticias was designed as the paper of the future for a burgeoning Hispanic population in the United States. It started as a tabloid with a few pages and evolved into a broadsheet with a splash of red and blue on the front page and a clean, straightforward design.

In 1984, when the Washington Times added satellite transmission capabilities, News World Communications decided that the Times' sister publication should beam along with it. On October 1, 1984, the first Los Angeles edition of Noticias del Mundo, with 24 pages, was published -- the initial step in what has become the only national Spanish-language daily.

In April 1986, the San Francisco and Chicago editions were published for the first time. There were plans to beam editions to other large Hispanic markets, including Miami, Texas, and Washington, D.C.

"Initially it was not viewed as much a business as a means of becoming a political force in a community that is growing so quickly," said Rafael Prieto, former Los Angeles Noticias editor and currently assistant national editor. "But there is no religious influence. There is no pressure in what to cover or where to play a story. Now I think News World Communications is interested in it as a business, and not just as a political force."

Unlike other national newspapers, Noticias is not the same product sold in different cities. New York, Los Angeles, and the satellite editions of Chicago and San Francisco are three separate publications, but they share an eight-page core section of editorial material produced in New York headquarters. This core material includes the same editorial, national, international, South American, Central American, and Mexican/Caribbean pages with little variation. If, say, the Los Angeles edition carries a smaller ad than New York on its national page, the New York staff adds a short story or a house ad to the Los Angeles edition on the national page.

The New York edition is a single-body paper "for the convenience of the readers in the subway," according to Prieto. The satellite and Los Angeles editions, on the other hand, are divided into the A Section -- with international, national, and local news -- and the B Section -- comprising sports, entertainment, and the classifieds.

Los Angeles sends its local news product -- layouts, stories, and photographs -- by landline to New York for paste-up. Then whole newspaper pages, sent as film negatives, are transmitted back to printing facilities in each of the cities.

"We are not a USA Today in Spanish," explains Jose A. Cardinale, national editor-in-chief. "We are not the same paper in each city. The community news is from our reporters, but we also produce general news that can serve all Hispanics."

All three editions are published Monday through Friday. In New York, circulation has reached 53,000. It is sold for 25 cents at 3,000 newsstands and retail stores in Hispanic neighborhoods in the New York/New Jersey metropolitan area. Most copies are sold in Queens and Manhattan. About 8,100 copies are sold in Brooklyn and almost 4,900 in Bronx. The New York edition employs more than 200 employees. Twenty-five of those are on the editorial staff as reporters, photographers and editors.

According to the newspaper's promotional literature, Noticias in New York has a pass-along factor of four -- that is, four readers per copy or a total readership of 200,000. Since it is not audited by an independent company, Noticias says it has its own team of specially trained inspectors who spot-check outlets to make sure the paper is sold.

Although New York's Hispanic community is still predominantly Puerto Rican with an increasing number of recent immigrants from the Caribbean and South America, a 1986 research report by Globe Research Corp. showed that the paper attracts a variety of nationalities in New York. Puerto Ricans make up 13 percent of Noticias' readers, but Cubans and Colombians also comprise 13 percent each. Ecuadorans, Dominicans and Argentines represent 12 percent of the readership each, Peruvians make up 11 percent, and Chileans, Hondurans, Spaniards, Uruguayans, and Bolivians round out the rest.

"It is not an easy task to cover the different communities," Cardinale said. "New York Hispanics used to be predominantly Puerto Rican, but that is changing and it is a very heterogeneous community. We try to reflect our community as much as possible. I would say that we have three levels of readers: the elderly Hispanics who can only read Spanish, the middle-aged who can read both but prefer Spanish, and the young who still feel more comfortable with English but read us for the content."

The Globe Research survey painted a composite picture of Noticias' New York readers. On the average, they were young, active readers with elementary-school-aged children, and they were better educated than the Hispanic community at large.

According to the research, Noticias readers were both loyal and involved. Sixty-five percent had been reading it at least three years or more. The average time spend reading the paper was 52 minutes, and 72 percent of the respondents said they looked at the advertisements all or most of the time.

In Los Angeles, a similar readership study was conducted in March 1986 by United States Research of Beverly Hills. Los Angeles' Noticias has a circulation of 30,000. Like New York, there are four readers per household for an approximate readership of 120,000 in Los Angeles, according to Noticias.

The study showed that 54 percent of the respondents were monolingual in Spanish and 43 percent were bilingual. Unskilled blue-collar workers made up the highest percentage of readers -- 38 percent -- while skilled blue collar came in second, at 28 percent. Seventeen percent had upper-white-collar jobs and 8 percent had lower-white-collar occupations. Seventy-percent of the respondents had a high school education or more, and 25 percent had attended college. An overwhelming 71 percent had children. The majority are Mexican.

"Our readers are recent arrivals or those who have been here some time but want to get more news from Latin America," Prieto said. "The people who arrived recently tend to be young. Some are bilingual but not completely. They can read English but naturally feel more comfortable in their native tongue. We do have second-generation readers who can read in English. They may read in Spanish to perfect the language."

The Los Angeles edition employs 70 people, 25 of those in the editorial department.

The satellite editions of Chicago and San Francisco have a circulation of 15,000 in each city. Noticias has plans to open local offices there, Cardinale said.

Advertising

Both national and local companies buy advertising in the Noticias editions. Everything from apparel to drugs to toiletries to food and beverages appears in the newspaper's pages. National advertisers include Cutty Sark, Stroh's Beer, Columbia Pictures, Warner Brothers, Seiko watches, Rolex jewelry, Coca-Cola, Pepsi-Cola, Wesson, and Oldsmobile. There are also international advertisers, such as Banco Bogota, Banco Nacional de Argentina, Peru, Aero Condor, Avianca Airlines, Dominican Airlines, and Lan Chile. Each edition has at least one page of classifieds.

However, it is local ads that dominate, including larger blocks for Spanish-language television and radio stations, middle-sized ones for lawyers specializing in immigration, and smaller ones for trade schools, travel agencies, and supermarkets.

The satellite edition carries the least amount of advertising. It had four ads in the A section of the June 3, 1986 edition, for example, but three of those were Noticias' own house ads.

News Coverage

Each of the Noticias del Mundo editions has standard daily sections of pages -- local (usually two pages), national, editorial (two pages), international, the South American page, the Central American page, and the Mexican/Caribbean page. There is also a large sports section in which one page is usually dedicated to baseball, another to soccer, and a third to various sports with an emphasis on boxing.

"We try to include a little bit of everything to appeal to everybody," Prieto said of the sports section. "It is the only way of meeting the various tastes of our readers."

Sports is by far the most popular section, according to both Prieto and Cardinale. The extensive coverage of the 1986 World Cup in Mexico City was a favorite with readers. An article on a match or player was usually teased on the front page. Sometimes it was the lead news of the day, played prominently on the front page and above the fold. For instance, the June 11, 1986 edition in Los Angeles had a picture of Argentine soccer hero Dieto Maradona in his team's match against Bulgaria. The lead story was the Mexican National Team's game against Iraq that day and there was a boxed sidebar rounding up the four World Cup games. The soccer coverage took precedence over a successful baby heart transplant in Loma Linda and the final acquisition of UPI by a Mexican.

Sports, however, is not the only reason Noticias readers buy the paper. The regular, daily coverage of the Caribbean and Latin America -- their home countries -- serves as a big draw. "The local, Anglo newspapers do not cover the Hispanic issues as thoroughly," explained Cardinale. "They cover Latin America when there is an earthquake or a volcano or a revolution."

The bread-and-butter news of Noticias as well as all Spanish-language newspapers is Hispanic America. What may appear as a brief item buried inside the local daily will be a full story in Noticias.

Prieto cites a recent example: The 1986 death of internationally known writer Jorge Luis Borges was published on page 17 of the Los Angeles Times. "We carried it on the front page plus we had additional coverage inside," Prieto added.

All Noticias editions of June 3, 1986, for instance, had at least two stories either directly from Latin America or about a U.S. Hispanic community issue. The satellite edition's lead story was about anti-Sandinista rebel Eden Pastora. The second story was about John Gavin, former U.S. Ambassador to Mexico, offering to buy some Spanish-language television stations. The Los Angeles edition led with a story about an immigration plan by Democratic Congressman Edward Roybal, and had four other front-page stories from or about Mexico. The New York edition of the same day had stories about former Puerto Rican Congressman Herman Badill's nomination for state controller and a story about the Puerto Rican senate's flurry of activity at the end of its session.

While Latin American events attract readers to Noticias, news from the barrios keeps them reading. The paper's policy is to reserve space on the front page for a local Hispanic story, Cardinale said. The April 17, 1986 edition ran a front page story, dateline New York, about a radio station's campaign to declare Puerto Rican pilot Fernando Rivas Dominich a national hero. Rivas Dominich died in the 1986 U.S. attack against Libya. The fourth annual convention of Hispanic journalists in Miami made it on the bottom of the front page of the Los Angeles edition on April 23, 1986.

In the Los Angeles edition, the back page of section A is reserved for one Hispanic nationality each day. The New York edition also dedicates a page per week to one of the local communities. "Some of this might never be published or it would be at the bottom of the heap," Cardinale said of the items. "But we publish it because it is important to the communities."

The New York edition has a business page on Tuesday, but neither the Los Angeles nor satellite editions do. Los Angeles, instead, carries a page on legal matters with guest writers from the community. Once a week there are literary, schools and education, and cultural pages. "Before Menudo was discovered in English," Prieto said of the popular teenage singing group, "we had covered them thoroughly in Spanish. We emphasize the cultural activities of our own communities. Readers will not find that in the English-language papers."

Noticias also publishes special supplements on historic dates. The Los Angeles edition, for instance, had a special edition for Cinco de Mayo, a patriotic day in Mexico. The supplement contained feature stories about the historic battle at Puebla, interviews with consulate officials, and news about Mexico today. The paper has also published supplements on the independence days of other Latin American countries.

About 50 percent of the news published by Noticias comes from wire reports, Prieto said. The newspaper uses UPI in Spanish and English, EFE, and Notimex. In addition, Los Angeles also receives AP in Spanish and two city wires in English.

Editorial Policy

"We are openly against dictatorships," Cardinale said, summing up the paper's editorial policy. "We cannot abide Marxism."

Cardinale and Prieto, who develop and write the editorials, opine on international, national, and local issues that affect Hispanics. They have taken stands against cuts in bilingual education and the deportation of undocumented workers. They have also written on a variety of topics -- contra aid, Hispanic television, elections in the Dominican Republic, education, and social services. The stands are decidedly conservative in international affairs and pro-Hispanic on domestic issues. As most Spanish-language papers, Noticias publishes its editorials in both Spanish and English.

While the New York edition has endorsed political candidates at the local level, the Los Angeles and satellite editions have made no political endorsements. Prieto said Los Angeles has plans to do so in the future. Endorsements, like the editorials, are pro-Hispanic. If two Hispanics are pitted against each other in a campaign, the newspaper refuses to endorse one "in order to promote unity," Cardinale said.

But, Prieto cautions, Noticias does not endorse a Hispanic politician simply because he or she is Hispanic. "I can tell you that if he wants to deport illegals or he has communist leanings, the paper will not back him," Prieto said.

The op-ed page carries columns on Hispanic issues and is as internationally oriented as the stories that appear on the news pages. Datelines appear from Miami, New York, Los Angeles, El Salvador, Costa Rica, Chile, Spain, Honduras -- to name a few. In the June 17, 1986 edition, for example, there was a column from Honduras on the labor movement in that country, a piece from Costa Rica on the need for free enterprise in Central America, a New York column on Tip O'Neill and contra aid, another from Los Angeles on bilingualism in the business world, and a piece from Miami on Panama's intelligence ties with Cuba.

The Business of News

Although Noticias was not operating at a profit in 1986, the paper could be profitable by 1988, Prieto said. The paper has several campaigns to attract readers and, consequently, bring in more advertising revenue. In Los Angeles, Noticias prints up 225,000 copies of one edition per month and gives them out free door to door. "The total market coverage campaign promotes the newspaper. It has been successful for us," Prieto said.

Noticias is aggressively pursuing more readers, according to newspaper marketing officials. In New York, the paper has promoted a Crazy Cash contest with posters and car cards in the subway system. There are weekly cash prizes of $250 and $500, plus a chance to win $10,000 every month. The paper also airs commercials on Spanish-language television stations and radio spots on Spanish-language radio.

El Diario/La Prensa

In 1913, a Spaniard by the name of Jose Campubre founded a Spanish-language newspaper for the Hispanic community in New York. He called it La Prensa. In the latter 1950s, Campubre sold the paper to Fortune H. Pope, an Italian who also owned a Spanish-language radio station now known as WJIT.

One of La Prensa's competitors was El Diario de Nueva York, a publication begun in 1948. In 1963, O. Roy Chalk, president of Diversified Media, bought El Diario and later that year also acquired La Prensa. A few months later, he merged both newspapers to form El Diario/La Prensa.

In 1981, the Gannett Company purchased El Diario/La Prensa from Chalk for a reported $9 million in cash "to gain access to the Spanish-language market," said Carlos Ramirez, president and publisher of El Diario/La Prensa. It became Gannett's first newspaper serving a specialized audience and the first Spanish-language newspaper of the media giant.

At the time of the purchase, Gannett chairman and president Allen H. Neuharth told reporters the purchase was "the first step toward providing more news and information to Hispanics all across the country."

The paper was then losing $2.5 million a year, but the company was determined to keep it and "Gannettisize it" into a profitable operation, Ramirez said. In 1985, after several cost-cutting and streamlining efforts, El Diario/La Prensa finally broke even. By mid-1986, the newspaper was turning a profit.

"We felt it was important to keep it going and there is a commitment to do so," Ramirez said. "The Hispanic community in the United States is the fastest growing segment of the market, and having a Spanish-language newspaper in New York establishes an access to a large market within the market."

El Diario/La Prensa publishes 60,000 tabloid copies six days per week, Monday through Friday and a weekend edition. It usually has at least 36 pages and, according to a 1982-83 study, a pass-along factor of five people, bringing the total readership to an estimated 300,000. Circulation is not audited. Most of the copies are sold for 35 cents in the Hispanic barrios of New York and New Jersey, but a few thousand are also shipped to Philadelphia, Washington, D.C., New Haven, and Bridgeport.

El Diario/La Prensa is printed in New Brunswick, N.J. and distributed to bodegas, newsstands, and retail shops. There are no home deliveries.

As a matter of fact, El Diario/La Prensa's most pressing problem is its distribution system. Unionized news distributors in New York often refuse to stop at the out-of-the-way bodegas which are the major sales points for the Spanish-language paper. In addition, since El Diario/La Prensa's circulation is smaller than that of other New York newspapers distributed by the drivers, the Spanish-language paper is often ignored, Ramirez said.

Twenty-five percent of the copies are distributed by gypsies (non-union drivers) because that is the only way the paper can reach the barrios, Ramirez said.

El Diario/La Prensa employs 150 people. Forty of those work in editorial positions.

Historically, most of El Diario/La Prensa's readers were Puerto Ricans who had come to the mainland for economic reasons. That influx, however, has slowed and New York's Hispanic community is growing more heterogeneous. There are more Dominicans, Cubans, and Central and South Americans. The fastest-growing readership is Colombian, and the most faithful are the Colombians and the Dominicans, Ramirez said.

"Puerto Ricans usually slide over to the Daily News," he added. "Our future readers will be more and more the South Americans and less and less the Puerto Ricans."

These South Americans, many of them recent arrivals fleeing both political and economic problems, look for news from their homelands as well as information from the new neighborhood. They want stories that will help them survive and become successful in the new country.

"Yes, they want to know what's going on back home, but they are also interested in what is happening in Jacksonville Heights and Queens and how it will affect them," Ramirez added.

Ramirez said that 35 percent of the paper's readers are Puerto Rican, 35 percent are Dominican. The rest are from Central and South America and the Caribbean. A 1982 Scarborough survey showed that 53 percent were women. Fifty-six percent of the adult readers are in the 25-to-54 age group and 13.5 percent have attended or graduated from college. Twenty-five percent are high school graduates.

Most El Diario/La Prensa readers are middle income. Only 10 percent make $30,000 or more per year, while almost 49 percent make more than $15,000.

Reader households tend to be larger than those of non-Hispanics. Sixty-four percent have three or more members. Forty-seven percent have at least one child. A little over 52 percent are married and almost 32 percent are divorced, separated, or widowed. An overwhelming majority -- 88 percent -- speak Spanish at home.

Advertising

In 1984, El Diario/La Prensa commissioned the Bravo arm of Young & Rubicam to launch a campaign to attract new advertisers. "Are you speaking to the Spanish market in a foreign language?" it asked. "Try Spanish." It was successful, and the newspaper plans to do another.

"It's getting easier now to bring the advertisers, the national accounts," said Ramirez. "They realize the purchasing power of the Hispanic market and how it is growing. They also know that many of these people do not use other English-language media and that the way to reach them is through their own language."

Forty-five percent of El Diario/La Prensa's advertising revenue comes from local accounts and 25 percent from national accounts, Ramirez said. The rest comes from classified advertising. The largest and most faithful advertisers are the local furniture outlets and appliance stores. Trade schools also buy many advertisements.

National and regional advertisers sell a broad range of products -- from whiskey to cars to airplane fares. In a typical 40-page issue in July 1986, for example, there were ads for Johnnie Walker Black Label, Chivas Regal, and Pan Am. These same companies advertised in a June edition, with the addition of Ford Motor Company.

However, it is the local retailers who fill El Diario/La Prensa's pages with full-page announcements of sales and specials. In the June 6 edition, Ford was the only full-page national advertiser; four other full-page ads were for local retail stores or government offices. Most of the businesses that advertise are Hispanic-owned or are located in predominantly Hispanic neighborhoods.

Advertisements for movies, concerts, and other entertainment events tended to have the strongest Hispanic connection. Except for a few ads for English-language movies and artistic events, announcements were, by and large, for upcoming shows of Hispanic performers, Spanish movies, and discos.

In a July 20, 1986 special supplement commemorating a Colombian patriotic day, ads were even more narrowly focused. There were ads for Colombian restaurants, trips to Colombian cities, and a show by a Colombian artist.

El Diario/La Prensa translates ads from English for its advertisers.

News Coverage

El Diario/La Prensa is very much a New York tabloid newspaper: colorful, splashy, with provocative front page headlines that lure the reader inside. For example: "She finds dead father in trunk of car;" "Another child falls through window;" "Commissioner Ward said: Those who shoot police should be executed."

The teasers on top of the masthead are often about sports stories in the back pages. The right corner of the masthead itself is devoted to sports results or, during baseball season, to Hispanic pitchers expected to start in the day's games. During the 1986 World Cup soccer match in Mexico, news about players and the games often dominated the page.

Yet, it is a traditional Spanish-language newspaper in many ways. In addition to its daily national, local, sports, and editorial pages, the paper carries two sections that are very popular with readers -- "Nuestros

Paices" (Our Countries) and "Nuestros Barrios" (Our Neighborhoods). They were added to the paper in 1984 after a readership study.

"If I had four more pages to add to the paper, I would automatically add them to 'Nuestros Paices,'" Ramirez said.

The sports section is the second most-popular, with "Nuestros Barrios" coming in a close third, Ramirez added.

There are other pages that appear once a week: Expanded sports coverage on Mondays, Business on Tuesdays, Food on Wednesdays, People on Thursdays, and "Que Pasa" (What's Happening) on Fridays.

El Diario/La Prensa emphasizes news from Latin America, but local Hispanic news takes precedence, appearing almost daily as the lead headline on the front page. The first four pages are devoted exclusively to local and state news, with "Nuestros Barrios" comprising the fifth page of local copy. That feature receives more space than "Nuestros Paices," and is second only to Sports. Page 2 always carries a round-up of local news that usually runs about three paragraphs. These items range from court news to police briefs to lottery information, all compiled from wire reports.

For example, Hispanic-oriented stories that appeared in the June 6, 1986 local and state pages addressed a refugee's dispute with immigration, the sentencing of a Hispanic convict, and a minister's accusations that the U.S. immigration service discriminates against Central Americans. But most of the local stories had no obvious or direct Hispanic angle; they could have appeared in any New York paper. All, Ramirez explained, were of such general interest that they would affect or interest New York residents, regardless of background. So there were stories about rent control, a fatal stabbing in a disco, a prisoner's escape, a heroin raid, and the discovery of a body in a car trunk -- to name a few.

It is on the "Nuestros Barrios" page where news of the Hispanic community is published daily. In the June 6 edition, for instance, there was a small item with a picture of a Jacksonville, Florida Hispanic. The item said the man had been offered a job in New York but once in the city had been abandoned without money by the prospective employer. The laborer turned to El Diario/La Prensa for help -- a reader donated fare back to Jacksonville, and Traveler's Aid gave him coupons for free meals. The headline: "This worries us." This type of news item runs when the case warrants it, Ramirez said. As a matter of fact, El Diario/La Prensa urges readers with problems to contact its offices.

Most other items that appear on the "Nuestros Barrios" page would probably not be published in the larger English-language press. Information about scholarships, an upcoming conference on "the urban adolescent of the '80s," the sixth annual Puerto Rican Fair in the Bronx, a weekend health fair, and a march against apartheid all appeared June 6. Aside from brief news items, there are full-length stories, with pictures, on social-service programs. On July 20, 1986, there were features on an education program for unwed mothers, and the search for Hispanic couples willing to adopt children.

Sometimes the paper also runs an editorial cartoon in the "Nuestros Barrios" page that deals with both international and local issues.

The popular "Nuestros Paices" section offers a wide variety of news from Latin America. With four pages devoted to news from south of the border and Spain, every Hispanic reader, whether from Argentina or Mexico or somewhere in between, is likely to find something to fill his hunger for information from home. Each story, considered the top news item of the day in the region, carries a "sig" with the name of the country for easy access.

While most stories are from wire copy, some are by El Diario/La Prensa reporters with foreign datelines. An El Diario/La Prensa reporter covered the fight for survival of three political parties in the Dominican Republic and another covered elections in Ecuador for the June 6, 1986 edition. However, the remaining stories -- a total of seven with datelines from around the hemisphere -- were obtained through the wires.

The last or second-last page of the "Nuestros Paices" section also carries a round-up column of international items that are not necessarily from Latin America or Hispanic oriented.

The weekly "Que Pasa" insert section, which includes upcoming events as well as feature stories on Hispanic entertainers, makes Friday's paper one of the better sellers, Ramirez said. The listings are divided by neighborhood and are easy to read. A short review with prices, showtimes, and telephone numbers is included.

Entertainment stories, like their news counterparts, have a strong Hispanic angle. In the June 6 issue, for instance, all stories in the nine pages of "Que Pasa" were about Hispanic artists, Spanish-language films, or productions.

The Sports section is perhaps the least Hispanicized section of the paper since the emphasis is usually on local teams. For example, there were three full pages devoted to the National and American Leagues, including stories and box scores, in a July 20, 1986 issue. The lead stories of the day, on the back page of the tabloid, were datelined from France and London. The story from London was about a boxing match, a sport Hispanics follow avidly. The story from France, about cycling, concentrated on the Hispanic riders.

Still, El Diario/La Prensa holds faithful to the idea of segmenting the news and drawing out the Hispanic angle. It carries two daily pages of "Nuestros Deportes" (Our Sports) with a country-by-country collection of the most important sports news of the day. A mid-Summer issue contained stories about soccer from Uruguay, a judo competition in Puerto Rico, a boxing championship in Spain, and a water skiing competition from Colombia. In addition, a full page was devoted to results of soccer matches of leagues around Central and South America, while results of local league matches took up another half page. The paper also carries a racing page with a local column, results of the day before, and selections by four different handicappers.

The special Monday sports section, like the daily, emphasizes baseball, soccer, and boxing, and stories do not necessarily carry a Hispanic angle. There was a story about baseball's Tony Perez in the special section of July 14, 1986, but the lead story of that day was about the starting pitchers for the All Star game. Of the nine stories in that edition -- excluding the "Nuestros Deportes" pages and the round-up -- four were about Hispanic players or games in Latin American countries.

Like most Spanish-language newspapers, El Diario/La Prensa publishes special supplements on the patriotic days of some Latin American countries. The supplements include features stories on customs, foods, and music typical to the land. On Sundays, El Diario/La Prensa also carries a wrap-around comics section with a weekly TV guide for the two local Spanish-language stations.

The paper uses AP (in Spanish and English) and DPA, the German news agency.

Editorial Policy

El Diario/La Prensa has a five-member editorial board comprised of one editorial writer, the editor, controller, the circulation director, and Ramirez. They span a broad range on the political spectrum, giving the paper "a definite independent editorial policy," Ramirez said. The paper provides two full pages of editorial material daily.

The primary focus of the editorials, without a doubt, is on Hispanic issues, whether local, national, or international. "If something comes up on immigration, we jump on it," Ramirez explained. "We have editorialized on the imprisoned Marielitos and that could be considered both a local and national issue. At the same time, we try to focus on New York City and what will directly affect our readers."

In a July 14, 1986 editorial, for instance, El Diario/La Prensa's editorial board chided U.S. attorney Robert Giuliani and New York senator Alphonse d'Amato for their theatrics in fighting drugs. "Enough clowning, gentlemen," it said. "It's time to get cracking. New Yorkers need to know that you mean business, not reelection."

Yet the "universal" Hispanic themes -- bilingual education, immigration, labor, and preservation of culture -- continue to provide plenty of fodder for comment. For example: In a July 25, 1986 editorial titled "U.S. English: The Hidden Agenda," the paper warned readers that Hispanics are the main target of the group that wants to make English the official language of the country. In a move that is likely to be held dear by Hispanics, El Diario/La Prensa urged voters to fight against an English-only proposition in California and expose the movement for what it is: "an effort to hold the great and beautiful English language hostage to the racist aims of a few zealots."

The editorials, as in many other Spanish-language newspapers, are published in both English and Spanish.

The paper endorses political candidates on the national, state, and local levels, but Ramirez claims the paper will not necessarily endorse Hispanic candidates.

"To be independent we have to call it like it is. You can have a non-Hispanic candidate represent Hispanics. That might hurt us in sales because of the mentality to stick to your own, but we strongly believe in the editorial independence of the paper," Ramirez said.

The columns, like the news stories, deal with a variety of Latin American topics and Hispanic issues -- from real estate in Miami to Nicaraguan-U.S. relations to education in New York City schools. Writers' backgrounds, too, are varied. New York Mayor Ed Koch has written for the paper. So has the New York school superintendent, a Cuban intellectual who lives in Spain, and a Colombian journalist from New York. The editor and managing editor of the paper also write columns.

"In a week's time our editorial pages will cover the spectrum of political opinion," Ramirez said. "The reader gets a balance, from the right wing to the left wing and the center."

Take some of the columns that appeared in the June and July 1986 issues as an example. One, written by a syndicated Cuban columnist, dealt with Fidel Castro's efforts to discredit a Cuban dissidents congress in Madrid. And on July 25, 1986, Carl Rowan, a News America Syndicate columnist, castigated conservative congressmen for leading Reagan in an "immoral" belief that the anti-apartheid movement in South Africa is led by communists.

The Business of News

From a peak of 75,000 copies in the early 1980s, El Diario/La Prensa's circulation plummetted to 35,000 in 1984 when the paper struggled to survive problems with its distributors. But in 1986, "the corporation turned the corner," Ramirez said. The newspaper has been able to turn a profit by increasing circulation and advertising revenue as well as streamlining manpower and operation expenses, he added.

"We're very confident in the future of the paper," Ramirez said. "We expect the growth from South American immigrants and our plans are to focus in that direction."

Diario las Americas

In 1953, when a young Nicaraguan lawyer named Horacio Aguirre decided to start a Spanish-language newspaper in Miami, Hispanics were a small minority of the population in this tourist town. It was almost six years before Fidel Castro's revolution would send tens of thousands of Cubans fleeing to America and more than 20 years before political and economic turmoil in Central America would prompt Central Americans to follow the Cubans to the Florida Peninsula.

In the 1950s, Miami was the playground for winter tourists. Few Latin American tourists visited and only 110,000 Spanish-speakers lived in Miami. But Aguirre, a former editorial writer for a Panamanian newspaper, thought that Miami, because of its strategic geographic location, would eventually become the gateway to the Americas.

On July 4 of the that year, Aguirre fulfilled his dream. He published 8,000 copies of Diario las Americas -- The Americas' Daily -- with the backing of a Venezuelan builder/investor and two Pensacola, Florida road-builders. He sold 4,000 copies; the rest he gave away. The issue had six pages, including a page with English translations of the news. Its motto: For Liberty, Culture, and Hemispheric Solidarity.

"Even in 1953, we considered Miami an important geographical location," Aguirre said. "It was before the time of the jets, but Miami was still only four hours away from many important Latin American cities."

The goal of the paper was to provide Miami's Hispanics, a group of well-educated, well-travelled people, with information about Latin America, something no other newspaper was doing at the time.

Less than a decade after Aguirre founded the paper, the first influx of Cuban refugees arrived in Miami. In 1960, only 5.4 percent of Miami's population was Hispanic. By the mid-1980s, it stood at 42 percent. And as Miami's Hispanic population grew steadily, so did Diario las Americas. Between 1975 and 1983, Diario's circulation increased 23 percent.

The paper is now published six times per week, Tuesday through Sunday. It is a broadsheet of at least 28 pages, and it sells for 25 cents. Aguirre says 66,000 copies are distributed in the Greater Miami area, with an average of 2.64 readers per copy. (Circulation is not audited.)

Two-thirds are home-delivered to subscribers and the rest is sold at some 1,200 newsstands and coin racks. Latin American tourists and businessmen read Diario: More than 1,000 copies are sold daily in or near hotels in downtown Miami, Miami Beach, and the airport area.

Diario also has mail subscriptions to several U.S. cities, including Chicago, Los Angeles, and Elizabeth, N.J., as well as all Central American capitals except Managua, Nicaragua.

Diario employs 100 people, excluding carriers. Twenty-six of those work on the editorial side of the paper.

Aguirre said Diario and its readers share not only the language of their homelands, but common traditions and heritage. Like other Spanish-language media, Diario tries to be a cultural vehicle, a shrine to the Hispanic way of life, Aguirre said. Reading it is a way of keeping in touch with what was left behind.

"Everybody is interested in what is happening in the world," explained Aguirre, "And in Miami, they are particularly interested in Latin America."

Diario readers, according to Aguirre, come from all walks of life. "We have readers who are quite wealthy and some who are the drivers who ride the laundry delivery cars," he said. They are young and they are old. Some are recent immigrants; other arrived more than two decades ago. But they all share one characteristic: "They have acquisitive power and have a certain cultural knowledge," Aguirre said.

In early 1985, Diario commissioned Strategy Research Corporation to conduct a study of subscribers and compare the data obtained with the research group's own Miami Latin-market survey. The average annual family income of Diario readers is $28,050, 20.7 percent higher that of the Miami Hispanic market as a whole. Accordingly, the educational level of the head of household was higher for Diario readers than for the Miami Hispanic market as a whole. Almost 30 percent had had some college compared to almost 25 percent of Miami Hispanics. The majority -- 58 percent -- were either owners of their own businesses or professionals.

Reflecting the Hispanic community at large, 88 percent of Diario readers were born in Cuba. The next closest country of origin, Nicaragua, accounted for only 5 percent. The average length of residency in the United States for the head of a Diario reader household was 16.8 years; residency in Dade County (Miami) was 14.5 years. And readers were loyal to Diario, too. Fifty-one percent had subscribed for five years or more, thirty-one percent for 10 years or more.

Advertising

Diario carries both national and local advertising. But it is the classifieds which Aguirre boasts about. "It is the thermometer of this newspaper's life," Aguirre said. The paper usually runs a minimum of five pages of classifieds. The real estate classified ads are particularly voluminous, perhaps because Hispanics account for more than 60 percent of all Dade County's housing sales, according to Aguirre.

National and local advertising is also plentiful. Among the national advertisers are Pan Am Airlines, Radio Shack, St. Pauli Girl beer, and Jack Daniels whiskey. But local and regional advertisers dominate, spanning the spectrum of goods from retail shops to movie theaters, from concert halls to tire sales.

"The number and size of ads have grown since the paper started," Aguirre said. "It is a reflection of the way this city has grown."

Diario also provides its advertisers with translations of their advertisements into Spanish at no additional cost.

News Coverage

Diario las Americas is comprised of two sections every day except Thursdays, when it has four sections, and Sundays, when it has six. Section A contains international and national news and sports. Section B is local and state news as well as feature articles and social and entertainment stories.

On Thursdays, Diario carries a food section, and women's news gets its own section. On Sundays, in addition to the women's section, Diario includes a social news section, a sports section, and a sixth section devoted to local Cuban society news.

A weekly feature page on financial and economic news often uses charts, graphs, and statistical data to accompany stories. Four times per week -- on Tuesday, Thursday, Friday, and Sunday -- Diario runs a "Mundos de los Negocios" (Business World) column which emphasizes Hispanic trade, commerce, and finance. For example, on July 29, 1986, the lead item of the column was about judicial proceedings against a well-known businessman in Spain. Other items in the column included information about Ginnie Maes, and PepsiCo's buy-out of Kentucky Fried Chicken. On another occasion, in the column of July 15, 1986, the lead item was about declining interest rates. The second item concerned the country's proposed budget.

Saturdays feature a weekly page on real estate news and a movie-review column called "Cinetemas" (Movie Themes). The paper's film critic reviews both English- and Spanish-language movies.

On Sundays, there is a two-page spread on books, literature, and art. This includes a book-review column as well as poems and profiles of writers and artists.

Whatever the section, the emphasis in on Latin American news. "We have news from other parts, but our specialty and focus is Latin America," Aguirre explained. "Our readers read us because we are written in Spanish, but also for the content. They get news from Latin America they can't find anywhere else."

That philosophy is nowhere more evident than in Section A of the paper. More than 90 percent of the front-page stories have datelines from Latin countries. While others are written from Washington, D.C., they usually have to do with U.S. policy in Central or South America. The July 19, 1986 edition, for example, carried six stories on the front page along with its daily "Al Cerrar la Edicion" (At the Close of the Edition), a column of brief, late-breaking news items. Five of those stories were from Latin America or dealt with a Hispanic issue.

The lead story of that day was a wire report from Havana on the government's probe into corruption. There were also stories about the vice president of the Episcopal Conference of Nicaragua, an upcoming U.S. Senate debate on anti-Sandinista aid, a Soviet communications system in Managua, and the 50th anniversary of the Spanish Civil War. The sixth story was about the liberation of a U.S. missionary in the Philippines.

Page 2 always carries a daily round-up column of news from Latin America, titled "Panorama de Iberoamerica" (Ibero-American Panorama). In addition, there are regular round-up columns of the same sort from different countries, particularly from Nicaragua and Puerto Rico. Pages 6 and 7 are usually reserved for news from Central America, with a strong emphasis on Nicaragua. Except for the editorial pages, Section A is made up exclusively of wire copy. In some cases, Diario will publish all wire versions of the same event.

"I think it is important that we give our readers all sides and viewpoints so they can form a more accurate picture of what is happening," Aguirre said.

The local and state section offers a smorgasbord of news, with stories from Miami, Tallahassee, and other major Florida cities. The emphasis again is on local Hispanic news. There is also a local daily column on Page 2, "Habla la Juventud," (Youth Speaks) that profiles a Hispanic between the ages of 18 and 35.

Civic, cultural, and charitable associations receive considerable coverage as well. On July 16, 1986, there were stories about the University of Miami's archives on Cuban exiles, a local festival, a dinner dance by a local organization, and a feature on a Cuban classical guitarist.

In sports, stories emphasize the Hispanic angle too, but the scope of coverage is somewhat broader. Diario regularly carries news about major professional sports as well as amateur athletics. To cater to Hispanics' interest, baseball, boxing, football, and soccer receive plenty of play.

There are also regular stories on the sports events of Cuban social clubs and local Cuban baseball associations, usually on Page 2. The July 26 edition, for example, included a story about a local baseball academy's victory in Tampa, a column about the Miami Dolphins, and a long round-up of local clubs' athletic exploits under the title "Por los Clubes Locales" (In the Local Clubs).

That day Diario also featured a daily page on thoroughbred racing, greyhound racing, and Jai-Alai as well as wire stories on cycling in France, soccer in Uruguay, Argentine tennis, and a Mexican boxer in Paris.

The feature section, called "Entre Mujeres" (Between Women) is devoted to fashions and home decorating. A poem by a Hispanic writer is published daily as well as features on theater, movies, and artists. There is, of course, the standard movie and TV listings, crossword puzzle, horoscope, and comic strips in Spanish. On Sundays, Diario also publishes features and news items about domestic and international tourist attractions.

By far the favorite of readers is the social pages, where baptisms and weddings, birthdays and graduations are recorded. On Sundays, in a section titled "Notas Cubanas Dominicales" (Cuban Sunday Notes), Diario features a second society section that focuses on the social comings and goings of the upper echelons of Cuban society, including coverage of fund-raising banquets and black-tie affairs.

"This is more than a thing of vanity or ego," Aguirre explained. "It's not just the trivial or frivolous. On the contrary. While this is common in Latin American countries, the social page has more significance here because in our case this is a community of exiles. And because of exile, it is a way of keeping up with people. If you want to know what happened to your old schoolmate's daughter, you can read it in those pages. It is a way of keeping together."

Diario publishes several special supplements every year to commemorate historic Cuban holidays and traditional Miami celebrations. In the past, it has produced supplements for Cuban Independence Day on May 20 and Grito de Yara, a Cuban patriotic day on October 10. The latter commemorates the start of Cuba's independence movement in the 19th century. Diario's promotional literature calls these issues "an ideal occasion to show an advertiser's solidarity with the Cuban community's continuing struggle for freedom."

There have also been special sections for Carnaval Miami, the largest Hispanic festival in the United States. This February supplement includes the traditional feature articles and photographs of the celebration as well as an information guide for spectators. Diario provided an extra press run of 20,000 supplements in 1986. In September, a special section celebrates the anniversary of the Latin Chamber of Commerce, and in October Diario helps the city celebrate the Hispanic Heritage Festival.

In a more sporty vein, Diario has also produced a special section for the Miami Grand Prix in February and another for the South Florida Auto Show in November.

The overwhelming number of stories that appear in Diario -- with the exception of local columnists and an occasional staff-written local story -- come from the wires. The newspaper uses UPI in both Spanish and English as well as Agence France-Press or AFP (the French news wire), ANSA (the Italian wire service), and EFE. The bulk of the wire stories used, Aguirre said, come from EFE and UPI in Spanish. Diario uses a number of feature syndicates, including Editors Press, King Features, Copley News Service, ALA, and International Writers Service.

Editorial Policy

"Since the fall of Cuba, we consider that one of the biggest problems we face is the Russian-Soviet border 90 miles from here," Aguirre said. "And now we have Central America in a precarious situation. The communists are in our own backyard."

Aguirre's political leanings are reflected clearly and eloquently in Diario's editorials. The paper's philosophy, according to Aguirre, is "in defense of liberty and the values of democracy." He labels it moderately conservative with a strong defense of individual rights. Aguirre has written the editorials since the inception of the paper, and he has dealt with a variety of themes -- from aid to the Nicaraguan contras to local street lighting and security to bilingual education.

There are at least two full pages daily of editorials and columns. Aguirre boasts that Diario has a unique editorial mix, for it carries the commentaries of top Spanish-language writers as well as translated columns of well-known American ones.

As in the news section, the emphasis of the editorial pages is on the international scene. On July 26, the anniversary of the Fidel Castro Revolution, Diario published an editorial with the headline "A Mournful Anniversary for the Cuban People."

"With exemplary patriotism, the Cubans in and outside the island are earnestly involved in and hope for the liberation of their country. Would to God that this be possible and that they receive the necessary help to carry out that noble feat," concluded the editorial.

In another editorial on July 15, 1986, Diario criticized former president Carter's opinions about Nicaragua, suggesting he remain "prudently and decorously silent." In a July 29, 1986 edition, the newspaper warned its readers about Communists who disguise themselves as democrats.

The editorials are written in Spanish and translated into English. "We do this as a courtesy to this country. If an English-speaking person wants to know our editorial position, he can do so even if he cannot read the rest of the paper," Aguirre said.

Columnists include well-known journalists and writers from Latin America speaking out on a variety of topics, from grammatical inconsistencies in the spoken language, to an election analysis, to a favorable commentary on a Reagan speech. Among the better-known American writers who have appeared in Diario's editorial pages is Jeane Kirkpatrick. In a July 20, 1986 column, the former U.S. ambassador to the United Nations talked about the Latin American debt crisis and a Senate plan to help resolve it.

Diario endorses candidates on the local, state, and national level.

The Business of News

Since the early 1980s, the number of total pages has more than doubled and is continuing at a rapid pace. Advertising lineage and circulation has also increased.

"People with surnames of Lopez, Martinez, Gonzalez, who at 17 weren't interested in reading in Spanish now discover their Spanish-speaking heritage," Aguirre said. "There will always be a public for the Spanish-language media."

El Miami Herald

In 1976, the Miami Herald made newspaper history when it published a Spanish-language newspaper insert, the only Spanish-language sister publication of a major U.S. metropolitan daily. Before its March 1976 debut, an in-house study noted that the time was ripe for a second Spanish-language newspaper in Miami. But the study, like many of its type, was filed away somewhere and forgotten -- until the paper got a new general manager. Bev Carter, now vice president of Knight-Ridder newspapers, was told of the study when he moved to Miami from Charlotte.

"He found it fascinating," recounted former El Herald editor Roberto Fabricio. "There was such a huge Spanish-language market that was being underserved at the time."

The concept of El Herald was discussed for months. Different formulas were presented, dissected, and then thrown out, until management decided on the present concept -- an insert, with independent sections, that would retain the qualities of its parent publication while catering to the Hispanic population.

"There were two areas that were very significant in the decision," Fabricio explained. "For one, this was a much more upscale market than New York, Chicago, Los Angeles. Hispanics here were also retaining their Spanish more than anywhere else. In addition, they didn't see an immediate erosion of that."

The idea, Fabricio added, was to sell the Herald to the growing Hispanic population. And to reach the market, Knight-Ridder would do so in Spanish.

The first press run of El Herald was 18,700 copies. All Herald subscribers with Spanish surnames, even those who could not read Spanish, received a copy. About 5,000 were sold on the street.

By 1979, the circulation had passed the 40,000 mark. For the next three years, it grew at a steady but modest rate. Since 1981, "the increase has been dramatic," a result of the sudden influx of Cuban refugees during the Mariel boatlift and a growing Central American population. Now, audited circulation is 84,000 on weekdays and 92,000 on Sundays.

El Herald, in many ways, has remained the same editorial product since its inception. It employs 24 people, all of them in editorial jobs, the same number since 1976. The broadsheet newspaper is still produced by Herald employees at its Miami offices.

Spanish-surnamed subscribers, as well as Anglos, can receive El Herald as a free supplement every day, Monday through Saturday, for the same 25 cents they pay for the Herald. It also comes with the 75-cent Sunday paper. Eighty percent of all El Herald subscribers receive the paper at home. The rest buy it from coin racks, at newsstands, and in bodegas in predominantly Hispanic neighborhoods. About two-thirds of El Herald readers also read the Herald in English, Fabricio said.

The number of daily pages has remained constant -- an average of 14 Monday through Saturday and 20 pages Sunday. Special supplements, however, tend to be much larger. For its 10th anniversary, El Herald published a 72-page special issue.

Though El Herald is published by a large American corporation, it resembles a Latin American newspaper more than its English-language sister, Fabricio said. Aside from the traditional emphasis on Latin America and Hispanic issues, El Herald provides a wealth of commentary and opinion columns.

"This town," explained Fabricio, "is more like Latin America than any other city in this country. And we are a product of that. Latins like to read ideas and philosophies and we tailor to them in that particular way. It's a paper that could be published in Caracas or Bogota or Mexico City."

El Herald readers, like the community at large, are predominantly Cuban and very middle class. About 8 percent of El Herald readership is comprised of Anglos.

Fabricio portrays typical readers this way: "On the average, they are under 42, have had some college education, make over $25,000 a year, and are most likely bilingual but prefer Spanish."

An in-house study of El Herald daily and Sunday readers showed that readership was evenly divided between women and men. The overwhelming majority, 67 percent, were married. Eighty-two percent of El Herald Sunday readers have lived in the county at least five years; 45 percent have lived there 10 years or more. About 50 percent own their own homes. Thirty-three percent of Sunday readers make $30,000 or more; of those, 12 percent make more than $50,000 a year.

The types of jobs held by readers varies. Twenty-three percent are employed in clerical or sales positions, while 18 percent are professionals, managers, or owners.

Advertising

Advertising lineage has remained relatively stable since about 1981, Fabricio said. Most of it is local, although national companies -- cigarette manufacturers, liquor companies, and airlines -- advertise frequently. Classifieds are not a big part of the advertising account. El Herald usually carries only one classified page daily, two pages Sunday. Real estate is the single largest account for the paper.

Merchants often buy a packaged advertising deal -- both the English and Spanish Heralds for lower prices than if bought individually. Full-page ads are rare. National advertisers tend to buy a quarter page or less. The same is true for local businesses that sell a broad range of goods -- banking services, shoes, clothes, schools, funeral homes, immigration help, and medical services. The Sunday paper, as one might expect, has the most advertising.

News Coverage

News from Latin America historically draws Spanish-speaking readers, but so does El Herald's coverage of the local Latin community, augmented by the staff of the English-language Herald.

The standard daily fare includes local news, sports, editorials, features, and a Latin American page. On Saturdays, El Herald runs a "people" page. Between 35-40 percent of the copy that appears in the paper is translated either from Herald reports or wire stories. Most of that translated material appears in the front pages -- the national, international, and local news. Features, sports, and columns are written in Spanish.

"El Herald cannot be all things to all people," Fabricio explained. "We have to serve the very special informational needs of a very specialized reading public."

Those needs, as defined by the paper, are news from Cuba, stories about Miami's Hispanics, and information about Latin America. "We will leave stories out in order to serve those needs. We are not a general-purpose newspaper. Our two mainstays are local Latin news and Latin American news," Fabricio added.

The play and space provided a story may differ dramatically from El Herald to the English-language Herald. When Reagan was shot in March 1981, for instance, El Herald was a single-issue paper. All news stories were related to the assassination attempt because the Cuban community in Miami is very pro-Reagan.

"General news will be briefer with us than with the main Herald because of the size of the paper," Fabricio said. "At the same time, some stories (about Latin America) will be played up in El Herald."

The August 8, 1986 editions of both newspapers provide a good example. The front page of El Herald led with a Hispanic organization's search for Cuban members. The second story concerned the new Colombian president, while other stories included one from Cuba about the distribution of Bibles, another about a Russian couple's defection, and a third about a tobacco heir's conviction in a murder trial. The English Herald, on the other hand, carried the story about the Hispanic organization on the bottom of the local page. The article on the Colombian president was carried on Page 3 of Section A, and the Cuban Bible story was on the feature section's front page.

Stories on the Russian defections and the murder conviction were the lead stories in the English-language Herald. Other stories on the main Herald front were about car-crash tests, a killer bee jungle attack, Andrew Young's visit to Angola, drugs tests for federal employees, and U.S.-South Africa policy. Only the killer bee attack and the federal drug-testing program were carried inside, in a much briefer form, by El Herald.

This is not to say that El Herald's front page will not carry a lead story from somewhere outside Latin America or Miami's Hispanic community.

On August 6, 1986, for example, the paper led with the increase of crude oil prices, a story that affects all Miami residents. The second item was about a U.S. offer to help other countries fight drugs, news that directly affects many Latin American countries.

Traditionally, El Herald's front page is a blend of international, national, and local news, with a heavy emphasis on Latin issues. Any news from Cuba is likely to get good play to satisfy the hunger of the Cuban-exile community. Front-page Latin American news is further supplemented by a daily Latin American page. Datelines on that page are from around the hemisphere. Most of the copy is provided by the wires, but often stories written by Herald foreign correspondents for the English-language side are translated for El Herald.

Page 2 is devoted to local news, again with the emphasis on the Hispanic community. The lead local story on July 27, 1986, for example, was about the burial of a Nicaraguan girl. On August 8, 1986, the lead story concerned the detention of three Cubans in an immigration camp. But El Herald follows the philosophy that news is news, no matter what language news-makers speak. So much of the local page is comprised of general interest stories written by main Herald reporters and translated into Spanish -- weather stories, court information, police briefs, and health articles. Monday through Saturday a round-up column of the news items runs down the left side of page two, titled "Miami y Sus Alrededores" (Miami and its Surroundings).

On Sundays, that column is replaced with another titled "Borrador" (Rough Draft), a sometimes sarcastic, often witty collection of names, places, and events of the past week.

A popular feature also carried on the local page is "Linea Directa" (Direct Line), a troubleshooting column for readers' immigration problems. It appears Wednesdays and Sundays. Occasionally, El Herald also runs a round-up column of international news under the heading "El Mundo en 24 Horas" (The World in 24 Hours).

Unlike the front of the news section, most stories in the "Galeria" feature section are written in Spanish by El Herald's own staff. Articles deal with Hispanic entertainers, local artists, health tips, and assorted feature items. El Herald has its own restaurant reviewer, film critic, entertainment writer, and local feature columnist. The emphasis, as expected, is usually on the Hispanic angle. "Galeria," usually two broad-sheet pages, also carries the traditional horoscopes, comics, and crossword puzzles.

Tuesdays are usually devoted to the social scene, with a collection of items or a full story on a particular fundraising or social event. There are always plenty of pictures of community leaders and politicians.

Thursday is the traditional food day. Although much is written about Latin foods and restaurants, El Herald critics do not limit themselves to that. The stories of August 7, 1986, for instance, were about diet desserts and a review of a Chinese restaurant. The third story on the page was about the death of a famous Mexican actor.

On Fridays, "Galeria" serves its reader a menu of upcoming entertainment events. There is usually one lead story about a Hispanic show or artist, and the traditional movie, art, or music review. The rest of the section is a handy reference to weekend events, including a local column about movies, theater, television, music, and miscellaneous exhibits. The inside "Galeria" page is also devoted to "Las Debutantes" (The Debutantes) -- pictures and brief items of Hispanic girls reaching the turning point of life -- "Los Quinces" (The sweet fifteen).

The People page on Saturdays, "Caras y Nombres" (Faces and Names), is a graphically pleasing, lightly written collection of items about the famous and infamous, the heartthrobs and the common-day folks.

Sports is usually packaged along with "Galeria" in one section. Like other Spanish-language newspapers, the emphasis is on baseball, boxing, and, to a lesser degree, soccer. (Miami's Hispanic community is comprised of diehard beisbol aficionados.) Coverage of Miami's only professional sports team -- the Miami Dolphins -- also receives a considerable amount of space during football season. For instance, the Dolphins' pre-season opener in Minnesota led the section on August 2, 1986; that story took precedence over a wire report about Cuba's threat to boycott the 1988 Olympics.

During baseball season, however, the sports pages are filled with news about Cuba's pasttime. When possible, the emphasis is on the Hispanic athletes playing in the major leagues. On August 3, 1986, for example, the entire front page of the sports section was devoted to baseball, including a column by a local writer and a story about the Oakland A's Jose Canseco, a homegrown Miami product.

El Herald publishes three special supplements a year -- on the anniversary of the newspaper, and on May 20 and October 10, two Cuban patriotic days. The special sections are invaluable sources of community goodwill. "It helps the public's perception of the paper," Fabricio said. "People talk about it for a long time."

El Herald subscribes to both AP and UPI in Spanish. It also gets both wires in English, through the English-language daily. Features and columnists are syndicated through EFE and ALA.

Editorial Policy

The most-read and best-liked section of the paper is the op-ed page, Fabricio said. "It is, far and above, the most popular feature of the paper," he explained. "Why? This is a town of exiles. This is a very politicized town. They are looking for orientation. They want to read what their favorite writers are writing. We have a strong stable of columnists. Not only do we carry the best writers from the Cuban community but also from around Latin America."

In addition to the politics, the op-ed page is of particular appeal to Latinos because "it is the only section that, for the most part, is not translated. The writers are real stylists of the language."

40

Columns cover a broad range of topics, but deal mainly with Hispanic issues. When dealing with politics, they tend to be anti-communist and conservative, a reflection of the overwhelming feeling of Miami's Cuban community. Columnists include poets, writers, former political prisoners, politicians, community leaders, and activists. Columns by the Miami Herald's publisher, executive editor, and other writers are translated, too. Some of the best-known names in Spanish literature -- including Jorge Luis Borges and Mario Vargas Llosa -- have appeared in El Herald's editorial pages.

On August 9, 1986, for example, there were columns by a Miami lawyer, a Cuban-born professor, a well-known Cuban poet, and a writer. Themes were varied: Mother Teresa's touching and poignant work with the poor; a report about the Cuban Intellectual Congress in Madrid; a long but entertaining recounting of the history of bilingualism in the United States; and musings about Scottie Fitzgerald, the daughter of the famous American writer.

Editorials are not written by El Herald writers, although Fabricio sits on the Herald's editorial board. Instead, the Herald's editorials are translated into Spanish, and appear the same day in both the English-language daily and in El Herald. Political candidates are also endorsed by the full Herald editorial board.

The Business of News

Though circulation has increased steadily, Knight-Ridder lost money on its El Herald operation for most of its first decade, Fabricio said. In 1986, the Spanish-language newspaper was breaking even.

THE TEXAS PRESS

Despite the growing number of Hispanics and this state's far reaching Latin roots, Texas does not have any major Spanish-language dailies. Dozens of smaller weeklies and monthlies are scattered around the vast state, in the border towns as well as the large metropolitan centers. Theories abound on why the area's Hispanic community has not supported a major daily.

Charles Kilpatrick, publisher and editor of the English-language San Antonio Express News, said there have been plenty of entrepreneurs willing to try. None has succeeded for a long period of time in his city.

"San Antonio Hispanics," Kilpatrick said, "are mostly second and third generation Latins. Many do not read Spanish, although they understand and speak it."

"For a long time, Spanish was not allowed in the schools, and we had these generations of Hispanics who could speak it but couldn't read it or write it," he said. "They can listen to Spanish radio, but they can't read a Spanish newspaper. The language they learned to read was English."

Others theorize that many of those who crossed the border were either illiterate or had very little education. They had never formed the newspaper reading habit in their own country. Struggling for survival, they came to the United States in pursuit of a better life.

However, recent immigrants from Central America who have made Texas and the Southwest their new home have come for political reasons. Many are well read and seek to maintain their culture and ties to their homelands.

La Aurora of Dallas, for instance, was started in 1984 by a Colombian journalist and two Chilean investors who aim their product at the growing South American population in that city.

"Around 1980-82 when I was in Miami, there was already too much competition to start another paper," said Fernando Escobar, publisher and editor of La Aurora. "But in the Dallas-Fort Worth area, the 400,000 Hispanics were being underserved. We knew there was established competition, but there was also a ready market."

La Voz de Houston

In 1979, Cuban refugee Armando Ordonez founded a weekly newspaper to serve the city's Hispanic population. Ordonez, an engineer by training, had done some serious dabbling in the Hispanic media earlier, helping to establish a Spanish-language radio station with a friend from Dallas. He wanted La Voz de Houston to be just that, the voice of the area's Latin population. More than a newspaper, he envisioned a publication that would help fellow Hispanics adjust to life in Texas. The first week's issue sold 5,000 copies.

"He saw the need the Hispanic community had for a newspaper that would serve to bring them a message and become a voice in their own language," said Olga Ordonez, owner and widow of the founder.

La Voz now has an unaudited circulation of about 40,000. She estimates that it has a pass along factor of about four readers, which could increase total readership to 160,000. It has come out every Thursday without interruption since its inception. Most of the sales are at bodegas, supermarkets, and other stores concentrated in predominantly Hispanic neighborhoods. There are "very, very few home deliveries," and these are by mail.

For 40 cents, La Voz's readers get a 16-page broadsheet paper with an eight-page tabloid magazine on entertainment and features.

La Voz's mission has remained the same throughout the years: to educate as well as to inform. "Readers look to us for orientation," Ordonez explained. "They often have nowhere else to turn to."

Most of La Voz's readers are Mexican, but a growing number are Salvadorans and other Central Americans. They are usually over 30, from working-class families. Although they know some English, they find it difficult to read in that language. Most are first-generation immigrants, some quite recent. "The continous influx is a good part of our readership," she said.

But there are also second-and third-generation Hispanics who read La Voz to practice their Spanish and to keep up with Houston's Latin community. These are Hispanics who identify with the paper because they feel their interests are being served, Ordonez said.

As in most small newspapers, individuals on La Voz's staff of 10 do a little bit of everything. Writers take their own pictures and Ordonez herself has covered and written stories for the paper.

Advertising is equally divided between national and local accounts, Ordonez said. National advertisers include cigarette manufacturers, beer companies, and food retailers. Coors beer is a frequent advertiser, often buying full-page announcements. Local advertisers include the traditional supermarkets, car dealerships, restaurants, and furniture stores as well as movie theaters and city-sponsored events. Ads run in both English and Spanish.

For example, all of the City of Houston's advertisements ran in English in the May 29 edition. These were wedged between ads, in Spanish, for a language school, a beauty academy, a chiropractor, and a pet shop. Another ad in the same edition by the Houston Community College System was in English, and one ad, for the U.S. Olympic Festival, was in both Spanish and English. However, the national accounts such as Marlboro cigarettes and Miller beer -- companies large enough to pay for their own translations -- ran their ads in Spanish.

The news is written entirely in Spanish, with a strong emphasis on Hispanic community news. Ordonez promises that readers will find out things about the local community that they cannot get anywhere else. And news of the Houston community at large has a different twist: The paper's stories on local government try to explain how municipal government in America works.

The standard weekly sections include local, Mexican news, "Cronica Roja" (police-blotter stories), Latin American, editorial, sports, and the special entertainment tabloid.

The front page is a blend of local and regional Hispanic news, and stories from Mexico. To a lesser degree, articles from the rest of Latin America receive space on the front page. In the May 29, 1986 edition, the top tease, stripped above the masthead, was about an accident that killed eight people in Mexico. A quarter-page picture displayed the new Miss USA, a Texan. Other stories on that page were about Hispanic astronauts, a fire in downtown Houston, a boycott in Mexico, the Hands Across America fund-raiser, and a Central American treaty signed in Guatemala.

This combination of local and Mexican news is the norm. In the June 12, 1986 edition, for example, the front page was packed with eight stories and one long cutline. All but one of the stories were from Mexico or about Hispanics. The exception was an article, datelined Washington, about the Rogers Commission report on the Challenger disaster, important enough news to warrant front-page play.

Local news takes up about four pages of each issue. Articles generally have a strong community angle. In the July 10, 1986 issue, for example, there were stories about the celebration of Colombia's patriotic day, a show that starred an idolized novela heroine, and the second anniversary of a local bar. Almost an entire page was devoted to the ordination of the new Houston bishop, with three large pictures of the ceremony.

The lead local story of the section on June 26, 1986 -- not counting the announcement of the new bishop on the front page -- was about "the meeting of two cultures," an entertainment event sponsored by the Ecuadorian airline. Other local stories included the anniversary celebration of a local supermarket, the naming of a Hispanic to a bank presidency, and the election of members to a local Hispanic group.

The weekly "Noticias de Mexico" (News from Mexico) page carries highlights of the most important news from that country. All stories are wire reports. The June 26 issue carried stories on the resignation of a cabinet member, a crop-threatening drought, the euphoria over the World Cup, and massive layoffs of oil workers.

Its Latin American page, like the News from Mexico, concentrates on the more important news of the week from that region. The attempt: to get a variety of news from different countries to appeal to the heterogeneous Hispanic community of Dallas. On May 29, for instance, stories with datelines from Nicaragua, Chile, the Dominican Republic, Peru, and Costa Rica appeared.

Sports, on the other hand, is a compilation of pleasant and short news stories about Hispanic sports heroes. Emphasis is placed equally on baseball, soccer, and local sports. If a Hispanic athlete plays on the team, so much the better. A regular feature, "Toques de Bola" (Touches of the Ball), is written by a staff reporter. In the May 29 edition, the column concerned the upcoming All Star game and it concentrated on the Hispanic players. On June 26, the feature was about Hispanic Baseball Players Day. Dodgers pitcher Fernando Valenzuela was pictured accepting an award.

For entertainment news, La Voz provides it readers with a weekly eight-page tabloid of news about their favorite actors and singers. A sampling from the May 22, 1986 tab: Miami Vice star Edward James Olmos' visit to Houston, an upcoming movie by well-known actress Sarita Montiel -- and Michael Jackson advertising Pepsi in Spanish. The tabloid's logo, printed above the masthead, sums it up best: "The latest news, gossip, and pictures of your favorite stars."

La Voz publishes special supplements, inserts of more than 50 pages on patriotic Mexican days and the Fourth of July, Mothers Day, and Christmas. It subscribes to UPI in Spanish.

La Voz's editorial page, as its news pages, is a reflection of the Houston Hispanic community. "We write about Hispanic issues," Ordonez said. "The newspaper supports that which we consider to be beneficial to the Hispanic community, but we also try to be objective. In the editorials we don't attack."

La Voz has editorialized on "general political issues as well as religious themes," she added. It has also endorsed candidates at all levels of government. The paper usually backs the Hispanic, "but only if we believe he is qualified for the job," Ordonez said.

Most of the time the newspaper's editorial page is comprised solely of columns, syndicated by Hispanic Link, which deal with national Hispanic issues.

El Sol de Texas

El Sol de Texas is one of the oldest surviving Spanish-language newspapers in Texas. It was founded in 1966 by Jesus and Sara Gutierrez, a Mexican-Argentine couple. In 1985, the Gutierrezes sold it to Editorial Hispana.

El Sol, which was once a twice-weekly, is now a weekly, published on Wednesdays. Recently the new management began translating editorials into English.

"Most officials here are Anglos," explained Marcos Nelson, former city editor. "Anglos want to know how the Hispanic community thinks and reacts."

The paper's unaudited circulation is 10,000. It is sold for 40 cents in predominantly Hispanic neighborhoods of Dallas, both in small bodegas and some larger Anglo supermarket chains.

The paper is directed at the Mexican population, "specifically the illegal, undocumented workers," Nelson said. He estimates that 85 percent of El Sol readers are in this country illegally. They tend to be young, although some readers are 60 and beyond. For many El Sol is the only newspaper they read.

"The only way they find out about issues that affect them -- immigration and labor -- is by reading our paper. We appeal to those who don't speak English, but at the same time we also have a group who knows English but prefers Spanish," Nelson said.

Of El Sol's 18 employees, four work on the editorial side. The circulation department also has four employees. In addition, the newspaper uses what management calls "intercambio," an exchange system with local photographers. Photographers cover an event and provide pictures in return for free ad space.

The advertising, as expected, is predominantly local. Announcements for immigration lawyers dominate. But national companies, such as beer and cigarette manufacturers, and regional government agencies also advertise. El Sol also sells the two "ears" at either side of its front-page masthead to local advertisers. They are usually bought by local Hispanic restaurants. Occasionally, one of the ears of the Section B masthead will also be sold. In the April 16, 1986 edition, for instance, that spot was taken by two lawyers specializing in labor and immigration law. One had a Hispanic surname.

In the same edition, the 10-page Section A had 28 ads, the larger ones -- quarter page and above -- were bought by local businesses. The back page was devoted to an upcoming concert sponsored by a local Spanish-language radio station. Supermarkets, banks, and clothing stores also advertised. One quarter page ad was for Miller beer.

Among the more frequent national and regional advertisers are Coors, Miller, Marlboro, and government agencies such as rapid transit, the local community college, and telephone and electric companies, Nelson said.

Although most of the advertising is local, El Sol emphasizes Mexican news, using two pages (usually facing pages) devoted exclusively to news from the homeland of so many of its readers. Regular weekly sections also include International, Sports, and Culture and Entertainment news. Even in these sections, the flavor is strongly Mexican.

Stories about immigration are the favorite of readers. When the paper did a series on immigration and the sanctuary movement "we got a lot of feedback," Nelson said.

The front page often uses full color. Teasers are in yellow, the masthead in blue. There are always four teasers to lure the reader inside -- to Mexican news, Latin America, National, and Sports. Again the emphasis is on news from south of the border. That is not to say, however, that national or international news of importance will be relegated somewhere else. On April 16, 1986, for example, the lead story was a follow up on the U.S. attack on Libya. A sidebar was about a speech by President Reagan. Of the remaining four stories, three were from Mexico and one was from Miami. The latter was a wire report about the increase of armed children in Miami schools.

Inside, at least two pages are devoted to local news. Occasionally one page will carry news from Fort Worth. On June 11, 1986, local stories included small features on a new Hispanic model, a protest against abortion at a local hospital, help for Hispanic children who do not speak English, the appointment of new lawyers at the Mexican consulate, and the results of a statewide test for public-school teachers.

The Fort Worth page of June 4, 1986, is as strongly community oriented. One story concerned the exemplary participation of the community in the May Fest celebration, the other was about an exhibit at a local museum. There also was a picture of a graduating class in the Japanese Gardens of Fort Worth.

Police News also takes up two pages, and includes crime news from around the country and Mexico. There is a weekly feature titled "Crime of the Week." It has, in the past, covered hit-and-run accidents, robberies, assaults, and murders. It always lists the Crime Stoppers phone number, encouraging readers to phone in tips or information.

Section A also carries "Sociales" (Social Page) and a national page. "Sociales" runs not only the traditional pictures of birthdays, graduations and weddings, but stories and columns aimed at female readers. In the June 18, 1986 issue, for example, there was a column about "a woman's place" and how to find it. In another issue, June 4, 1986, the column dealt with peer pressure and how women are often influenced by third parties.

The National Page, on the other hand, offers up a smorgasbord of hard news from around the country. A June 18, 1986 sampling: a Supreme Court decision in favor of abortion, a protest in New York against South Africa's apartheid policy, a possible Reagan-Gorbachev meeting, a prediction of a rise in AIDS cases, and a report about the increasing number of bank failures.

The first page of Section B usually carries hard news from the wire services. The emphasis is on Mexican news for the first page and Latin American stories inside. These pages, said Nelson, might be the best read in the paper.

Entertainment and Sports make up the last three to four pages of the section. The entertainment section is perhaps the least Hispanicized section of the paper, carrying articles and a regular gossip column about Hollywood and U.S. stars. Of course, stories about Julio Iglesias and other famous and less-known Hispanic artists are standard fare.

In Sports, "soccer is better than baseball," according to Nelson. So the sports pages are full of news about soccer matches and players, particularly from Mexico and the rest of Latin America. Boxing also remains a favorite among readers, particularly stories about Latin champions. On April 16, 1986, for example, of the six stories in the two pages of sports, three were about boxing and the rest about soccer.

El Sol obtains most of its news through wire services. It subscribes to EFE, Notimex, and, for features, it receives Washington-based Hispanic Link and ALA. Some stories, Nelson said, are also translated in part from the English-language newspapers, particularly the Dallas Times Herald and the Dallas Morning News.

Editorials comprise one page every week, usually the third page of Section A. Editorials concentrate on local issues. About 25 percent could be considered Hispanic-only issues, Nelson said. The rest are general themes of interest to the community at large.

Syndicated columnists also deal with a variety of topics, from drug abuse to the clash of the two cultures. A standard weekly feature titled "Un Mensaje a la Conciencia" (A Message for the Conscience) is written by "Brother Paul" and sometimes takes the form of a parable or an entertaining story to carry a message of the Christian way of life.

Nelson selects topics and writes the editorials. In a June 4, 1986 editorial, he said that a local school board member had almost pushed the board into a racial and ethnic battleground. It urged him to meet with a local group of Hispanics, the Hispanic Coalition. "Together they must come up with an agenda of items that concern the Hispanic community..." the editorial said.

In another editorial, on June 11, 1986, El Sol talked about Hispanics' growing political power after two Latin candidates won a local election runoff. "Make your vote count," it concluded.

Nelson is optimistic about El Sol's future. "We will definitely grow because immigration continues," he said. "At the same time Hispanics are maintaining their cultural ties. It's very promising."

La Aurora

This Dallas-Fort Worth weekly was founded July 17, 1984 by a Colombian journalist and two Chilean investors. "I looked at the cities that were Hispanic markets and looked at the numbers (of Hispanics)," said Fernando Escobar, editor and founder of La Aurora. "There were plenty of big ones but not one was like Dallas."

In this Texas town, Escobar and investors Jose Palomo and Jorge Arellano sold 5,000 copies of the paper's first issue. Now La Aurora publishes 25,000 copies. About 80 percent are sold for 25 cents at bodegas, supermarkets, 7-Elevens -- "anywhere there are Hispanics," Escobar said. About 1,200 are home subscriptions and another 800 are sent by plane to San Antonio. The rest are given away.

The paper, published every Tuesday, has 16 to 18 broadsheet pages. Special editions include more -- 24 to 28 pages. At least three special editions appear each year -- on the Mexican patriotic days of May 5 and September 16, and on Christmas. In 1985, special issues marked the Fourth of July as well as the paper's first anniversary. In 1986, La Aurora published a special section for the 150th anniversary of Texas. Each special edition included articles on historical events, features, and columns.

La Aurora employs 18 people, five of whom are on the editorial side.

The paper's slogan is "Educar es Redimir" (To Educate is to Redeem). "We're doing it in the South American style, very educational, with the emphasis on information and teaching," Escobar said.

Escobar estimates that about 70 percent of La Aurora's readers are Mexican; the rest are South American. There are probably more men, since immigrants tend to come over alone and then send for their families after settling into a new life. Both Mexicans and South Americans, though they come to this country for different reasons, seek information about the new land as well as a bridge to their own culture. Most readers probably do not read English and La Aurora may be their only source of written information.

To conduct a survey of reader preferences, La Aurora employees distributed newspapers at a local soccer field. Most read the sports page first, followed by entertainment and the editorials, Escobar said. (Perhaps it is not surprising that people gathered for a soccer match would turn first to the sports page.)

Advertising is predominantly local. According to Escobar, about 15 percent are national advertisers. Advertisers range from restaurants to lawyers, trade schools to medical services, supermarkets to radio stations.

"It is mainly Hispanic businesses. They also tend to buy the smaller ads, but they buy. The larger ads are for the Anglo businesses," Escobar said.

In the 16-page August 6, 1986 edition, for example, more than 90 percent of the ads were for Hispanic businesses. But there also were ads for 7-Eleven, Fayva, the City of Dallas Fair Housing Office, and Dallas County Community College.

On the editorial side, La Aurora offers its readers a little bit of everything. One page per week is devoted to Dallas news, another to Fort Worth. Other regular weekly pages include editorial, national, international (with emphasis on Latin America), entertainment, women's news, and children.

In every issue there are two pages of sports and two pages in which science and education alternate. Specialized columns -- on Social Security, consumer issues, and "Mundo Curioso" (round up of human interest and unusual events) -- are very popular with readers.

La Aurora also runs short features on local Hispanic merchants who advertise in its pages.

But the emphasis is clearly on Mexican and Latin American news with a generous dose of local and regional stories. Three of the six stories on the front page of the August 6, 1986 edition were about Mexico, including the two lead stories: U.S. economic aid to Mexico and hazy Reagan Administration threats to close the Mexican border. The stories not about Mexico dealt with Chile, the OPEC meeting, a national campaign against drugs, and a possible strike by U.S. actors.

Inside, the local page is strongly community oriented. Stories about local presentations at the library and city parks often appear. In the July 30, 1986 edition, the top local story was about Reagan's declarations in Dallas. The three other stories dealt with a photographic exhibit on display in the public library, protests over the increase in telephone fees, and in-fighting among Dallas city-council members.

The International News Page is actually devoted to Latin American news. La Aurora readers can find the most important news of the week from anywhere in the Southern Hemisphere. An August 6, 1986 sampling: Ten brief stories (no more than five paragraphs each) from Bogota, Brasilia, Guatemala, Lima, Panama, Managua, Asuncion, and La Paz.

The entertainment page carries the traditional horoscope, crossword puzzles, "Chistes de la Semana" (Jokes of the Week) and other reader games. The Women's Page -- "Femeninas" (Feminine) -- contains features on fashions, hair, and food. The traditional Social Page appears occasionally to chronicle (with photographs) the baptisms, birthdays, graduations, and weddings of the Hispanic community.

The stories in the alternating Scientific and Education pages, like the others, are mostly taken from the wires. The stories prove to be compelling reading. Again, from the August 6 issue, were articles about estrogen's effects on heart attacks, the mysterious disappearance of a ship, a column about quitting smoking, and news about AIDS.

Sports, like the news pages, carries a strong Mexican angle. Soccer reigns supreme and there is little, if any, coverage of local or Texas professional teams. In the July 30, 1986 edition, for example, with baseball season well underway, two of the four full stories were about soccer, a third about boxing, and the last on cycling. "Capsulas Deportivas" (Sports Capsules), a round-up of sports items, also emphasizes soccer.

Escobar estimates that more than 65 percent of the copy comes directly from the wires. About 15 percent is locally written. The rest is information provided by organizations and printed verbatim. La Aurora uses EFE and UPI in Spanish.

Columns for its editorial pages are also supplied by EFE, although La Aurora has its own columnists in Miami, Los Angeles, and Hollywood. Jorge Arellano, president of the company and one of the Chilean investors, writes "El rincon de Jorge" (George's corner). Columnists' themes are varied, from authoritarian regimes in Argentina to the stigma of being Colombian in a world that suspects all Colombians of being drug dealers.

Editorials are not translated into English. An editorial board comprised of the owners decides the topic each week and Escobar writes the piece. About 70 percent are on international politics, with the rest on domestic issues that affect Hispanics, such as immigration.

"We have a conservative tendency without being a party paper," Escobar said. "We are conservative in the sense that we are friends of democracy and enemies of dictatorships. We criticize what happens in Cuba, Nicaragua, Chile."

The paper refuses to endorse candidates at any level of government. "That is something we agreed upon from the very beginning. We are a young newspaper. If we take sides, we may debilitate ourselves before getting strong," Escobar said.

La Aurora's management planned to turn a profit by the latter part of 1986 "with a lot of sacrifices," according to Escobar. The paper's ultimate goal is to become the first statewide Hispanic paper in Texas. La Aurora already has opened a small office in Fort Worth. In 1986, it had plans to do the same in San Antonio, Houston, and Austin.

II. Spanish-Language Television

Television is an integral part of the Hispanic culture in the United States. As is true in English-language households in the United States, television is by far the most popular medium of all time.

According to a Strategy Research Corporation report, more than two-thirds of all U.S Hispanics interviewed said they had watched Spanish-language television on the day before they were interviewed. Compare this to 47 percent who had listened to Spanish-language radio and 21.5 percent who had read Spanish-language newspapers. Television was most popular in New York, where 76.8 percent stated they viewed Spanish TV. It was least popular in Texas and Southwestern markets, which also recorded the lowest level of listenership for Spanish radio and readership for Spanish newspapers.

Viewers spent an average of about two and one half hours per day watching Spanish television. According to the Strategy Research 1984 report, U.S. Hispanics between 18 and 34 watched about the same, on average, as those between 35 and 40. Hispanics' faithful television viewing may be due partly to the pervasiveness of the medium. The average number of TV sets per Hispanic household is 1.91, and at least 24 percent of households have cable television, the Strategy Research report said.

Unlike newspapers and radio stations, most of the fare on Spanish-language television is not tailored for a particular audience. The Mexican-American usually sees the same soap opera in Los Angeles as the Puerto Rican in New York and the Cuban-American in Miami. Such programs often contain regional dialects that may sound foreign to some U.S. Hispanics. There may also be references to little-known cities in the country where the show was produced. But executives believe this is a small price to pay. Audiences put up with the occasional unfamiliarity to watch shows that are in their native tongue and more sympathetic to Hispanic values and mores.

Although the overwhelming majority of the programs aired on Spanish television are imported, most stations have their own news programs and talk shows. A few have also produced weekly variety shows and specials on topics of interest to their communities.

Novelas (soap operas) are the bread and butter of Spanish televison, drawing the largest audience of any format. Soaps are scheduled both during the daytime, for the largely female audience, and during prime time. Unlike their English-language counterparts which can continue for years, these novelas have between 120 and 160 installments and are completed in four or five months.

For those stations that have ventured into production, the rewards are many. Univision-affiliate WLTV-Channel 23 in Miami began producing a three-hour, weekly game/interview show in April 1986. The station persisted despite the high cost -- $20,000 per show -- and the uncharted territory -- a staff that had never worked in production of this type. By late 1986, "Sabado Gigante" (Giant Saturday) was the station's top-rated show, reaching 70 percent of Miami's Hispanic population, according to Channel 23 executives. It was expected to be syndicated in 1987.

Other stations have done well by offering an alternative to the novelas. KVEA-Channel 52 in Los Angeles offers Spanish-language movies (and a few dubbed from English) to its viewers. During a May 1986 showing of a Mexican movie hit, KVEA garnered 65 percent of Hispanic viewers. Likewise, WNJU-Channel 47 in New York offers mini-series and variety shows along with novelas -- a blend that beats the competition.

But for all its monetary and rating successes, Hispanic television is at a crossroads. 1986 proved to be a year of problems and promises. Univision -- formerly SIN -- dominated the airwaves but it also encountered unprecedented mishaps and changes. With the sale of its principal affiliates -- the SICC stations -- Univision faces what will be perhaps the toughest battle of its 25-year history.

The New York-based network is owned by Televisa of Mexico, which, in turn, is controlled by the wealthy Azcarraga family of Mexico. Televisa's move in late 1986 to take over Univision's news show has raised concerns in journalism circles. Televisa's jockeying, critics said, cast a shadow over the integrity and professionalism of the U.S. newscasts.

Televisa's takeover of the then-SIN "Noticiero" (News Show), which reaches 6 to 10 million people, has had a ripple effect. When vice president and news director Gustavo Godoy was fired in the fall of 1986, a mass resignation of the network's journalists ensued. More than 15 key employees walked out to protest the Mexican government's influence over the news show and Godoy's firing.

But Univision rebounded. Its news division, ECO, is led by former UPI chief Luis Nogales. ECO continued to produce the nightly news show and planned to sell news programming to national and international subscribers. In addition, Univision began the first weekend Spanish-language news show, produced in Miami, and the first late night national news show, from Los Angeles.

Still uncertain, however, is the future relationship between the SICC stations and Univision. If the sale of the SICC stations is approved by the Federal Communications Commission (FCC) as expected, new owners Hallmark and First Chicago Venture have agreed to continue buying programming from Univision for two years. Univision, however, will not continue to be the station's national sales representative.

"At this point in time we cannot say who will be or what will happen," said Charles Hucker, Hallmark vice president of public affairs and communications, in January 1987. "The future course hasn't been determined."

This could mean that Hallmark will represent the stations itself or hire a large advertising representative. It could also mean that after two years Hallmark and First Chicago Venture might also try their hands at Spanish-language television programming.

At the same time, the new kid on the block, Telemundo, has challenged Univision on turf the latter network long dominated. Telemundo has a nightly newscast that goes head-to-head with Univision's. The network is owned by Reliance Capital Group, with stations in the three top U.S. Hispanic markets -- Los Angeles, New York, and Miami -- where Univision affiliates also exist. It also has a station in San Juan, Puerto Rico.

Telemundo buys its newscast from Hispanic American Broadcasting Corporation, formed by disgruntled employees who left Univision. Godoy serves as president of Miami-based HBC, which planned bureaus in California, Texas, Washington, D.C., New York, and Mexico City.

Although Reliance sold some of its English-language radio and television stations, it kept the Spanish-language outlets. This is a strong indicator of Reliance's faith in the Spanish-language market.

Henry R. Silverman, president of Reliance Capital, has said publicly that the stations will have common ad sales representation as well as joint programming. WCIU-TV in Chicago is expected to join the four other stations.

"We believe that Spanish-language television is the fastest-growing segment of the television industry," Silverman said, "and we are committed to serving it with high-quality programming."

Univision (formerly SIN Television Network)

This television network aimed at Hispanic viewers was founded in 1960 by the Azcarragas, one of Mexico's wealthiest families. In addition to Univision, the Azcarragas own almost 60 percent of a huge Mexican broadcasting company called Televisa and, through Televisa, have controlling interest in four television stations, five radio stations, Mexico City's only cable system, and several production facilities.

About a year after Univision's founding, KWEX-TV, Channel 41 in San Antonio, became the first station to affiliate with the network. The first Univision affiliate to turn a profit was KMEX, Channel 34 in Los Angeles.

For two decades Univision climbed the heights to virtual domination of Spanish-language television broadcasting in the United States. By 1970 it became the first U.S. network to offer live coverage of the World Cup Soccer Championship, a big hit among U.S. Hispanics. It also launched GALAVision, the first Spanish-language pay television service in the United States and, a year later, made its debut into the low-power television station market with an affiliate in Denver.

Univision nows offers programming 24 hours per day, seven days per week, including the first evening network news program in Spanish in the United States. Its ECO news operation began producing the nation's first weekend Spanish-network news show, based in Miami, and the first late-night national Spanish news show, from Los Angeles. This one-hour evening show features sports, entertainment, and human interest segments. It replaced a Mexican newscast "24 Horas" (24 Hours), that many Univision affiliates carried.

Clearly, this is evidence of Univision's increasing interest in U.S.-based productions for the U.S. Hispanic market. However, aside from its news programs, most of its programming is imported from Mexico and other countries in Latin America. Univision executives say the network can reach more than 80 percent of the Hispanic residents in the United States.

As of this writing, the network had more than 405 affiliates, including 12 UHF outlets in major cities and 14 low-power outlets. It changed its name from SIN to Univision in January 1987. The jewels in its crown are stations once owned by the Spanish International Communications Corporation (SICC), including those in such major markets as New York, Los Angeles, and Miami. However, SICC was sold in late 1986 (see next section), raising questions about the future of both the network and the station chain so vital to Univision.

Rene Anselmo, a Massachusetts-born businessman with ties to the Azcarraga family, at one point owned 25 percent of Univision, along with about the same percentage of the SICC stations. He also served as president of both companies. In 1986, he resigned those posts and sold his shares of Univision to Televisa, which already owned 75 percent of the network. Emilio Azcarraga took over as president of Univision.

Although Univision long dominated the Spanish-language market, that is likely to change. Hallmark and First Chicago Ventures, new owners of the

SICC stations, agreed to buy programming from Univision for two years after the sale. However, Univision will not be the stations' national sales representative, a lucrative position. And Hallmark officials are not saying what the company will do about programming after two years.

The bulk of Univision programming is purchased from producers in Mexico, but Venezuela, Puerto Rico, Spain, Argentina, and other countries are quickly focusing on the profitable television production market. Because of its rapid growth, Univision has become the most important outlet for programs produced in Latin America.

Soaps are the most popular programs Univision provides its affiliates. In the spring of 1986, for example, there were 11 different novelas programmed by the network. Six of those were from Mexico, two from Venezuela, and one each from Brazil, Puerto Rico, and Spain.

According to Rosita Peru, who heads the network's programming division, the Mexican novelas are the most popular because of the large number of Mexican-Americans in this country. Yet, Peru said she must also find novelas that will appeal to all of the nationalities that make up the polyglot Hispanic population in the United States.

"I must be particularly careful in picking novelas because the tastes and reactions of the viewers on the East and West Coasts are so different," Peru told Broadcast Daily.

Soaps, by no means, are the only staple of Univision's menu. In 1986, one of the network's biggest events was its coverage of the World Cup in Mexico. With the exclusive rights to the games for Spanish-language television in the United States, it was able to televise two live and one taped games per day.

Univision also offers specials, mini series, comedy, musical, and variety shows. In early 1986, Univision aired an eight part-miniseries in prime time, "Teresa de Jesus" (Teresa of Jesus), which traced the life of the Carmelite nun who resisted the Spanish Inquisition. The series was filmed at 150 different locations.

Another series Univision purchased was a six-parter, "Estamos Unidos" (We are Together). The first installment was shot in Miami and included appearances by Julio Iglesias and Bo Derek. A third special -- this one produced by Univision itself -- was the coverage of the Statue of Liberty festivities during the July 4, 1986 weekend.

For its predominantly female audience, Univision has broadcast specials on Latin fashion designers Oscar de la Renta and Adolfo, and carried the annual International OTI Song Festival in November.

But not all programming originates in Latin countries. Univision has aired "Follow Me," a series of educational programs designed to teach English, and produced by the BBC. "El Sumaurai Fugitivo" (The Fugitive Samurai) was a Japanese-produced two-hour weekly series on the adventures of a samurai warrior. The program was dubbed into Spanish in Peru.

Until 1987, before the addition of the late night newscast and the weekend news show, the only two shows produced by Univision were the national evening newscast and a morning talk/variety show. In late 1986, Univision announced that its five-year-old half-hour "Noticiero" would be absorbed by a new agency, ECO, headed by a Mexican newsman. ECO is owned by an investors group headed by Emilio Azcarraga, who planned to move to New York at the time of this writing. "Noticiero," based in Miami, ran weekdays in the 6:30 p.m. slot. The new show took over the same time slot, and most of the staff was absorbed.

Originally, the news agency, ECO, was scheduled to be headed by Jacobo Zabludovsky, who anchored and directed the nightly news show for the Azcarragas' Televisa for 16 years.

Zabludovsky's Mexican news show, "24 Hours," is the primary nightly news show on Mexican TV. Some SIN affiliates in the United States carried it before Univision produced its own late night newscast. But when critics began complaining about Zabludovsky's objectivity, the Mexican newsman did not take the job. Instead, Univision hired former UPI chairman Luis Nogales to head ECO.

Zabludovsky's initial appointment, however, resulted in some staff shakeups in the news division. Gustavo Godoy, who served as "Noticiero's" news director for five years, was asked to resign by Univision executives in October 1986. What followed was a mass resignation by producers, journalists, and technicians who said they objected to Zabludovsky's journalistic ethics. This group formed Hispanic American Broadcasting Corporation, which sells its news program to Univision's competing network, Telemundo.

In 1986, before ECO took over, "Noticiero" had bureaus in New York, El Salvador, London, Puerto Rico, Argentina, and Jerusalem plus stringers in other countries. "Noticiero" provided extensive coverage of Latin America, including exit polls in Latin American elections.

"We cover Latin America like no other news media," boasted Godoy before his resignation. "We cover it like a day-to-day beat."

"Noticiero" also covered national news, concentrating on reports that would affect Latins in the United States directly. Its information programming went beyond the nightly newscast as well. It broadcast five news updates during the day and night. During the contra-aid-package discussion in Congress, for example, "Noticiero" provided special reports throughout its programming.

"Noticiero" reached at least 4 million Hispanics in the United States in 1986. Stations in Argentina, the Dominican Republic, Honduras, Guatemala, Costa Rica, Peru, Bolivia, and El Salvador also carry "Noticiero," for a total of 6 to 10 million viewers.

"A common language unites us, but terminology differs from nationality to nationality," Godoy said. "We have to be conscious of using a very universal Spanish."

With the creation of ECO, Univision expanded its news coverage. It opened national news bureaus in Los Angeles and San Antonio. It planned international bureaus in Mexico City, Madrid, and the Middle East. And it expected to sell its product to other subscribers.

The network's two-and-a-half hour morning variety talk show, "Mundo Latino" (Latin World), premiered in January 1986. Much like the morning shows on English-language stations, it features news and weather, interviews, exercise classes, travel tips, and cooking segments. It transmits live from Miami and Los Angeles, and includes live reports via satellite from New York, Washington, and Mexico.

In 1985, Univision -- then SIN -- took in $55 million in ad revenues, according to published reports.

Spanish International Communication Corporation (SICC)

Spanish International Communication Corporation's first station went on the air in San Antonio in 1961 as an affiliate of the then-SIN Television Network. In addition to KWEX in San Antonio, SICC later became the licensee for four other UHF stations: WXTV in Paterson, N.J.; KMEX in Los Angeles; WLTV in Miami; and KFTV in Fresno, California. It also owns low-power stations in Philadelphia, Denver, Bakersfield (California), Hartford, and Austin. More than 50 percent of the Hispanic population lives in areas served by these stations.

Until early 1986 Rene Anselmo, a U.S. businessman, served as president of the company and president of Univision Television Network. He owned 25 percent of SICC and 25 percent of Univision. The powerful Azcarraga family of Mexico owned another 20 percent of SICC, the maximum a foreigner is allowed to own according to U.S. law.

Anselmo resigned from both posts in 1986 and sold his 25 percent of Univision to the network. Emilio Nicolas, who heads the SICC station in San Antonio, took over as president of the chain. Several months after Anselmo's resignation, Hallmark Cards and First Chicago Venture Capital bought SICC's 10 stations for $301.5 million. Each of the companies was buying 50 percent of SICC, putting up $75 million in cash jointly, and borrowing the rest. The sale was pending approval from the FCC in early 1987.

Hallmark, the world's largest manufacturer of greeting cards, and the Chicago company said that they would keep the Spanish-language format of the stations for the two years required by the sales contract. Executives of both companies went even further, stating they had a "long-term commitment to the Spanish-language format of the stations." Management of each of the stations was expected to stay the same.

If the Hallmark and First Chicago Venture sales go through, Univision is expected to continue supplying programming for two years. Univision will not, however, remain as the station's national sales representative, Hallmark officials said in January 1987.

Both Anselmo's resignation and the sale of the SICC stations was the culmination of an FCC ruling and years of haggling in a dissident shareholders' suit. In 1980 a group called the Spanish Radio Broadcasters Association, an organization of radio-station owners, complained to the FCC that the Azcarraga family's backing provided an unfair advantage that made their own stations less competitive because they didn't have similar foreign financial help. The FCC's Mass Media Bureau investigated the complaint under Section 310 (b) of the Communications Act, which prohibits aliens or their representatives from controlling broadcast or common-carriers licenses or from owning more than 20 percent of a licensee.

Although the Azcarragas owned 20 percent of SICC, within the legal limits, an administrative law judge concluded that Anselmo was acting as a representative of the Azcarragas' interests. The FCC agreed to drop its opposition to SICC's request for license renewals if it sold its stations.

In a separate suit, minority shareholders had also accused Anselmo, SIN (now Univision), and Televisa of fraudulently using the stations for their own purposes instead of the good of the shareholders. In 1983, the SICC countersued. The shareholder lawsuit focused primarily on Anselmo's dual role as president and part owner of both companies.

All allegations and suits were expected to be settled by the sale of the SICC stations. However, several groups had protested the sale of the stations at the time of this writing. Thirteen U.S. Congressmen introduced a bill to short-circuit the Hallmark deal. They wanted the FCC to invoke a "minority distress-sale policy," so the stations could be sold at 75 percent of their fair market value to a minority purchaser. A disgruntled group of rival bidders also charged that the Hallmark-SICC bidding process was tainted by collusion between both groups. The accusing company, TVL, challenged the sale in federal court. Hallmark has denied the charges.

Five community groups in Los Angeles also challenged the sale because they felt there was no long-term guarantee by Hallmark to retain the Spanish-language formats. The bill died, but other complaints remained unresolved in late 1986.

In the fall of 1986, the FCC's Review Board renewed the licenses of SICC's stations for the purpose of transferring them to a new owner. However, FCC officials said this decision did not directly affect the Hallmark purchase, which will be reviewed separately.

Rick Sowa, assistant general manager of KWEX-Channel 41 in San Antonio, said he expected the sale to go without a hitch. Employees at SICC stations had been told the new owner would not change the station's programming or operations significantly.

Management also expects the SICC stations to continue buying about 80 percent of their programming from Univision while maintaining their editorial independence.

In early 1987, Univision still served as the advertising representative for the SICC stations on both the local and national level. In 1985, SICC stations earned $65 million in ad revenues, according to published reports.

Telemundo

Telemundo Group Inc. became the nation's second Spanish-lanaguge television network -- and the only U.S. owned -- when it aired its first broadcast in January 1987. Formed the year before by New York-based Reliance Capital Group LP, Telemundo has stations in the top three U.S. Hispanic markets. It has an interest in KVEA-Channel 52 in Los Angeles, and owns WSCV-Channel 51 in Miami/Fort Lauderdale and WNJU-Channel 47 in New York. It also owns WKAQ-Channel 2 in San Juan.

Reliance purchased WNJU for $70 million in late 1986 and officials said they expected to acquire other stations.

Its first national broadcast was the half-hour "Noticiero Telemundo" weeknights at 6:30. It goes head to head with Univision's national newscast. "Noticiero Telemundo" (Telemundo News Show) is produced by the Hispanic American Broadcasting Network.

Reliance officials, however, said the newscasts would not be the only domestically produced shows the new network would try to offer.

"Our plans call for greatly increasing our number of broadcast hours and eventually airing our own domestically produced programs, which will be specifically targeted for the U.S. Hispanic community," said president Henry Silverman.

Two of the Telemundo stations are profiled here:

WNJU-Channel 47

WNJU has been airing Spanish programming since 1966. In late 1986, Reliance bought the station from Norman Lear, Jerry Perenchio, and Bud Yorkin for $70 million. WNJU is the top-rated Spanish-language station in the New York market. According to a Spring 1986 report, WNJU reached 144,000 homes Monday through Friday from noon to 12:30, one of the highest rated periods. A 9 p.m. novela garnered 382,000 homes, as did a 7 p.m. novela.

Almost half of the station's audience is Puerto Rican, according to Carlos Barba, president and general manager under the Lear-Perenchio venture. About 15 percent come from the Dominican Republic, 10 percent from Cuba, and the rest from around Latin America. Because such a large percentage of its viewers come directly from the Caribbean, "We concentrate on programming that would appeal to them," Barba said.

Barba attributes the station's success to its counterprogramming policy. Since so much of Univision-affiliated station programming is novelas, much of it from Mexico, Barba tries to use more movies, mini-series, and variety shows. Of course, novelas are still a staple -- 50 percent of the programming.

About 80 percent of WNJU's programming is in Spanish, and the rest is sold to groups who broadcast in languages such as Japanese and Greek. The latter programming is done in the very early morning and weekend slots, when the Spanish-speaking audience is light.

"The intent of our programming is to create habit," Barba said. "Tele-novelas are still the most popular shows, but viewers are also hooked on the musical variety, the public service shows."

Summer 1986 programming, for instance, included a lively and colorful half-hour cooking show at 11:30 a.m. Hosted by a husband-and-wife team, it was appropriately titled "Friendo y Comiendo" (Frying and Eating). The sample recipes included both Caribbean and continental dishes, and Hispanic stars introduced their favorite recipes and offered tips on food preparation.

The noon show -- a musical variety program -- brought to the screen interviews of and performances by some of the best from the Latin entertainment world. The 1-4 p.m. slot was devoted exclusively to soap operas, produced in Venezuela and Puerto Rico. A one-hour musical "The Every Day Show" was wedged into the 4 p.m. slot but soap operas continued until 9 p.m., with two-minute news bulletin updates every hour.

Musical programming takes up the rest of weekday night programming, save for the half-hour news show at 11 p.m. and a 10 p.m. soap. Late night and weekend programming did not include any soap operas. All are sports, talk shows, musical variety, comedy shows, movies, and action/thriller series.

As expected, many of the shows are produced in Caribbean countries. For example, the 5 p.m. Saturday talk show is produced in Santo Domingo, a half-hour comedy series at 8 p.m. comes from Puerto Rico, and the 8:30 p.m. slot also goes to Puerto Rico's top comedy show.

There is, of course, the station's share of American-produced shows dubbed in Spanish. The 3 p.m. Saturday show, "Mr. Solo," is an action series starring Robert Vaughn as a secret agent. The 8 p.m. Sunday movie shows American, Canadian, British, and Australian films.

The station's locally produced news show, "Informador 47" (The Informer), airs Monday through Friday from 11-11:30 p.m. It is supplemented with two-minute news-bulletin updates every hour in the afternoon and evening.

The emphasis of "Informador 47" is on local news, although reports from Latin America, particularly the Caribbean, are also aired prominently. WNJU employs 12 reporters and camera people on its news staff. The total staff numbers 92. It supplements its own reporting with AP and a business wire. According to a Spring 1986 rating, 93,000 homes tuned to the news.

WNJU airs editorials, but not frequently. "We try to provide orientation, to resolve problems, and to suggest solutions," Barba said. Themes include education, housing, immigration, and other social issues.

Like other Spanish-language media, WNJU promotes itself with public-service programming and community activities. In October 1985, for example, WNJU sponsored a telethon "Nosotros con Puerto Rico" (We With Puerto Rico) for victims of a mudslide. The station raised more than $1 million.

About 60 percent of WNJU's advertisers are national accounts, Barba said.

"The idea is for companies to buy Spanish-language advertising, not as part of their national accounts but as part of their international budget," Barba said. "If you're investing $10 or $15 million in Venezuela, why not use part of that money here? If I have been shaving with Gillette before coming here, I'll continue doing so here too."

KVEA-Channel 52

KVEA signed on in November 1985, the brainchild of Joe Wallach, a former network executive in Brazil for 15 years. The station is owned by Reliance Capital Group, SFN Company, and Wallach, who also serves as general manager.

"The number of Hispanics in Los Angeles is enormous," said Frank Cruz, who left his post as an anchor in the city's NBC affiliate to join the new station as vice president. "Four million is a conservative number, yet there was only one station (an Univision affiliate) serving this entire community. Mr. Wallach asked: 'Why not another one?'"

In the February 1986 Arbitron ratings, KVEA had 37 percent of the total Spanish-language TV audience on Monday through Friday from 8-11 p.m., compared to rival KMEX's 63 percent. KVEA scored high with male viewers -- 58 percent of the TV market.

Cruz attributes this success to its movie programming during prime time and throughout the rest of the day. For example, on May 20, 1986, when the station ran a Mexican blockbuster adventure, KVEA garnered 65 percent of the Spanish-language viewers.

"Our viewers," said Cruz, "want to see something other than novelas. We have our own novelas, of course, but they want to watch something that will finish in one night."

The station broadcasts 14 hours per day, until midnight. It offers more than five hours of movies weekdays and even more on weekends. Most of the movies are American-made, but others are from France, Spain, Italy, South America, and Mexico. A sampling of June feature films: "Hour of Hell" with Richard Harrison, "Days of Fury" with Vincent Price, "Mutiny on the Bounty" with Marlon Brando, and "Singing in the Rain" with Gene Kelly. There were, of course, movies produced in Spanish as well.

KVEA begins programming at 10 a.m. with a one-hour musical show Monday through Friday. A half-hour novela, a cooking program, and an astrology show are also in the morning lineup. The first novela of the afternoon starts at 1 p.m. At 2 p.m. the station runs movies until its 5:30 p.m. news show. The soaps run from 6 to 9 p.m., with a movie fitted into the 9-11 p.m. slot, before the second weekday news show. The final slot, at 11:30 p.m. hosts a novela. On weekends, there are action series, cartoons, comedy and variety shows, as well as religious, public service, and sports programming.

The two half-hour news programs are supplemented with three breaks for headline news in the evening. Cruz said the newscasts do not concentrate on one particular type of news.

"They're action packed, much like the format of an 11 p.m. newscast in the English-language station," he added. "Whatever is the breaking story of the day will lead. It could be local and it could be international."

The station has three reporters and four camera crews. It subscribes to AP and UPI in both Spanish and English. KVEA also has an international satellite feed of news from Mexico, Imevision. Of the 105 station employees, between 30 and 40 work on the editorial side.

KVEA has a three-member editorial board that decides which issues to address and stands to take. Cruz writes the editorials which have dealt with subjects such as English-only bills, bilingual education, and immigration.

"We feel that there are quite a few issues of importance to Hispanics and that it is our duty to talk about them," Cruz said.

During the week of July 1, 1986, the station aired an editorial that was received warmly by its audience. "We feel that Gov. George Deukmejian overlooked the Hispanic community when he elected a Russian and Armenian immigrant to represent our state at the July 4th Centennial Ceremony of the Statue of Liberty in New York," Cruz wrote.

About 65 percent of the station's advertising accounts are local companies, from doctors to car dealerships to supermarkets, Cruz said. "Our selling point in this market is that we offer a different product. They do this, we do that. They have soaps, we have movies. They have women, we have men," he added.

III. Spanish-Language Radio

Like television, radio is also dependent on material that is primarily produced for audiences outside the United States. However, it does more domestically produced talk, news, and entertainment programs than television. It gives recent arrivals and long-time immigrants not only information in their own language but the music of their homelands as well. The sounds prove to be sweet to both listeners and station owners. Radio stations are generally quite profitable. And their numbers are growing, particularly in the larger, more affluent Hispanic cities.

The increased competition is forcing some old-timers to change their formats or to take a long, hard look at their products. General managers predict that Spanish-language radio will become more segmented and specialized as the number of stations increases.

"There will be less of a shotgun approach and more of a sharp-shooting approach," said Frank Flores, general manager of New York's WJIT-AM. "The competition forces you to say, 'This is where I am going, this is who I am going to appeal to, and this is how I am going to do it.'"

Radio is a popular medium with Hispanics. According to a Strategy Research Corporation report, almost half of all Hispanics listen to Spanish-language radio stations. But a 1985 study conducted by Arbitron Ratings says many more listen to radio each week -- 98 percent of all Hispanics. According to the report, Hispanics spend 30 hours per week with radio, 20 percent more than the general population. It is more popular with women 18 to 49, but men 50 and older listen more to radio than women in the same age bracket.

Listenership is highest on Saturdays from 10 a.m.-3 p.m. -- more so than the 6-10 a.m. Monday-through-Friday slot, which is peak listening time nationally. According to Arbitron, Hispanics use both AM and FM radio. Eighty percent of AM listeners spend two-thirds of their time with AM radio and 91 percent of all FM listeners spend the same amount of time with FM radio, making them a very loyal audience.

Older Hispanics seem to rely on Spanish-language radio more than their younger counterparts. In the Arbitron study, 73 percent of all Hispanic adults 55 and older who listen to radio tune to a Spanish-language station. Compare that figure to 28 percent of adults 18 to 34 years old.

Formats vary in each city, but musical programming -- whether adult contemporary or folkloric Mexican -- dominates. It is only in Miami where more than half of the seven radio stations have news/talk show formats. Newscasts are generally limited to drive time with hourly updates of three to five minutes. Many stations depend on the wire services for their information; others admit that they simply read the local newspaper on the air. Those that have longer newscasts -- 30 or 60 minutes -- employ their own news staff and often call on their on-the-air personalities to double as reporters. A few have successfully simulcast a translation of a local English-language news show. Some emphasize Latin American news, but most agree that their listeners are also interested in stories from the barrio.

Few stations editorialize. Generally, the stations prefer to air programs in which members of the audience are encouraged to call and voice their opinions.

Where music is concerned, general managers tailor musical programming to the audience. In California and Texas, for example, even the international-hit stations play a good deal of rancheras and nortenas. In New York and Miami, the beat is salsa because the majority of radio listeners are from the Caribbean countries of Cuba, the Dominican Republic, and Puerto Rico.

As is true with the larger newspapers and television outlets, there are few minority-owned radio stations. The two largest Spanish-language chains -- Tichenor and Lotus -- are not owned by U.S. Hispanics, although this does not mean the companies are less sensitive to coverage of the Hispanic community. Spanish Broadcasting, owned by a father-son Hispanic team, added two stations -- an AM and FM -- to two other holdings in 1986.

Like many of the newspapers that are not audited, most stations do not subscribe to Arbitron, a broadcast ratings service. Some claimed that such ratings services undercount Hispanics. Others, particularly the smaller, privately owned stations, complained that it was too costly. Instead of using a ratings service to help sell advertisements, many stations often sell radio spots based on their in-house surveys.

Whether FM or AM -- and the overwhelming majority are AM -- all stations are community oriented, sponsoring events such as blood drives, health fairs, and concerts. Their public-service programming follows a common thread, too: helping recent immigrants and longtime residents alike find their way through social-service agencies and the job market. Many have raised funds for victims of disasters, such as the Mexican earthquake; others have helped local charities through radiothons.

Although several station managers fear that unbridled growth in some cities -- particularly Miami and Houston, with seven stations each -- may saturate some markets, all expressed optimism in Spanish-language radio's future. Many expect young Hispanics who now listen to English-language rock stations to return to their roots as they grow older and start families. That, along with the steady influx of refugees, guarantees them a captive audience.

"When I was growing up, I didn't listen to Spanish radio," said Maria Alonso, program director of KEDA-AM in San Antonio. "I grew up on rock and roll. But when you get married and settle down, you go back to it. Before, you didn't even want to speak Spanish around your friends. But once you get into that melting pot and feel comfortable with the Anglo culture, you have more confidence to go back. You don't neglect that part of you."

LOS ANGELES RADIO

The Los Angeles area is the number-one-ranked Hispanic market in the United States, with an estimated 3,614,000 Latins. About 75 percent live in Los Angeles County. Orange County is the second and San Bernardino the third most Hispanic-populated counties. At least 32 percent of Los Angeles County's population is Hispanic. And if one were to include estimates of the number of undocumented workers, the number would increase to 40 percent.

According to a Strategy Research Corporation report, the Hispanic population in Los Angeles grew 128 percent between 1970 and 1980. This was due partly to immigration from across the border and a higher fertility rate among women of Mexican origin.

Los Angeles Hispanics tend to be young. Almost 40 percent are under 18 years of age, and 71 percent are under 35. Those 65 and older make up only four percent of the population. Fifty-seven percent of the Los Angeles elementary school enrollment is of Spanish origin.

By virtue of the city's geographic location, 70 percent of Los Angeles Hispanics are of Mexican descent. Seventy percent speak Spanish at home and 10 percent say they use both languages, according to a 1987 Strategy Research report.

Los Angeles Hispanics are solidly middle class. Strategy Research reports that 30 percent of Hispanic heads of households work in white-collar professions, 22 percent in blue-collar, and 29 percent as laborers.

Five full-time Spanish-language stations serve Los Angeles:

KALI-1430 AM

Maryland-based United Broadcasting Inc. bought KALI in the early 1960s. It was already a Spanish station playing contemporary music. United, which owns nine other stations, including Spanish-language WKDM in New York, wanted to share in the growing Hispanic market of the West Coast. In November 1985, management changed the format to include more news, but kept its predominant music programming. Now the 24-hour station, which broadcasts at 5,000 watts, airs two records followed by one-minute newscasts 24 hours a day.

"Our listeners are never more than eight to 10 minutes from the news," said Gary Mercer, the station's operations manager.

The format change, Mercer added, is an experiment. Instead of fighting to keep an eroding audience base, KALI decided to go for listeners in the 35-44 age group who are more interested in news but also want to hear music.

KALI continues to play Spanish contemporary hits as well as golden oldies. And if the news events of the day warrant more time, newscasters have the freedom to extend reports beyond the minute mark.

The station is attracting more men and a more upscale market in general with its new format, Mercer said. He estimates that 80 percent of KALI's audience was either born in Mexico or is of Mexican descent, and about 70 percent speak only Spanish.

The one-minute newscasts are aired 24 hours per day, up to seven news stories per hour. The most important news from Mexico and Central America is given priority "without losing sight of local events," Mercer said. In addition to its own news programming, KALI also translates simultaneously the 11 p.m. news from KNBC television.

The news department has five full-time employees, out of a total of 35. Deejays often double as street reporters. The station also uses AP in English, Notimex, and the Los Angeles city wires.

KALI offers a good deal of public-service programming as well. Taped comments from callers on selected topics are aired throughout the day in "La Voz del Pueblo" (The Voice of the People). Twice per day, Monday through Saturday, five-minute segments present community, club, and association news. On Sundays there are several public-service and religious programs, including one produced by local high-school students.

About 80 percent of KALI's advertisers are local, Mercer said. The station limits its commercial time to 15 minutes per hour.

KLVE-107.5 FM, KTNQ-1020 AM

KLVE and KTNQ were bought by H & W Communications in 1985. Both stations carried Spanish-language programming at the time of purchase, KTNQ since July 1979 and KLVE since 1975. H & W, based in Hawaii, operates six stations. The two in Los Angeles are the only ones with a Spanish-language format.

KLVE, "Radio Amor" (Radio Love), broadcasts at 34,000 watts 24 hours per day. In 1986, it was the only FM station serving the Los Angeles Hispanic community in its own language. KLVE's format, according to promotional literature, is "music, music, music." Indeed, deejays play Latin international hits and aim them at the 25 to 49 "white collar, affluent, upwardly mobile Hispanic," according to Jeff Liberman, operations manager. Although the largest percentage of its audience is of Mexican heritage, the station also tries to attract Central and South Americans, Puerto Ricans, Dominicans, and Cubans.

KTNQ, at 50,000 watts, appeals more to the Mexican-American. The station plays typical Mexican music -- rancheras and nortenas, for example. KTNQ is targeted to the 24-plus age group. The audience is more blue collar than that of its FM sister.

In the Monday to Sunday 6 a.m.-midnight slot, about 353,100 people listened to KTNQ, according to the Winter 1986 Arbitron ratings. Some 32,800 tuned in at some point in an average quarter hour.

71

In the same rating period, KLVE had 348,800 listeners in one week. In an average quarter hour, 22,800 tuned in.

KTNQ carries news broadcasts on the hour and half hour and weather and traffic reports 24 hours per day. Broadcasts at the top of the hour last five minutes; at the half hour, they are limited to headline news. KTNQ also provides its listeners with four traffic reports per hour during morning and afternoon drives, for a total of 28 reports.

The typical five minute broadcast contains three local stories, two regional, two national, and two international, plus weather and sports. "The lead is whatever is the most important news that day," Liberman said. "We try as much as possible to give a fair shake to everybody."

Still, the emphasis is on Mexico. KTNQ features a five-minute broadcast at 7 p.m. Monday through Friday directly from Mexico.

Both stations also use UPI in Spanish and English and the local news wires.

The FM station, KLVE, is "more music, less talk, less news," by Liberman's definition. Newscasts run three minutes at 45 minutes after the hour during the drive time slots -- 6-9 a.m. and 3-7 p.m. The FM station carries 21 traffic reports per day, or three reports per hour during the morning and afternoon drive times.

In addition to music and news, KTNQ-AM carries the Los Angeles Dodgers baseball and Los Angeles Raiders football games. Both stations air employment opportunities seven days a week. KLVE changes its format slightly on Thursday during "Mini-Concierto" (Mini-Concert), playing three songs in a row by one artist.

H & W Communications, Liberman said, favors audience-building promotions. In 1986, it gave away four automobiles in two months. It also commissioned several television and billboard advertisements in an effort to attract more listeners.

About 30 percent of the stations' advertisers are national companies. The rest are local and regional accounts. "We have everything, from the beer companies to the local mom-and-pop stores," Liberman said.

Both stations employ 48 people.

KSKQ-1540 AM

Spanish Broadcasting System of California bought KSKQ in 1984 and immediately converted it to a Spanish-language contemporary music station, playing everything from soft rock to ballads to Mexican rancheras. Spanish Broadcasting System also owns WSKQ in New York and WCMQ-AM and WCMQ-FM in Miami.

Nicknamed "Super KQ," the station broadcasts at 50,000 watts. About 70 percent of its listeners are Mexican, 15 percent Salvadoran, 5 percent

Cuban, and the rest Central American, Puerto Rican, and Dominican, said Raul Alarcon Sr., chairman of the board. But on-air personalities make a conscious effort not to slip into local idiomatic expression.

"We use an international Spanish," Alarcon Sr. said. "That is our appeal. That is what we stress. We don't use 'Spanglish' or words in Spanish that don't exist and have been taken from English."

In the Winter 1986 Arbitron, 239,600 people listened to the radio station in one rating week. At some point in time during an average quarter hour, 18,200 different people tuned in.

Weekdays from 6-7 a.m., KSKQ airs "El Gran Noticiero" (The Great News Show). The station also broadcasts five-minute newscasts on the hour and three minutes on the half hour, 24 hours per day. These include weather and traffic reports.

Alarcon estimates that 60 percent of the news is from or about Mexico. The station employs four correspondents in Central America as well as several in the Caribbean and South America. "Local and California news is important, too, but we must keep in mind our audience when we give the news and they are interested in their country of origin," Alarcon said.

Of the 40 people employed by the station, 10 are on the editorial staff. The station receives AP and UPI in Spanish and English, the local Los Angeles city and traffic wires.

The station also has special short broadcasts on patriotic days. On January 28, the birthdate of Cuban hero Jose Marti, for example, the station discussed the man and his philosophy, quoting from his poetry. Management also writes editorials on local and national issues "when the case warrants it but not on a regular basis," Alarcon said.

While music is the predominant format, the type of music the station plays varies. International hits are played throughout the day. After 7 p.m., however, the music turns more upbeat in an effort to appeal to a younger audience. At 1 a.m., the music softens into romantic melodies. Sunday mornings are reserved for community and religious programming.

Like other Spanish-language stations, KSKQ tries to maintain a level of community involvement. During the 1985 Mexican earthquake, the station scrapped all regular programming to raise money, food, clothing, and medical supplies for earthquake victims.

National companies comprise about 60 percent of KSKQ's advertising, Alarcon said. This balance, however, varies according to the time of year. In the summer, national accounts tend to buy more spots, but this wanes in the fall.

KWKW-1300 AM

"La Mexicana" (The Mexican), as KWKW is called, has been a full-time Spanish station since 1959, although it debuted in 1942 as an English-language station. Lotus Communications, which also owns six other Spanish-language stations, bought it in 1962.

Transmitting 24 hours at 5,000 watts, KWKW plays a variety of music, from typical Mexican rancheras to hits, from well-known balladeers Julio Iglesias, Rafael, and California groups.

The station's target audience is the young adult and its main appeal is to women 25 to 54 years old. "The attraction is the romantic music," said Alfredo Rodriguez, program director. "But we are not interested in teenagers. They listen to the English-language stations."

About 252,100 people listened to KWKW during a given week in the Winter 1986 Arbitron ratings. In a quarter hour, 19,000 tuned in.

KWKW limits its news broadcasts to five minutes at the top of every hour, seven days per week. "We emphasize whatever is more important or relevant at the time and that doesn't necessarily have to be from Mexico," Rodriguez said. "But we do focus on Latin America and Mexico in particular."

The five-minute 5 p.m. newscast, "Panorama Latino" (Latin Panorama), for example, is devoted exclusively to Latin American news. Most of the information is obtained through UPI in Spanish and English, and local feeds from the UPI/EFE radio network. Four of the station's 60 employees are full-time reporters or newscasters.

The station's most popular program is the Saturday music show, when deejays play Mexican folkloric songs, including rancheras, cumbias, and mariachi music by the best-known groups. Another well-received program is "Hablando con La Comunidad" (Speaking with the Community), a Sunday night remote broadcast from local restaurants with community leaders and experts as guests. Diners are asked to participate.

National and local advertising is evenly divided, Rodriguez said, although local accounts tend to buy more spots in December.

NEW YORK RADIO

New York, long known as the home of wave after wave of immigrants, is second only to Los Angeles as the U.S. city with the most Hispanics. In 1985, according to Strategy Research Corporation, 2,442,300 Hispanics lived in the Big Apple -- or 14 percent of the entire U.S. Hispanic population.

Two-thirds of all Hispanics lived in five areas -- Bronx, Kings, New York, Queens, and Richmond. Between 1970 and 1980, the Hispanic population more than doubled. Between 1980 and 1985, about 378,100 more were added to that number. In contrast, the non-Hispanic population in the 28-county area which makes up greater New York showed a decrease of 9.5 percent.

In the past, New York's Hispanics were predominantly Puerto Rican. However, this group is making up less of the total population. Where Puerto Ricans once made up more than 80 percent of the Hispanic population, they now comprise 46.5 percent. Dominicans rank second with 26.7 percent, Central and South Americans 16.5 percent, Cubans 7.2 percent, Mexicans 2.2 percent, and Spaniards less than 1 percent. "While the massive influx of Puerto Ricans into the city has ended, other Hispanic newcomers have taken their place," says a Strategy Research Corporation study conducted for New York's Channel 41.

New York Hispanics are young, although not as young as the Los Angeles Latin population. About 36 percent are under 18 years old and 70 percent under 35, according to Strategy Research.

According to the 1980 census, 12.5 percent of New York Hispanics in the labor market held professional or managerial positions. That is slightly higher than the overall rate of 12.2 percent for the U.S. Hispanic population. The median income of Spanish households, according to a Scarborough Report for the New York Market-1980, was $16,300. Total household median income was $20,000.

There are four full-time Spanish-language radio stations in the market:

WADO-1280 AM

WADO has been transmitting Spanish programming since the early 1960s, in a news/talk/music format. In 1986 Tichenor Media System purchased the station for $20 million from Nelson Lavergne of Command Broadcast Associates Inc., who had owned it since October 1978. The purchase price was the highest paid for a stand-alone AM station in the history of broadcasting, and brought to eight the number of Spanish-language radio stations owned by Tichenor.

Although the sale was pending FCC approval in late 1986, executives at the station expected to continue the successful format. The station broadcasts 24 hours per day at 5,000 watts, with the slogan "La Isla del Norte" (Island in the North.)

The station's audience is primarily women over 25 "although we also get our share of males," said Albert Cameron, executive vice president of Command Broadcast Associates.

In the Winter 1986 Arbitron ratings, 371,700 people tuned into the station during Monday through Sunday, 6 a.m.-to-midnight. In an average quarter hour, listeners numbered 48,300. That made it the top-rated Spanish station in New York.

Cameron attributes the station's success to the blended format. During its music programming, the station does not play salsa music, although a majority of New York Hispanics are from the Caribbean. Instead, it plays the international hits of Latin America.

Weekday news broadcasts are five minutes on the hour, and 30 minutes at noon. On weekends, the five-minute broadcasts remain on the same schedule but there is no half-hour news show. The station also carries daily five-minute live feeds from correspondents in Puerto Rico, the Dominican Republic, and Miami. The emphasis, of course, is on Latin America.

"We also give national and local news certainly but we provide the news our listeners want from Latin America," Cameron said.

WADO management airs editorials -- about 10 a year -- on topics of interest to Hispanics, Cameron said. "We don't do it every day, not even every week, but as necessary," Cameron said.

WADO subscribes to EFE and AP in English and Spanish. Of the station's 40 employees, one is a full-time news director.

One of the station's more popular shows is the 10 a.m.-3 p.m. "No Solo Para Nosotras" (Not Only for Us Ladies), which includes music, horoscopes, and interviews, as well as news.

Also every weekday morning, WADO features a consumer specialist from Cornell University talking about safety, credit, consumer rights, nutrition, and other consumer-related issues. According to promotional literature, the consumer show is designed to "ease marketplace decisions for Spanish-speaking people in the Metropolitan New York area."

Monday through Thursday, from 3-8 p.m. the station opens its doors and microphones to the public in "Puertas y Microfonos Abiertos" (Open Doors and Microphones). The show features live interviews with personalities, and the audience is encouraged to participate.

The station's format changes on Friday, when all interviews and talk shows are suspended and the day is devoted to music of yesteryear.

About 60 percent of WADO's advertisers are national companies, Cameron said.

WJIT-1480 AM

WJIT (then known as WHOM) was founded in the mid-1950s by an Italian named Fortune H. Pope, who also happened to own a Spanish newspaper. The station is now owned by Infinity Broadcasting which changed the call letters to WJIT.

In April 1986, after two newcomer stations began to erode its audience base, WJIT changed its format from Spanish urban contemporary to easy listening. Its old nickname "Hit Radio" was changed to "Soft Sound."

"It is a boleros, ballads, oldies selection, actually very much a light FM station format," said Frank Flores, general manager.

Like the three other Spanish-language stations in New York, WJIT transmits 24 hours a day at 5,000 watts. Its target audience: 25- to 49-year olds.

Although WJIT used to play a great deal of salsa music, its new format calls for a broader appeal to the growing Central and South American population in New York. "We no longer have a predominance of one type of Hispanic," Flores explained. "Since the migration from Puerto Rico has stopped, it is difficult to program for the New York Spanish market. You have to please everybody. We literally have a hodge-podge."

In the Spring 1986 Arbitron ratings, 177,800 people tuned in to WJIT at some point during the week. The average quarter hour listenership was 11,500.

WJIT broadcasts three news reports per hour -- every 20 minutes -- during the 6-9 a.m. drive-time show. After that, the station's newscasts are limited to 60 seconds on the 35-minute mark.

"We key to what we figure our listeners want to hear. Sometimes we air live reports from Puerto Rico and the Dominican Republic, but we also do local news. When the bus fare goes up from 90 cents to $1.50 our audience certainly wants to know," Flores said.

The station has one full-time news reporter -- the total staff numbers 43 -- and correspondents in Latin America. It also uses AP and UPI in Spanish.

Listeners' favorite show, Flores said, is the 6-10 a.m. program. Although the music played is similar to that played the rest of the day, the morning drive "is more topical and has more news so it is more of a necessity," Flores said. The station has promoted special news features in this time slot to increase listenership. In the Spring of 1986, for example, WJIT heavily promoted a feature on crack, a form of cocaine, which aired on the morning-drive program.

Weekends are partly devoted to public-service programming and shows discussing local issues and consumer problems. These types of shows are particularly important in the Hispanic community, Flores said.

"They feel the radio station belongs to them. They are very, very sensitive to any changes," he added.

WJIT has always been profitable, but the station in 1986 targeted several categories of advertisers -- national and large local companies -- in the hope of increasing ad revenues. To increase listenership, WJIT also launched an ad campaign aimed at Hispanics in the 25- to 49-year-old group. "The noise has ended," the slogan said. "Come to the new soft sound."

WKDM-1380 AM

WKDM had run part-time Spanish programming for several years before it went full-time in September 1984. The station is owned by United Broadcasting. It transmits at 5,000 watts 24 hours per day.

"We continually survey and play the top romantic ballad stars who have familiar and well-loved songs," said Joseph Schweighardt, vice president and general manager. "We play the latest hits and the younger oldies."

WKDM's audience is mostly women in the 18- to 49-year-old group, but there is also a strong 18-to-34 male listenership. Both groups are solidly "working class, blue collar," according to Schweighardt. About half are bilingual with strong cultural ties to Spanish and music from the homeland.

About 272,000 people listened at some point during the week of the 1986 Spring Arbitron ratings. In an average quarter hour, 29,800 had their dials on WKDM.

Morning drive newscasts run twice an hour for five minutes each. After 10 a.m., news is limited to 90 seconds, but also twice an hour. About 50 percent of the broadcast is local news, the rest international and national, Schweighardt said. "What is more germane to the audience, what will affect them the most, is the lead story," he added.

In addition to its three-member news staff, WKDM has regular live feeds from Puerto Rico, Ecuador, Colombia, and the Dominican Republic -- countries from which the majority of New York Hispanics come. The station also uses AP and UPI in Spanish. It employs 40 people.

As most other Spanish-language stations, WKDM does not editorialize. It does, however, encourage listeners to phone in their comments. Six to seven times per day, WKDM airs community opinions on topical issues in a program called "The Community Speaks."

But by far the audience's favorite show is the morning drive program, Schweighardt said. Three disc jockeys host that show, playing music, reading news, and giving the weather report "in a very light, lively banter."

WKDM's advertising has "a heavy national dimension," according to Schweighardt, although the station carries a strong share of local ads.

"It's getting more and more sophisticated," he said. "Ten years ago, national business was few and it was considered a token buy. That has made a 180-degree turn."

WSKQ-620 AM

Spanish Broadcasting System bought this station in 1983 and changed its format from nostalgic American to Spanish-language modern contemporary music. Spanish Broadcasting also owns KSKQ in Los Angeles and WCMQ-AM and FM in Miami.

About 30 percent of "Super KQ's" audience is Puerto Rican, 30 percent Dominican, 10 percent Cuban, 10 percent Colombian, and the rest Central and South American, said Raul Alarcon Sr., chairman of the board. The station's strength is with young adults, 18 to 34 years old. Fall 1985 Arbitron ratings showed WSKQ reaching 36,400 Hispanics between 18 and 49 in an average quarter hour.

In the Spring 1986 Arbitron ratings, 341,800 people listened during the Monday-to-Sunday 6 a.m.-to-midnight slot, and 27,500 during an average quarter hour.

WSKQ's programming is similar to its sister station in Los Angeles, but with two differences: New York's music has more of a Caribbean touch and the news show is an hour longer than on the West Coast.

WSKQ's broadcast, "El Gran Noticiero" (The Great News Show), runs from 6 to 8 a.m. Monday through Friday. Like its music, the emphasis is on the Caribbean, particularly Puerto Rico and the Dominican Republic. Local and national news is also part of the newscast, and depending on the type of news, it is often given in headline form. In addition to this two-hour show, there are five-minute newscasts on the hour and three minutes on the half hour 24 hours a day.

"We try to give the listener the news that is important to him," Alarcon said. "You don't have to go to the English-language stations for information if you listen to us. At the same time, we will give you Latin American news that will not be covered by another station."

There are about 10 editorial employees out of a staff of 50 at WSKQ. There is at least one newsperson on every shift. The station also supplements its own newsgathering with UPI and AP in Spanish and English, as well as the New York and New Jersey metro-service wires. New York has three mobile units and often exchanges news stories with its Los Angeles sister station.

News stories are not the only thing the two stations share. A special series on unwed teenage mothers, a 20-part program produced by the Los Angeles staff, was also aired in New York. Editorials are the same and so is some of the community programming. For example, when KSKQ went into special programming to raise money and supplies for Mexican earthquake victims in 1985, WSKQ launched a continuing appeal coordinated with the Red Cross. WSKQ also relied on KSKQ's reporting for coverage of the disaster.

WSKQ does have its own public-service shows. A Sunday morning program, "El Medico y Usted" (The Doctor and You), has earned high ratings in the New York market, according to Alarcon. The one-hour show gives panelists a forum to discuss medical problems and issues. Another public service show,

"Casos y Cosas de la Comunidad" (Cases and Matters of the Community), invites community leaders to discuss problems that directly affect New York Hispanics.

WSKQ markets itself along with its sister station in Los Angeles. By having stations in the two largest Hispanic markets in the country, Alarcon said his company is ready to build a Spanish-language radio chain.

"Hispanics tend to be unified as far as maintaining cultural ties," said Alarcon about why his chain could be successful. "It is the only group that is not melting into the pot."

SOUTH FLORIDA RADIO

An estimated 936,200 Hispanics lived in the tri-county area of South Florida in 1987. Most, 92 percent, were concentrated in Dade County (Miami), although Broward County (Fort Lauderdale) has a growing Hispanic population. In 1987, that was estimated at 70,000. Monroe County (the Florida Keys), which has a well-established Hispanic tradition because of its proximity to Cuba, has about 7,700 Hispanics.

Dade County, where the major tri-county Hispanic radio stations are based, is 43 percent Hispanic. That has been increasing steadily since the 1960s. In 1970, the Hispanic population was 299,200. In 1980, it was 664,500. Five years later, it had climbed to 805,800.

According to a 1985 Strategy Research Corporation report, the Latin population in this tri-county area increased 188 percent between 1970 and 1985. Eighty percent of the Latin households were headed by persons of Cuban origin, a number that has decreased slightly as more and more Central Americans seek political refuge in the area. Central American households now make up over nine percent of the Latin population.

Miami's Latins tend to be older than the U.S. Hispanic population at large. Men 18 years and older made up 32 percent of the Hispanic population, while women 18 and older made up almost 40 percent.

About 30 percent of heads of households were employed in white-collar professions and about half in blue-collar jobs, according to Strategy Research.

Spanish was by far the language of preference at home but it was spoken least often in the workplace, according to the report. More than nine out of 10 spoke Spanish at home, an increase from the 89 percent that reported doing so in 1983.

There are seven AM and FM radio stations serving the Dade County Hispanic community. More than half are news stations, an unusually high number particularly when compared to other U.S. Hispanic markets.

"That is what the Hispanic community of Miami wants," said Salvador Lew, president and general manager of WRHC-AM. "They seek information."

WAQI-710 AM

The newest Spanish-language radio station in Miami, WAQI, went on the air in Spanish for the first time in October 1985 with the slogan "Radio Mambi." It was purchased by a group of Cuban businessmen who formed Mambisa Broadcasting Co. to buy the former English-language WGBS. Amancio Victor Suarez owns 51 percent of the stock and serves as president and chairman. Armando Perez-Roura, the station's general manager, is also its top commentator and 20-percent owner. The rest of the company is owned by three other investors.

Being the new kid on the block has not hampered WAQI. In the Spring 1986 Arbitron ratings, WAQI was the third-ranked Spanish-language radio station. It broadcasts 24 hours a day.

"There is enough room for all of us," said Perez-Roura. "We have demonstrated that. The growth of Hispanics in this community is phenomenal."

WAQI broadcasts at 50,000 watts day and night. Perez-Roura claims Hispanics can listen to it as far away as Tampa.

In the Miami-Hollywood-Fort Lauderdale area, WAQI is 14th of 34 stations. An estimated 156,200 people listened to the radio station in an average week, which means that of all persons 12 and over listening to the radio, 3.2 percent tuned into WAQI, according to Arbitron. The average listener spent 13 hours and 15 minutes per week with the station. The Monday-through-Friday 6-10 a.m. drive time show was the most popular time slot for the station. During that time, the station ranked fifth in the market.

WAQI's audience, Perez-Roura said, comes from all walks of life, and it ranges from teenagers to the very old. "We try to have something for everyone," he added.

Listeners tune in to WAQI for news, commentaries, and talk shows. News broadcasts are, as Perez-Roura explained, "our ABCs." The station provides 12 hours of solid news programming Monday through Saturday, without counting the headline news every hour on the hour when there are no newscasts. The news programs run from 4-10 a.m., noon-2 p.m., 4-6 p.m., and 9-11 p.m. Among the special features of the news broadcast is the time and weather report every minute.

WAQI also broadcasts a one hour novela (soap opera), a daily astrology program, several talk shows, and a half-hour comedy segment by a popular Cuban comedian. Sundays are reserved for musical programming.

"It may not be the most cost-effective way of delivering radio," said Perez-Roura of the high cost of news-station programming, "but the information we provide is indispensable."

Almost half of the station's 70 employees are on the news staff, Perez-Roura said. And that does not take into account freelancers and staff correspondents throughout Latin America and Europe. The emphasis is on international news, especially from Latin America and more specifically from Cuba and Nicaragua. Local news is also covered thoroughly because "it has immediate impact on our listeners," Perez-Roura said.

If news is the station's bread, commentaries are certainly its butter. Two news/commentary programs, "La Mesa Revuelta" and "En Caliente," are very popular with the audience, Perez-Roura said. In the latter program, he and another broadcaster argue the pros and cons of several issues. Editorials are usually conservative and anti-communist. Issues range from international topics to local themes. They often concentrate on Latin America.

The station subscribes to AP and UPI in English and Spanish, and to the EFE newswire.

Like other Spanish-language stations in Miami, WAQI prides itself in taking an active part in community activities, helping listeners cut through bureaucratic red tape, and sponsoring fundraising marathons.

Because of its relative youth, "Radio Mambi" was not making a profit in mid-1986, but it was reaching the break-even point at eight months, as its management had expected. Local advertisers are the station's main accounts, but Perez-Roura said the sales staff will be going after national companies now that listener surveys have given them something to show to prospective clients.

WCMQ-1210 AM, WCMQ-92.3 FM

Herbert S. Dolgoff purchased WCMQ-AM in 1972 from Dynamic Broadcasting. Two years later, he also bought WQXK and turned it into the first full-time Spanish-only FM station in South Florida. Now it is known as WCMQ-FM. In 1986, Spanish Broadcasting bought the two stations from Dolgoff.

WCMQ-1210 AM broadcasts at 25,000 watts in the daytime and 3,000 at night. The FM at 92 khz has 50,000 watts. Both stations share offices and employees, about 30 workers in all. Half of those are deejays and news people.

In the Spring 1986 Arbitron ratings, WCMQ-FM was the second-ranked station in the market. About 173,200 people listened to the station on an average week. The average time spent listening: 14 hours and 15 minutes per week. Of all persons listening to the radio during the surveyed time, 3.9 percent were listening to WCMQ-FM, making it the eighth-most-listened-to station in the Miami-Fort Lauderdale area. The Monday-through-Friday, 10 a.m.- 3 p.m. slot was the most popular, garnering 4.8 percent of the total radio listening audience.

WCMQ-AM, though less popular, has an intensely loyal audience. In the Spring of 1986, 79,100 people listened to the radio station on an average week. Time spent listening: 13 hours and 45 minutes per week. Of all persons listening to radio, 1.7 percent were tuned to WCMQ-AM. It ranked 25th out of 34 stations, according to the Arbitron ratings of the Miami-Fort Lauderdale-Hollywood area.

Both stations are on the air 24 hours per day. Both are considered contemporary Spanish-music stations, but each has its own characteristics. The AM, known as "Radio Alegre," has slightly more news, and the FM specializes in debuting hit songs aimed at a younger audience.

Antonio Arias, director of public relations and community affairs, said both stations' news programs are characterized by the absence of political commentary. "We present the news as impartially as possible. Yes, we call Castro a dictator, but we don't harp on it," he said.

WCMQ-AM carries three minutes of news every hour 24 hours per day. In morning drive time, from 6-9 a.m., its every hour and half hour. The FM broadcasts three minutes of news at 45 minutes past the hour between 6-9 a.m. After that it drops to two minutes until 7 p.m.

Unlike other Spanish-language stations in Miami, the two WCMQs do not try to emphasize news from Cuba or Central America. "We open the broadcast with the most important event, whatever that may be," Arias said. About 30 percent of the broadcast news is local, 30 percent is from Latin America, and the rest is international and national, Arias said.

The overwhelming majority of the broadcast comes from UPI in Spanish and English. Arias said the stations also depend on listeners to call in news tips. Although the stations have no local reporters, a staff member will attend a press conference if necessary.

The news, however, is not why listeners tune to the two stations. "We are in a city that is very newsy," Arias said. "But eventually those who hear news seek an alternative. They turn to music."

And music is what the stations give them, along with the witty, per-sonable talk from deejays. The FM has two programs that are very popular with its audience, Arias said. One -- "Nocturno 92" (Nightly 92) -- is a one-hour Monday-through-Friday-night show that plays only 1960s music. It takes its name from a popular Cuban radio show in the 1960s that played "foreign" rock music, the only radio show that aired music from abroad in the communist-controlled island.

The second show, "Notimusicales" (Musical Notes), is a 10-minute show that airs every Monday through Friday at noon. Like the English television show "Entertainment Tonight," it gives a rundown of what's happening in the artistic world.

"The audience calls a lot, to ask questions, to request songs. They like participating in the contests and, of course, we encourage that," Arias said.

Aside from Spanish contemporary music, the AM station also airs public-service programs on Sunday. The programs deal "with anything from bus routes to health issues, whatever is of interest to the public," Arias said.

Because of their tendency to attract a younger audience, the two WCMQs have more national advertising, including airlines, beers, and auto manu-facturers, Arias said. But local business, particularly Anglo super-markets, shoe stores, and condominium developers, also advertise.

WOCN-1450 AM

Union Radio Inc., a group of Cuban-American investors, bought this station from Minority Broadcasting in 1983. It transmits 24 hours a day at 1,000 watts.

It is one of four news/talk radio stations in Miami's Spanish-language market. Most of the audience consists of men between 25 and 54 years of age, according to Jorge Luis Hernandez, news director.

In the Spring 1986 Arbitron ratings, 56,800 people tuned to the station at some point during the ratings week. The average quarter hour listenership was 4,000 people. Its highest-rated time slot during that ratings period was the 10 a.m. to 3 p.m. time segment, with 5,400 listeners tuned during an average quarter hour.

WOCN devotes six hours of its programming time to news broadcasts, from 4 to 8 a.m. and noon to 2 p.m. The rest of the programming consists of talk shows, except for a two-hour interval of music from 10 a.m. to noon. Most of the talk shows have a political slant, concentrating on national, international, or Cuban news. There is also a daily one-hour health show, a religious show, and another aimed at women.

In the news broadcasts, news from Cuba and Latin American take precedence, but national news is also emphasized.

"We concentrate on the battle between democracy and communism," Hernandez said. "That is what our audience demands. If we were a station in rural Oklahoma, agrarian news would take precedence."

Of the 40 station employees, about 10 are on the news staff. The station also relies on UPI and EFE news wires as well as daily UPI live feeds every half hour until midnight.

About 90 percent of the advertising is local, Hernandez said.

WQBA-1140 AM, WQBA-107.5 FM

In June 1966 Susquehanna Broadcasting Corp. bought an AM radio station at 1140 on the dial and within a year tapped into the Spanish market. The station used WQBA as its new call letters and called itself "La Cubanisima" (The Most Cuban). It was so successful -- WQBA has been the top Spanish-language radio station in the Miami area for years with the exception of a few rating periods -- that its parent company bought an FM country music station and turned it into a sister Spanish-language station with a twist.

The FM station, "Super Q," was the first bilingual station in the market. It plays one contemporary song in Spanish, the next in English. Disc jockeys speak Spanish, but sprinkle their banter with English words and idiomatic expressions.

"We based the station on what we saw happening to the Latins in this community," said George Hyde, general manager. "They go through an Americanization phase, but when they get a little older and start a family, they return to their roots, to the language and Spanish music. That's the premise of 'Super Q.'"

While the AM station's format is news and commentary with some music tucked in between noticieros, the FM is adult contemporary in both languages. Advertising is, even on the FM, always in Spanish. The AM broadcasts at 50,000 watts daytime and 10,000 at night, the FM at 100,000 watts.

In the Spring 1986 Arbitron ratings, WQBA-AM was the third-rated station overall in the Miami-Hollywood-Fort Lauderdale market. About 210,300 people listened to the radio station in a week. That meant that of persons listening to radio, 5.6 percent were listening to WQBA. Like other Spanish-language stations, "La Cubanisima" has an intensely loyal following. The average listener spent 17 hours tuned to the station, the longest time spent by an audience for any station in the market. The top-rated station in the area, an English-language one, had 391,600 listeners in one week and they spent an average of 14 hours tuned in.

The AM was rated tops in the market during the 6-10 a.m. weekday time slot, beating the English-language competition, according to the Spring 1986 Arbitron ratings. In the combined drive time -- 6-10 a.m. and 3-7 p.m. -- it was rated second.

WQBA-FM was the fifth-rated Spanish-language station and 20th overall in the market, according to the Arbitron ratings. About 145,800 listeners tuned in during an average week and spent nine hours, 30 minutes listening.

Hyde attributes the AM station's success to its news product and to "a real community sense of everybody in the organization." WQBA has sponsored fund raisers for victims of the Colombian earthquake, for instance, and in 1986 sponsored a 12-hour radiothon for the South Florida Blood Service. The station's efforts helped Dade County break a national record for blood contributions.

WQBA-AM provides plenty of news every day, beginning at 4-10 a.m. with its "Radio Reloj" (Clock Radio) <u>noticiero</u>. Broadcasts also air at noon-2 p.m., 4-6 p.m., and 9-11 p.m. Monday through Saturday. During the rest of the time, headline news is aired on the hour and half hour. The station also broadcasts six hours of music daily, several talk shows, and the standard radio soaps. During football season, it carries live the Miami Dolphins football games.

Among the favorite talk shows is "Microfono Abierto" (Open Microphone) Monday through Friday from 6-8 p.m. Typical topics for this live call-in program include local, national, and international politics and immigration, medicare, and social security. From 8-10 p.m. listeners are encouraged to call in for discussion of personal problems in "What's Your Problem?"

While the AM station is heavily news oriented, news plays a minor role on the FM. Five-minute broadcasts are heard on the hour from 6-8 a.m. and 4-6 p.m. Monday through Friday. There are no political commentaries or editorials.

While news from Cuba is always of primary interest to its audience -- the AM has a daily news feature "Cuba por Dentro" (Cuba from Inside) -- WQBA also tries to serve other constituencies within the Hispanic community. "What is increasingly important here is Nicaragua," Hyde said. "We need to get the news here and get it first and get the most."

Needless to say, the emphasis in the news program is on Latin America as well as Washington news that may affect Hispanics and Latin America. Though it employs correspondents throughout Latin America, the station also subscribes to AP in Spanish and English and UPI in Spanish.

"This community has an insatiable thirst for news, particularly about Latin America," Hyde said. "Politics permeates every discussion -- and it's talk about international politics."

The station editorializes about a variety of issues. Hyde, the station manager, and news director form the board that decides editorial policy. On international issues, the station is strongly pro-democracy and fiercely anti-communist.

Both stations employ 90 people. The news staff accounts for 35. About one-third of the advertising is national, Hyde said.

WRHC-1550 AM

WRHC was bought in November in 1973 as a brokered station. Villa Broadcasting Company, the owners, changed the call letters from WRIC to WRHC and reserved afternoons for Spanish programs. RHC stands for Radio Havana Cuba and its nickname is "Cadena Azul" (the Blue Network), which was the name of a popular pre-Castro radio station. Four of the five major stockholders grew up together in the same town in Cuba and their dream was to have a full-time Spanish-language station.

Two years after the purchase, WRHC went all-Spanish during the daytime. In 1983 it began broadcasting 24 hours per day, 10,000 watts daytime and 500 at night.

Salvador Lew, company president, general manager, and part owner, said listeners are 18 and older. Some are recent immigrants; others have been in Miami since the early 1960s. All share one thing in common: "They're interested in news from their countries," Lew said. "If they listen to an English station, they get very little about Latin America. When the Anglo stations do something from Nicaragua, it's 30 seconds if that."

In the Spring 1986 Arbitron ratings, WRHC was the fourth-rated Spanish-language station in the market. About 104,700 listeners tuned in during the week from 6 a.m. to midnight. The average listener spent 13 hours and 15 minutes a week with the station. Its most popular time slot was the weekday 6-10 a.m. drive-time program.

One of four Spanish-language news stations in the market, WRHC emphasizes local news although its attraction for many is information from Latin America. Lew estimates that 80 percent of the station's broadcasts are devoted to local happenings. The noticieros run from 4-10 a.m., noon-2 p.m., and 4-6 p.m. Monday through Saturday. The noon news program includes a one-hour remote broadcast from a local restaurant.

In addition to the news, WRHC airs community-oriented talk shows, political commentary, comedy programs, and even poetry readings in the evening. One of its more popular shows, Lew said, is a daily one-hour program by a Catholic priest called "Conflictos Humanos" (Human Conflicts). A 3-4 p.m. daily talk show focuses on social security, housing, equal employment, and other local issues. On Saturdays, a two-hour sports show deals with baseball, football, boxing, and soccer.

Lew is the station's chief editorialist. His main objective: "To make Miami a better community." He labels the station's political philosophy as "pro-democracy and pro-freedom." Though the station's stance is often against communism in Cuba and Nicaragua, it has also criticized Latin dictatorships of the right, Lew said.

About 30 of the 55 station employees work in the editorial department. The station also has two reporters in Washington. It subscribes to EFE and UPI in Spanish and English.

The station is profitable and "the great majority" of advertisers are local businesses, corporations, and merchants.

WSUA-1260 AM

In 1982, Herb Levin and partner Enrique Landin bought the former "Radio Hit," a contemporary Spanish-language music station, and converted it to WSUA, or "Radio Suave." WSUA transmits 24 hours a day at 5,000 watts.

Its format is mellow, easy listening with some international hits blended in.

Most of its listeners are women between 25 and 54, according to Lourdes Perez, sales coordinator. A Strategy Research study commissioned by "Radio Suave" shows that the typical WSUA listener had an annual income of $29,347 and 53 percent had a white collar job. More than half owned their own home.

In the Spring 1986 Arbitron ratings, 81,200 people tuned into the station at some point during the ratings week. The average quarter listenership was 6,800.

Newscasts run every hour five minutes before the hour from 6 a.m. to 5 p.m. Although the station employs three out of its 30 staff members in a news capacity, most of the news is obtained through UPI and AP, Perez said.

"We try to cover international, national, and local news. We don't emphasize one over the other. What is the biggest news event of the day will get the play," she said.

In addition to its regular newscasts, WSUA also airs three to five minutes of business news Monday through Friday at 4:43 p.m. Every morning and afternoon drive, the station plays traffic reports and, three times a week, an agenda of city happenings.

One of the audience's favorite shows is the 6 to 10 a.m. morning drive. News about the entertainment world is interspersed among the easy listening songs. Every evening from 9 to 10 p.m., during the International Hits hour, songs in French, English, Italian, and other languages are also played.

About 60 percent of the station's advertising is local, Perez said.

TEXAS RADIO

SAN ANTONIO

San Antonio, the frontier town known for its fierce fight for independence from Mexico, is a city with a Hispanic majority. There are about 889,300 Latins. Most -- or 73 percent -- are concentrated in Bexar County. From 1970 to 1980, there was a 51-percent increase in the Hispanic population, according to Strategy Research Corporation. In the five years after that, the number of Hispanics grew by 22 percent. From 1985 to 1987, the population grew by almost 14 percent. Hispanics comprise about 48 percent of the market.

Local officials and community leaders say the Latin population is actually much larger if one counts the undocumented workers in the area. According to a 1976 U.S. Immigration and Naturalization study, there were an additional 330,000 undocumented Spanish-speaking people.

Hispanics in San Antonio tend to be young and to live in larger households than non-Hispanics. More than 41 percent are under 18 years of age and 69 percent are under 35, according to Strategy Research Corporation. The average number of Hispanics per household is 3.4 versus 2.9 for non-Hispanics.

As one would expect from San Antonio's proximity to Mexico, 90 percent of the city's residents are of Mexican descent. Many are second and third generation, which may explain why only 28 precent prefer to speak Spanish at home. About half of San Antonio Hispanics speak both English and Spanish at home. According to Strategy Research, about 86 percent of Hispanic heads of households have lived in the area for more than 25 years.

San Antonio has three full-time Spanish-language radio stations:

KCOR-1350 AM

KCOR signed on as the first Spanish-language station in the United States in 1945. It was owned by a Mexican-American named Raul Cortez. The station changed hands three times before Tichenor Media Systems, based in Harlingen, Texas, bought it in 1975.

The station, with 5,000 watts of power, features a spectrum of Hispanic music -- ballads, mariachi, rancheras. "We stay very contemporary," said Nathan Safir, vice president and general manager. "But we don't do a lot of rock."

KCOR's listeners are slightly older than the average San Antonio Hispanic. Those 35 years and older make up 50 percent of the audience. Twenty-five years and older make up another 25 percent. Many are second- and third-generation Mexican-Americans whose ancestors arrived in the early 1900s, although the continuous immigration from Mexico guarantees the station a permanent audience.

Safir classifies the typical KCOR listeners as "loyal Catholics who like a lot of church news and who listen because we have a more melodic sound and still love Mexico and want to be reminded of it."

In Arbitron's Spring 1986 ratings, 104,900 people listened to the station during the week. About 10,700 tuned in during an average quarter hour.

Because KCOR's audience is predominantly Catholic, the rosary is recited on the air every day. At noon, the local archbishop leads the audience in prayer. The station sends cards to the families of the recently deceased having Hispanic surnames, announcing that a requiem mass for the relative will be said on a certain date. The station arranges the masses with the San Antonio Archdiocese.

KCOR also tries to involve itself in the daily lives of its audience, Safir said. It sends out congratulatory cards to the mothers of every Hispanic-surname baby born in San Antonio, and carries news of marriages within the Hispanic community. Every two weeks it sponsors a concert in a city park. And once a year, it produces the Hispanic State Fair, an all-weekend festival that attracts more than 50,000 people.

Two public-service programs -- "Esta Semana en Los Barrios" (This Week in the Barrios) and "El Pulso de San Antonio" (The Pulse of San Antonio) -- are aired on Sundays. Experts on these shows discuss local issues and answer questions from the audience.

News broadcasts are aired for five minutes on the hour and three minutes on the half-hour 24 hours per day. There is a ten-minute round-up at 6 p.m. daily, with special sport reports at 7:45 a.m. and 5:45 p.m.

The typical newscast is 60 percent local news, 10 percent state, and the rest national and international, Safir said. "We try to go with a local story because we feel they can get plenty of international and national news from TV," he said.

The station has a five-person news staff (out of 35 employees) and three mobile units. It also uses four correspondents in Mexico for live feeds, UPI in Spanish and English, and the radio reports produced by UPI/EFE.

Depending on the news, KCOR management will also run commentaries on local issues. In the Summer of 1986, for example, KCOR supported a referendum to put flouride in San Antonio's water. It also went on record against a spending cap for the city budget.

About 60 percent of the station's advertisers are national accounts.

KEDA-1540 AM

With a hot jalapeno pepper as its logo and the nickname "Spanish Voice of the San Antonio Area," KEDA has been a full-time, 24-hour Spanish-language station since March 1966. It is owned by Manuel Gonzalez Davila, who also owns a Spanish-language station in Corpus Christi.

When the station was first founded, it played only conjunto -- music by a band of fewer than six people and led by an accordion. It can be thought of as the country western sound of Chicano music. More than any other type of music, conjunto is the marriage of South Texas and Mexican and European melodies.

Conjunto music is still played but international songs and mariachi are also aired, giving this station a uniquely Hispanic flavor. KEDA, with 5,000 watts of power during the day and 1,000 watts at night, also plays Tejano music recorded in English.

KEDA's audience is mostly second- and third-generation Mexican-Americans, said program director Maria Alonso. They are primarily 18 to 49 years old, bilingual, and solidly working class.

"If they come straight from Mexico, they might not listen to us. We are more geared to the local community. Our disc jockeys often use Tex-Mex idiomatic expressions. You have to live here a while to understand. They listen to us because we have the music that is uniquely San Antonio," Alonso said.

In the Spring 1986 Arbitron ratings, 74,200 listened to the station during the Monday-through-Sunday 6 a.m.-midnight slot. In an average quarter hour, 8,100 tuned in.

Five-minute newscasts are aired Monday through Friday 10 minutes before the hour, from 5:50 a.m. to 5:50 p.m. Two of the newscasts are devoted entirely to agricultural news from the local extension service. While sports is included in the main newscast, weather reports are given at the quarter and three-quarter hour.

A typical broadcast may have about eight local stories, five from Mexico, and the rest from national and international sources. "Whatever affects our listening audience we emphasize," Alonso said. "It could be local, it could be regional. We try to concentrate on the local because of its immediate impact, but if the national story affects us more, then that takes precendence."

KEDA employs one news director and one part-time news person out of a total staff of 20. It gets the bulk of its news from wire services -- UPI in Spanish and Notimex from Mexico. It does not air editorials.

The station's biggest attraction is its on-air personalities, Alonso said. One of the audience's favorite programs is the afternoon drive-time show hosted by Richard Davila, the station owner's son who is also known as the "Guero Polka." (Guero is a Tex-Mex expression for a light-skin Chicano or Gringo.)

Another audience favorite is a Sunday afternoon music program, "Jalapeno con Salsa" (Jalapeno with Sauce). KEDA takes a break from its traditional Tejano music to play salsa for two hours.

Monday through Friday from 10-11 a.m. listeners are invited to call the station and give job-opportunity information off the air. The employment ads are then aired at 11:30 a.m. and 7:20 p.m. Six days per week, KEDA also broadcasts five-minute public-service announcements of upcoming events, community programs, and social services. "Our listeners are very tuned in to the information we provide," Alonso said.

About 60 percent of the station's advertising is national, Alonso said. A list of regional and national advertisers provided by KEDA covers a wide range of goods and services -- from Allstate Insurance to Busch Beer, from Huggies diapers to Pennzoil.

KXET-1250 AM

Lotus Communications bought KXET in 1983, changed its call letters, and switched its format to Spanish-language music. The station, at 1,000 watts, plays a varied list of hits -- rancheras, nortenas, ballads, cumbia, and Chicano.

The station's music research department monitors request lines, San Antonio record-store sales, and publications in Texas, Mexico, and the rest of the United States to come up with a 600-song play list.

More than 90 percent of its listeners are of Mexican descent, according to general manager Manuel Perez. The audience is a mix of new immigrants, mainly from the northern towns in Mexico, and third-generation Hispanics. The 35- to 64-year-old group is KXET's target audience, and women between 35 and 49 are the station's strength.

"They are the ones who still listen to Spanish radio, and the younger ones are usually the ilegales from Mexico," Perez said.

In the Spring 1986 Arbitron ratings, 50,800 tuned in to KXET during the survey week. About 4,500 listened during an average quarter hour.

The music on KXET "Radio Exito" (Success Radio) varies according to the time of day. Monday through Saturday from 6-10 a.m., a music/variety show features callers wishing loved ones a happy birthday on the air. The station also plays the "Mananitas" (Happy Birthday) song in accompaniment.

From 10:30-11 a.m. "Las Favoritas" (The Favorites) focuses on the best Spanish-language artists and their hits, from Julio Iglesias to oldies by Pedro Infante. "La Hora de los Novios" (Lovers' Hour) runs from 6-7 p.m., with listeners phoning in dedications. That is followed at 8 p.m. by an hour of classic hits by trios from Latin countries in "Guitaras Americanas" (American Guitars).

News is broadcast twice an hour, five minutes before the hour from 6 a.m.-10 p.m. and six times per day on weekends. The emphasis is on local news, followed by state news. A typical broadcast, for example, will have three local stories, two regional reports, one from Latin America, and a national story, Perez said.

Of the station's 22 employees, one works as its news director and is in charge of obtaining local stories, or about 30 percent of the news stories aired. The newscast is supplemented by AP in Spanish and the UPI/EFE live feeds. The station does not editorialize.

However, KXET's policy calls for community involvement and public service. "KXET en la Comunidad" (KXET in the Community), a Sunday show, deals with housing, social services, employment, and other issues. To promote community goodwill and to increase it own listenership, the station has sponsored a summer concert series to assist nonprofit organizations.

KXET also has its own in-market promotions, such as How Many Frijoles in a Taco, Guessing the Mystery Melody, and a Worker's Lunch Raffle in which local businesses register to participate.

The station's advertisers are evenly divided between national and local accounts, Perez said.

HOUSTON

As the seventh-largest Hispanic market in the United States, the Houston area was home to 706,500 Latins in 1987. From 1985 to 1987, the Hispanic population experienced almost a 16 percent increase, according to Strategy Research Report. Although they make up only 15 percent of the Houston metro-area population, Hispanics comprised 41 percent of the Houston Independent School District in 1985.

Seventy-five percent of the Hispanics live in Harris County, which includes the City of Houston. Most have lived in the area for some time. The average length of residency, for example, is 15 years. About one-third have lived in the Houston area for more than 20 years.

The majority are quite young -- almost 74 percent are under 35 years of age. About 27 percent are children under 12, according to Strategy Research Corporation. Hispanics also live in larger households; the average household size is 3.7 persons, compared to 2.8 for their non-Hispanic counterparts.

Interestingly, about three-fourths of Houston's Hispanics are U.S. citizens, according to Strategy Research Corporation. This suggests that, given the youth of this market, many are citizens by birth.

About 90 percent of the Hispanics are of Mexican origin. The rest are Salvadorans, Cubans, Puerto Ricans, and other Latins.

About two-thirds of Houston's Hispanics speak Spanish at home; the rest speak both languages. The educational level is slightly higher than other Hispanic areas in Texas. More than 40 percent are high-school graduates, and 20 percent graduated from college.

There are at least seven Spanish-language radio stations in the area:

KEYH-850 AM

In the Summer of 1978, KEYH experimented with its format by providing half a day of Spanish programming on Saturdays. The pilot programming on the all-news English-language radio station proved to be so popular that management expanded Spanish programming, first to all day on Saturdays and then to full time on weekends.

The station, which is owned by 10 local investors, finally went all Spanish in February 1979. Nicknamed "La Ranchera" for the type of music it plays, KEYH transmits at 10,000 watts from sunrise to sunset.

Listeners come from all walks of life and ages, according to David Armstrong, general manager and one of the owners. But most are Mexican, primarily from the northern border towns, who like to listen to Tejano and ranchera music but enjoy Latin American hits as well. About 60 percent of its audience is composed of women.

"We have a little bit of everything, people who own businesses to blue-collar workers to laborers," Armstrong said.

In the Spring 1986 Arbitron ratings of the Houston-Galveston area, 45,800 people reported listening to KEYH during the Monday through Sunday 6 a.m.-midnight slot. In an average quarter hour, about 4,000 tuned in.

Newscasts are aired for five minutes on the hour plus headline news on the half hour from 6 a.m. to sign off. The station also has a five-minute prerecorded sports show weekdays at 5:15 p.m. Latin American news receives a little more play, but not necessarily at the expense of other stories. "Whatever is more imperative, more newsworthy, we carry," Armstrong said.

KEYH airs editorials, but not on a regular basis. In the past, management has spoken out on immigration, bilingual education, and "anything that would have a big impact on our community," Armstrong said.

The station employs 21 people but it has no news staff. All of its news comes from AP in Spanish and English.

The station's efforts are directed at its music programming. Golden oldie programs and cooking and recipe shows are interspersed with international music and a daily hour of tropical music. As for public-service programming, KEYH airs employment opportunities daily at 8 a.m.; a one-hour noon show, "La Voz del Pueblo" (The Voice of the People), deals with a variety of topics from medical problems to social-service issues. An audience favorite is "Platica De Houston" (Talk of Houston), hosted by a Texas-born Anglo who grew up in Mexico City. Subjects range from politics to religion to schools.

About 60 percent of the advertisers on KEYH are national accounts. That number has been increasing steadily since the station changed its format, Armstrong said.

KFRD-980 AM

This station was founded in 1948 by a Texas businessman. Although its programming was in English, there was a 15-minute block of Spanish every day. That increased over the years as did Houston's Hispanic population. In November 1985, the station went full-time Spanish.

KFRD transmits at 1,000 watts from 6 a.m. to sunset. It is owned by Fort Bend Broadcasting Company, a local, privately owned company. It plays Tejano music primarily, but adds some international Latin American music as well.

Disc jockeys sometimes use English phrases and will occasionally play English-language songs, mostly by singers such as Julio Iglesias who have crossed the language barrier.

KFRD's audience is the second-generation Hispanic who has developed a taste for Tejano music, a blend of Mexican and U.S. sounds. Most of its listeners are in the 30-to-50-year-old age group, said George Thompson, executive vice president and general manager.

News is broadcast for five minutes every hour and half hour during daytime programming. The emphasis is clearly on Houston-area news, with reports from Texas a close second. "We actually have very little news from Mexico and Latin American," Thompson said.

The station shares 23 employees with its English-language FM station (KFRD-104.9), including its three news people. Most of the news is supplied by UPI wires.

One of its more popular community-oriented programs is a half-hour show on Sunday mornings. "Lo Nuestro" (Ours) is a prerecorded program that features lawyers, Army recruiters, welfare officials, school board employees, and a host of other community leaders, discussing various topics.

About 60 percent of the station's advertising comes from local companies, Thompson said.

KLAT-1010 AM

Tichenor Media Systems bought this station in 1984. It had been broadcasting in Spanish, at 5,000 watts 24 hours per day, for four years with a varied music format.

"La Tremenda" (The Tremendous), as the station is nicknamed, plays rancheras and regional music about 80 percent of the time, said news director Mariano Garcia. This reflects the station's listenership, which is about 85 percent Mexican.

Garcia estimates that the overwhelming majority of the station's listeners work in the service industries (hotels, restaurants, construction, etc.) and have less than a high-school education. Most are recent immigrants and some form a transient population that comes to the Houston area looking for work and leaves when there is none. They are middle class to lower-middle class and tune in "because most of them don't speak English and we are their source of information," according to Garcia.

About 87,700 people listened to "La Tremenda" during the week of the Spring 1986 Arbitron ratings. The average quarter hour listenership was 6,000.

Although KLAT's music is the primary attraction, the station offers a fair share of news. In addition to the newscasts of five minutes every hour, from 5:56 a.m. to 8:56 p.m., KLAT has a 15-minute news block during the morning drive. It also airs a daily simulcast of the local NBC affiliate's 10 p.m. news show. Listeners need only turn down the sound of the television to hear the translation on KLAT. Garcia said this is an important source of news for area Hispanics because there is no Spanish-language TV with local programming in the evenings.

Aside from the traditional weather, sports, and traffic reports, KLAT also features daily feeds from its correspondent in Mexico City. The emphasis, however, is on local news, then reports from south of the border. "We try to be as flexible as possible and, of course, if you have a news item like the U.S. attack on Libya, that takes precendence over every-thing," Garcia said.

KLAT has a three-member news staff among its 33 employees. The bulk of the news is obtained from AP in Spanish and English, local newspapers, and television.

The station has editorialized on traditional Hispanic issues, such as immigration, police abuse, and housing, but it has done so sporadically, Garcia said.

Most of the community-service programming is reserved for the weekend. A 15-minute Saturday night show, "En Houston" (In Houston), focuses on community events and social happenings with short, lively interviews. KLAT also does a considerable amount of remote broadcasting from malls and neighborhoods on weekends. Since December 1985 the station has sponsored the "Festival of the Super Stars" along with several national companies. More than 36,000 Hispanics filled the Astrodome in 1985 to watch the show.

Weekdays, there is a one-hour noon show, "La Voz del Pueblo" (The Voice of the People), which features an open line with community leaders, busi-nessmen, and politicians. At 9:30 a.m. "La Tremenda" has its own version of want ads with "Mercado del Aire" (On-the-air Market).

The audience favorite is the morning drive show from 6-9:30 a.m. titled "Cada Loco con su Tema" (Every Fool with a Theme). Four deejays exchange verbal jabs, jokes, and philosophy between songs and newscasts.

KLAT has more national advertisers than local advertisers. Garcia attributes that to the recession in the area. "When the boom went bust, a lot of local businesses failed," he said. "Our management had the fore-sight to see beyond the local companies and go for the national accounts."

KLVL-1480 AM

Felix H. Morales founded this station in 1950, the first Spanish station in the Houston area. Although its license is approved for 24 hours, "Radio Morales" actually transmits at 1,000 watts from 5 a.m. to midnight.

Most of its listeners are bilingual but prefer to speak Spanish, said news director Pedro Gomez. Many are recent immigrants, having arrived within the last 10 years. But another sizable segment of the station's constituency is the Mexican-Americans who have listened to KLVL since the station signed on.

"The common denominator is their Hispanic roots," Gomez said. "They want to listen to music in Spanish."

KLVL plays rancheras as well as ballads, salsa, and cumbia music. The idea, Gomez said, is to appeal to everybody without losing the station's faithful Mexican-American following.

From 7 a.m.-5 p.m. every day, KLVL listeners hear five minutes of news every hour on the hour. The newscasts include not only weather and sports but missing-persons reports. A typical broadcast emphasizes local news first with at least two local stories per hour, Gomez said.

There are two news employees out of a total staff of 20. Practically all the news is obtained from UPI in English, which Gomez translates. The rest is taken from the local Houston dailies.

The station editorializes, although not frequently. "We do so because we think that part of our job is to orient people and let our opinions be known," Gomez said.

The station tries to serve as an educational link in the acculturation process for Houston's Hispanics. In addition to its employment ads and religious programming, Houston police officers man the microphones 15 minutes every Tuesday to talk about drugs, crime protection, and police service. Also on Tuesday, from 2:15 to 2:30 p.m., representatives from the public library talk about programs and about the types of books, films, and tapes available to the community. On Thursdays, a nonprofit community-service organization gives similar information about medical and social services.

Most of the advertising comes from local businesses, Gomez said.

KXKX-106.5 FM

KXKX has been the only FM Spanish-language station in Houston since 1983, when Mar Broadcasting purchased the station and changed its English-language rock-music format. For 24 hours, at 100,000 watts, the station plays a blend of international hits, romantic easy-listening music by leading Hispanic vocalists, and rancheras.

"We play the top 20 hits from Mexico City, from Bogota, from Caracas," said station manager Bruce Miller Earl. "We pride ourselves in breaking new ground. No matter where the Hispanic comes from, he will feel at home with us."

KXKX targets its music to the 14-to-45-year-old group and a more affluent audience. Most of its listeners are Mexican, but "we're not a Chicano station," Earl said. The station also tries to maintain an international flavor with its disc jockeys, who are from Honduras, Colombia, and Mexico.

In the Spring 1986 Arbitron ratings, 58,200 people tuned in during the week. The average quarter hour listenership was 3,400.

KXKX has five-minute newscasts 20 minutes after the hour every hour from 6:20-9:20 a.m. and from 3:20-5:20 p.m. It also translates simultaneously the local CBS affiliate's news program at 10 p.m. Monday through Friday.

A typical broadcast features about 10 stories in headline fashion, along with weather and sports. At least four of those stories are local. The

99

station employs 20 people. Of those, one is a news person -- the news director -- who delivers the morning and afternoon drive newscasts. Most of the news is obtained from UPI in Spanish and from listeners' tips.

On Special patriotic days -- Mexican, Colombian, and Cuban Independence days, for example -- the station airs short vignettes about the history of the country and its heroes. However, KXKX does not editorialize on any issues.

It broadcasts a two-hour public-service program on Sundays, "Linea Abierta" (Open Line), in which experts talk about drugs, child abuse, and other social issues.

About 70 percent of KXKX's advertising comes from national accounts. But the station carefully screens its customers. "If you advertise on this station and we get a complaint that you burn someday, that's it, Jack," Earl said. "Radio is a trust sort of thing, particularly Hispanic radio. We want to build a confidence with the audience."

KXYZ-1320 AM

Infinity Broadcasting, which also owns a Spanish-language station in New York, bought KXYZ in June 1983. At that time the 24-hour station, which transmits at 5,000 watts, had been programming full-time in Spanish for about 18 months. Before that, it had a religious format.

KXYZ is a soft-listening adult contemporary station that often plays "sophisticated rancheras," said program director Eleazar Garcia. About 70 percent of the station's listeners are Mexican, but there is also a sizable number of Salvadorans and Colombians. Listeners are 18 to 54 years old and are primarily working class. Many are bilingual and second-generation U.S. Hispanics. "They may listen to other English-language stations, but they come back to listen to us for music and sports," Garcia said.

In the Spring 1986 Arbitron ratings, about 73,600 people listened Monday through Sunday from 6 a.m. to midnight. About 5,100 listened during an average quarter hour.

Weekdays KXYZ has a one-hour block of news at 6 a.m. Five-minute newscasts are heard every hour throughout the rest of the day until 10 p.m. The station also carries news every hour on Saturdays from 9 a.m.-8 p.m. Sports is an important ingredient in the newscast. During the 1986 World Cup in Mexico City, for example, there were up-to-date bulletins throughout the day. One week, the sportscast originated from Mexico City.

The station obtains most of its news through UPI in Spanish. It employs one newsperson and a staff of more than 30 people.

The audience's favorite show is the morning drive, "Todo en Uno" (All in One). Three disc jockeys tell jokes, read the news, and discuss entertainment events from 6-10 a.m. "Chandeliers" (Candlelight), another popular show in the 7-10 p.m. weekday slot, encourages listeners to call in with requests for the most romantic ballads.

100

KXYZ also publishes a monthly magazine which is distributed by 35 merchants in Latin neighborhoods. About 20,000 copies of "Revis 13" (Magazine 13), are given away to entice listeners to participate in contests with prizes of cash and merchandise.

The station's local and national advertisers are about evenly divided. But Garcia expects some growth in the local market. "Probably in two years, we'll see the local economy coming back," said Garcia in mid-1986. "There will be a better economy and an increasing number of Hispanics and more business for us."

DALLAS-FORT WORTH

About 383,700 Hispanics lived in the Dallas-Fort Worth area in 1985, an increase of 18 percent in two years. Dallas-Fort Worth is the 12th largest Hispanic market in the United States. The majority of Hispanics, 56 percent, lived in the Dallas County area. Tarrant County, adjacent to Dallas, had another 26 percent of the population, according to Strategy Research Corporation. About 90 percent are of Mexican descent.

Like other Hispanic groups, Dallas Hispanics tend to be young but have lived in the area for some time. Forty percent are under 18, and 34 percent are between the ages of 18 and 34. The average household head has lived in the area for 16.5 years.

The average Hispanic household in the area is also 37 percent larger than the non-Hispanic home -- 3.7 persons per home to 2.7, according to Strategy Research. At home, 41 percent speak Spanish most frequently and 29 percent speak both languages.

KESS-94 FM

"La Fabulosa" (The Fabulous) KESS has been a full-time Spanish station since 1964. Its present owner, Mark Rodriguez, is the son of former owner Marcos Rodriguez, Sr. of Latin American Broadcasting. Rodriguez, Sr. started as a disc jockey and salesman, was promoted to director of programming, and then to general manager. In 1976, Rodriguez bought the station. In mid-1986 he passed controlling interest to his son and stayed on as a consultant and radio supervisor. His son also bought the other Spanish-language station in the Dallas-Fort Worth area -- KSSA-AM. The sale is pending FCC approval.

KESS, transmitting at 100,000 watts, directs it musical format at the heavily Mexican population of the area, playing nortenas, rancheras, and other Mexican folkloric melodies. A great percentage of its listeners are bilingual, most are 25 years old and up, although the station does attract some teenagers, Rodriguez said.

"They listen to us for information about the Hispanic issues of the community because that concerns them directly," Rodriguez said. "But we are also a reminder of their roots and culture."

In the Winter 1986 Arbitron ratings, 93,700 people reported listening to KESS during a given week. About 13,700 tuned in during an average quarter hour.

News is broadcast at the hour and half-hour for five minutes every Monday through Saturday from 6 a.m.-10 p.m. Preference is given to local news. "But whatever is news gets in and may lead the broadcast," Rodriguez said. "We have news from everywhere, national and international."

The station, which employs 31 people, has a two-person news staff. It also uses AP in Spanish and English and the UPI/EFE live feeds.

Like many Spanish-language stations, KESS often serves as an employment agency for its immigrant listeners. At 3:45 p.m. every day, job opportunities are broadcast during a 15-minute program called "Busco Trabajo" (Seeking Work). In addition, a daily program at 9:30 a.m. helps the audience buy and sell items on "Linea Abierta" (Open Line).

A more typical community-service program is the 30-minute "Fabulosa en La Comunidad" (Fabulous in the Community) on Sundays. Community leaders and experts are invited to discuss issues, with an emphasis on local happenings.

The station's management editorializes occasionally, "when it is necessary," Rodriguez said.

Most of KESS' advertisers are local companies. The station, however, does not accept ads for liquor, wine, card readers, or astrologers.

"A big part of our audiences places a lot of trust in this station and we want to keep a certain image in the community," Rodriguez Sr. explained.

KSSA-1270 AM

KSSA began its 24-hour Spanish programming in 1983, when it changed its format from a soft listening sound. Marcos Rodriguez Jr. of Latin American Broadcasting bought the station in mid-1986 and, at the time of this writing, the sale was pending FCC approval.

"Radio Variedades" (Variety Radio), as the station is called, transmits at 5,000 watts. The overwhelming majority of its audience is Mexican-American, many of them third generation. There is, however, a growing number of Argentines, Peruvians, and other South Americans in the area who tune into the station, said general manager Al Brooks. For each of these groups, KSSA plays a variety of Latin music.

In the Spring 1986 Arbitron ratings, 36,100 people reported listening to the station at some point during the week. During an average quarter hour, 2,800 people listened.

News is aired every hour on the hour for three to five minutes. While the station tries to provide a range of stories, the emphasis is clearly on local and Mexican news. KSSA also carries a lot of sports -- baseball, boxing, and soccer news.

Of the 25-member staff, two are full-time news people. KSSA also uses AP in Spanish, and Notimex.

The station has always been profitable with the Spanish-language format, Brooks said. It has both national and local advertisers who buy time on the station because "it is a way of reaching an audience they might not reach otherwise."

CHICAGO RADIO

Chicago is the nation's fifth largest Hispanic market, with 753,700 Hispanics in 1987. Yet, Spanish-language radio is in its infancy in the Windy City. Two of the three Spanish stations signed on in 1985. The third has been broadcasting since 1968.

"Chicago is one of the major markets for Hispanics and yet there are so few stations," said Chuck Brooks, vice president and general manager of WIND, which debuted in December 1985. "We wanted to be in Chicago and we were looking for the right opportunity."

The Chicago Hispanic population has been growing steadily in recent years. In 1970, Latins totalled 368,300. A decade later that had almost doubled to 640,200. Between 1980 and 1987, the Hispanic population grew by about 18 percent, according to Strategy Research Corporation. The City of Chicago, in Cook County, is home to nearly 70 percent of those Hispanics; surrounding counties with sizable Hispanic populations include Lake, Kane, DuPage, and Will.

Chicago Hispanics tend to be quite young, according to a 1984 Strategy Research Corporation report. Forty-one percent are under 18 years of age and 75 percent are under 35. Most -- 63 percent -- are of Mexican descent. Puerto Ricans make up 22 percent of the population and Cubans another 3 percent. Central and South Americans comprise the remaining 12 percent.

Chicago's Hispanics have a lower average educational level than the Hispanic population at large, but have higher family disposable income, according to the 1984 Strategy Research study.

In 1986, there were three full-time Spanish-language stations:

WIND-560 AM

Tichenor Media Systems, based in Texas, bought this station in 1985 from Westinghouse and converted it from a news/talk format to Spanish-language adult contemporary. It broadcasts 24 hours a day at 5,000 watts.

The music selection tends toward international hits with songs from Mexico, Puerto Rico, and the Dominican Republic. Disc jockeys also play ethnic music -- salsa, rancheras, and cumbia -- as well as traditional ballads.

General manager Chuck Brooks said the station has made a conscious effort to go after the female audience. He estimates that about 55 percent of WIND's listeners are women.

According to the Winter 1986 Arbitron ratings, 147,900 listeners tuned to the station between 6 a.m. and midnight during a given week. Fifty-seven percent of those were Hispanics and nine percent were black. In an average quarter hour, 11,400 persons listened to the station at any given point, according to Arbitron.

WIND conducts frequent promotional campaigns to attract Hispanics, Brooks said. But that is not the station's chief attraction. "There is a great incidence of those who don't speak Spanish. And an English-language radio station doesn't play music in Spanish," Brooks said.

The station also tries to maintain its community involvement. A new in-house program features United Way and Red Cross volunteers manning phone lines off the air three days per week to help callers. On Saturdays, a half-hour program discusses "anything that affects the local market -- education, jobs, or politics," Brooks said.

News broadcasts are limited to three minutes every hour from 6 a.m. to midnight Monday through Sunday. The emphasis is on headline local news. The station has four staff reporters who double as reporters and on-air personalities. (There are 40 full-time employees.) The news staff supplements the broadcasts with AP in English and UPI in Spanish and English.

Ninety percent of WIND advertisers are local merchants advertising everything from cars to banking. Many are Anglo-owned businesses. The station also airs remote broadcasts from malls and business centers to attract advertisers and to increase its profile in the community.

WOJO-105 FM

WOJO, nicknamed "Radio Ambiente" (Radio Ambience), carried Spanish programming since 1968 as a brokered station before going to a Spanish-only format. It is owned by the privately held Broadcast Communications.

For many years, WOJO was the only full-time Spanish outlet catering to the predominantly Mexican population. While its format is adult contemporary music, there is also a heavy emphasis on news. The station plays a bit of everything, including rancheras, and its listeners are attracted to it because they prefer to listen to Spanish or simply because they do not understand English.

"There is a very strong tie to the culture among Hispanics," explained Mary McEvilly, the station's public-relations manager. "A good two-thirds prefer to use Spanish. That is the language they feel comfortable in."

WOJO was the top-rated Spanish-language station in the Arbitron Winter 1986 sweeps. Over 162,000 people tuned in during the week between 6 a.m. and midnight. Ninety-five percent were Hispanic. In an average quarter hour, 15,600 people listened to the station.

McEvilly said the station is "very middle of the road." It does not editorialize or take stands on issues. "The news," she added, "is reported as the news. We are objective."

The eight-person news department and its stable of correspondents puts together three news broadcasts -- 6-7 a.m., noon-12:30 p.m. and 4:30-5 p.m. WOJO also broadcasts five minutes of news on the hour and headline news on the half hour.

Newscasts carry a variety of stories, including national and local news, but international news tends to emphasize reports from Mexico. The station also gets feeds from the AP.

"What we highlight depends on what is news," McEvilly said. "During the earthquake in Mexico, a lot of our news program dealt with that, more so than, say, NBC or CBS."

In addition to the news broadcasts, WOJO carries a one-hour community-oriented talk show on Mondays. "You and the Law" focuses on regulations and laws that affect Hispanics, from immigration rulings to labor laws. Other popular shows include a weekly gong-show type program called "The Stairway to Fame," which features live performances of local amateur artists.

Every year the station stages its own festival, "Con Sabor a Mexico" (With the Flavor of Mexico), an event that attracts 150,000 Hispanics over three days. WOJO also has the rights to the Spanish-language broadcasts of the Chicago Cubs baseball games.

The majority of WOJO's advertising clients are local businesses, but the station also has major national accounts, such as breweries, soft drink companies, and car manufacturers, McEvilly said. The station employs 47 people.

WTAQ-1300 AM

WTAQ, "Radio Fiesta," signed on August 1, 1985, shortly after being purchased by Lotus Communications. Before it became full-time Spanish-language adult contemporary, it was a brokered station providing the programs in several languages. WTAQ transmits at 5,000 watts.

"The market is large enough to support another Hispanic radio station," said general manager Joe Newman. "Fifty percent of the Hispanics in Chicago are bilingual, but their music is ingrained as they are growing up. They want to listen to their music. A large number also want to listen to community news and events that are not covered by the general media."

WTAQ's main audience is Mexican, although the programming is not limited to them. Most listeners are between 18 and 34 years old. "Radio Fiesta's" secondary market is the 35-to 49 year-old group. Most listeners are blue-collar working people "who haven't integrated as much because they are the newer immigrants," Newman said.

WTAQ carries news on the hour and half hour 24 hours per day. Five minutes in length, the broadcasts carry local, national, and international news supplied mainly by UPI and EFE. The station, however, also has its own news director, assistant news director, and seven stringers. The emphasis is on local news.

"They want to listen to the news from the barrios," Newman said. "This is the type of information that cannot be gotten anywhere else."

The popular shows, however, are the music and audience-participation programs. One program, "King of the Hill," features two music groups battling it out while fans call in to vote for their favorite. The morning drive show, from 6 to 9 a.m., is the "Blooper Hour" when deejays tell jokes and talk to callers between songs.

In addition to music, WTAQ provides extensive sports coverage. It carries Chicago White Sox baseball and the Chicago Sting soccer games. During the World Cup, it broadcast several matches live.

Newman said the station stresses its community involvement and its eagerness to serve as a forum for the local Hispanic community. Twice a day, seven days a week, the station airs comments by callers in a program called "The Voice of the People." The station has promoted voter registration and aired panel discussions with eight city council candidates. It sponsored a health fair with 60 health-care providers, and a sidewalk sale with local merchants.

WTAQ management does not editorialize. "We would rather have the audience say what the problems are than pontificate," Newman said.

"Radio Fiesta" is "very profitable and very successful," he added. Advertisers run the gamut from national food makers to major local department stores. The station employs 23 people.

IV. Wire Services

The wires are the main -- in some cases, the only -- source of information for the Spanish-language media. Yet not one news service is owned by a U.S. Hispanic. Only Hispanic Link News Service is a homegrown product -- but it is a column syndicate, not a news service.

AP and UPI have Spanish-language wires, which move stories written by Hispanics. EFE, also written in Spanish, is subsidized by the Spanish government. Most Spanish-language customers of these three wires are in Latin America. Those in the United States are simply a secondary market and there is no consistent coverage in Spanish of events that interest them. In other words, news concerning Hispanics in the United States does not take precedence over news from Latin America.

News executives agree that this creates a void in the coverage of the U.S. Hispanic community. Many newspapers, radio stations, and television outlets must buy the English-language wire and go through a tedious translation process to obtain a substantial amount of domestic news and sports coverage.

Some have suggested that the ideal solution would be a news service by and about U.S. Hispanics. The immense cost, however, makes such a venture unlikely in the near future.

EFE

Spanish-language EFE was started in 1939 as a national and international wire service for newspapers in Spain. In its beginning years, it bought international news from AP, UPI, and Reuters, and also supplied those wire services with news from Spain.

In 1966, EFE expanded its foreign service, opening a bureau in Buenos Aires; later it opened offices in every Latin American country. With a staff of its own in Latin America, EFE stopped buying news from the other wire services. In 1973, EFE helped found the Central American News Agency, with headquarters in Panama. EFE now owns 51 percent of that organization. In 1979, EFE inaugurated its English-language service for English-language clients in Europe. In 1986, it had nine clients.

EFE's American operations are headquarterd in Washington, D.C., where there are 12 correspondents. Two other reporters are based in New York, and one in Miami. The service also employs stringers in Los Angeles and Houston in addition to the bureaus in Latin American countries.

To date, the majority of EFE's clients are Latin American newspapers. EFE has about 600 newspaper, television, and radio-station clients in both American hemispheres. Customers also include embassies and government agencies -- anybody, that is, who may be interested in Hispanic America.

"America continues to be one of our most important clients. In addition, the news that comes from this continent is always very important," said Victor Olmos, general manager for the United States and Canada.

EFE, explained Olmos, is a state agency but unlike other news agencies controlled by the government, such as the Soviets' Tass, "it does not answer to the dictates of the Spanish government," Olmos said. Though subsidized by the government, "it is an independent informational service," he said.

Media outlets subscribe to EFE because of the information and special insights the wire service can provide, Olmos said. The Spanish agency gives its clients a different perspective on Hispanic America: news from Latin America and the United States through the eyes, voice, and writing of Spanish speakers.

"EFE's information on Central America is very complete, and in Cuba we are vital because no U.S. wire agency can get much information," Olmos said.

EFE moves an average of 300 news items a day. The two most important criteria, Olmos said, are speed and complete objectivity. Special news summaries are sent to morning and afternoon newspapers.

In addition to news from Latin America, EFE has a domestic service covering all of Spain. A condensed version of this service is offered to foreign clients in Spanish, English, and French.

The EFE sports service handles both domestic and foreign news. Subscribers get special soccer reports during the soccer season as well as stories on domestic and foreign sports tournaments -- the Olympics, World Soccer Cups, Formula I races, and cycling tours.

Like other wire services, EFE has its own photo department, which employs more than 400 photographers in Spain and correspondents in the bureaus. EFE also maintains special exchange agreements with almost 50 other wire services.

In 1983, EFE and UPI agreed to form "Nuestras Noticias" (Our News), a special live broadcasting service with 18 feeds per day. EFE provides the personnel and UPI the technical operations. The emphasis in the seven-minute broadcasts of "Nuestras Noticias" is on Latin American news -- political, cultural, and human interest.

"Radio stations throughout the hemisphere had been asking for live feeds by Spanish-speakers," Olmos said. "For them we play a different role than other services. We provide news that is reported, investigated, and written by somebody in their own language. Our Latin clients notice the difference."

Aside from the traditional daily news coverage, EFE also doubles as a feature syndicate. Members can subscribe to its "Grandes Firmas" (Great Signatures) service. Well-known Hispanic writers -- Mario Vargas Llosa, Octavio Paz, the late Jorge Luis Borges, Alejo Carpentier, among others -- have written about religion, politics, philosophy, and sociology.

EFE also has a weekly service called Stories and Tales. Guest short-story writers include Jose Luis Acquaroni, Francisco Ayala, Vicente Soto, Francisco Umbral, and others.

Olmos is very optimistic about the future of EFE in North America. A growing Hispanic population, he says, can only mean more television stations, more radio stations, and newspapers -- all potential clients for his wire service. "This market can only grow," Olmos said. "And we believe EFE can grow along with it."

Hispanic Link

In 1980, when Charlie Ericksen began to dream of a syndicated feature service in Spanish, there were no Hispanic syndicated columnists. "There was a real frustration on the part of Hispanic journalists and a voice in the media," said Ericksen, who has worked for two Los Angeles newspapers and three television stations.

That year he and his Mexican-born wife, Sebastiana, founded Hispanic Link News Service. The Washington, D.C.-based Hispanic Link has two separate functions: providing columns to newspapers three times per week, and publishing Hispanic Link Weekly Report newsletter.

The syndicated column service provides columns in both English and Spanish. It has 200 clients, about 50 of which are Spanish-language newspapers, mainly in the Southwest. Clients range from small Spanish-language weeklies to major metropolitan dailies in English such as the San Diego Union. A client can order a column in both Spanish and English.

Hispanic Link has used the works of about 80 different authors, from mayors to journalists to people who smuggle aliens. In the past, it has used well-known names -- such as Vice President George Bush, 1982 Nobel Prize winner Gabriel Garcia Marquez, and San Antonio Mayor Henry Cisneros. It also has regular contributors, including a humor columnist from California and an Arizona-based writer who does analysis of Latin American issues.

"We are a showplace for the best Hispanic minds and writers," Ericksen said.

The criteria used to select columns is simple: What will interest Hispanics around the country? The service does not shy away from controversial topics. Subjects include Central American politics, police brutality, lack of Hispanics in American newsrooms, immigration, and desegregation of barrio schools. During elections, Ericksen has asked Republican and Democratic leaders to voice their opinions in paired columns.

"We try to provide a cross-section of Hispanic views, with a lot of pros and cons," Ericksen said. "We don't try to sell editors on one Hispanic viewpoint. There is no such animal."

English-language clients have become increasingly receptive to the service in the past years, yet they prefer certain types of columns. "The English-language media likes the soft, gentler column, the one that reminisces about growing up in the barrio, for instance. They will also take something if it's a hot issue and it's timely, but getting them to do that has been something of a weaning process," he added.

Spanish-language clients, on the other hand, are eager for any type of column. They prefer ones that contain hard information, opinions, and analysis. In either case, Ericksen looks for a column that will provide a different angle on an event, something that establishment newspapers have not already got.

The service's most successful columns have done precisely that. In May 1980, dozens of English- and Spanish-language newspapers ran a powerful first-person story by Diego C. Asencio, the U.S. Ambassador to Colombia taken by terrorists who occupied the Dominican Republic Embassy in Bogota. In the account, he told how he used his Hispanic heritage to ameliorate the explosive situation.

"At one point, during a debate with the guerrillas about multinationals and Yankee imperialism, I made a sharp comment, 'How can you talk? You're all middle-class. I'm the only son of a working man here.' When a culture is part of you, you know when to press and how far," he wrote.

In a more sentimental vein, another popular column was written by Cesar Chavez's son in "A Father's Day Message to Cesar Chavez."

"Material things meant nothing to him, but we always had something to eat. Sometimes we got it picking potatoes in the fields after the crew had been through them.

"'I want you to learn what farm labor is like,' he said. But we'd have enough potatoes for weeks. A used couch or used TV was as good as a new one, he'd tell us," wrote Fernando Chavez.

Ericksen occasionally writes columns himself although he prefers not to. "The people with real sensitivity and depth are out there," he said. In a poignant column that poked fun at many stereotypes, Ericksen wrote about his experiences raising five bicultural and bilingual children. "Somehow, Spanish became the family language of laughter. English we used to make assignments and to discipline," he wrote.

The Hispanic Link Weekly Report, the second component of the Ericksen organization, was started in 1983. By mid-1986 it had 1,000 subscribers who paid $96 per year. The overwhelming majority of subscribers are Hispanic leaders and some American firms with a stake in knowing what is happening in the Hispanic community.

The English-language newsletter "assumes a greater sophistication on the part of the reader. This is for people who don't have the time to read 20 tabloids, the movers and shakers who have an interest in keeping up with the Hispanic community at large," Ericksen said.

The newsletter is written much like a newspaper: tightly, objectively, and to the point. It employs an editor and two reporters who gather information from politicians, other journalists, media outlets, and Hispanic organizations. The weekly report is usually full of statistical information about unemployment, farm population, and other trends. "We are constantly looking for trends because that is what interests our readers," Ericksen said.

Weekly Report usually runs about six 8-1/2x11" pages. The front page carries four stories along with a standard department called "Making the News this Week." The lead story of the newsletter is always longer than the others and focuses on an issue of national importance. For example, in the February 3, 1986 newsletter, the lead story was about the Hispanic population growth over the past five years. The story reported that it had increased by 16 percent compared to a 3-percent growth in the total population. The story jumped to page two, citing more statistics on unemployment rates, poverty level, median age, household size, and gender of heads of households. The story included a small chart on the front page and, inside, two full pages of statistics provided by the U.S. Bureau of the Census.

That same week, the three other front-page newsletter pieces were no more than three or four paragraphs each. One was about Red Cross fraud in Puerto Rico, another was on a poll of Hispanic churchgoing, and a third on a sting operation by the Immigration and Naturalization Service in El Paso.

This variety of topics and wealth of statistical information is typical of front pages of the Weekly Report. In the April 28, 1986 issue, for example, a report on the growing number of Hispanics registering to vote was the lead story. It also included three charts of voter registration by geographic region, presidential voting, and number of eligible voters. The only other story on that page was a four-paragraph obituary on a well-known Hispanic journalist who had covered Fidel Castro's early revolutionary activities.

The standard "Making the News This Week" is a roundup about newsmakers around the country. It includes information about politicians, scientists, entertainers, businessmen, and athletes. For instance, the June 30, 1986 issue listed the names of Hispanic students honored during a Presidential Scholars ceremony, announced the appointment of the first Hispanic to the University of Wisconsin Board of Regents, and included sports results for golfer Chi Chi Rodriguez, boxer Hector Camacho, and swimmer Pablo Morales.

On page two, a lively and cutting feature is "Sin Pelos en la Lengua" (Without Hairs on the Tongue), which contains funny (and embarrassing) news items. In a February 3, 1986 column commenting on a Census Bureau report, a Weekly Report writer said: "In all of its reports on persons of Spanish origin in the United States, the Census Bureau obstinately refuses to include those in Puerto Rico, even though they are U.S. citizens and there's a constant flow between the island and the mainland."

In another column, on April 28, 1986, the writer reported that San Antonio Mayor Henry Cisnero, who won 72.9 percent of the vote when last elected, sent Clint Eastwood, who received 72.2 percent, a telegram welcoming him to "the good, bad, and ugly world of local government."

In addition to this regular feature, page two usually carries two or three short reports on a variety of topics. A sampling from the February 3 newsletter: few Hispanic lawyers in the nation's largest law firms; a new program for undergraduate Central American students; the decline of Hispanics serving on public-school boards; and a U.S. Supreme Court ruling against a group of Chicago Hispanic police sergeants.

Weekly Report also runs several other departments in every issue: Collectables, Calendar, Arts & Entertainment, and Media Report. Collectables tells readers where to get more information on topics that were covered in the newsletter. The other sections as their names imply, list the latest news on those topics.

Every issue also contains a short classified section for corporate and managerial positions.

United Press International (UPI)

UPI's Latin American wire can trace its roots back to 1919, when La Prensa newspaper of Buenos Aires started United Press service. Sixty-seven years later, in 1986, Mexican businessman Mario Vazquez Rana bought 95 percent of the ailing wire service along with Houston developer Joe E. Russo, who owns five percent. This prompted some critics to worry that Vazquez Rana would promote the national interests of Mexico.

Vazquez rebutted those concerns: "I didn't buy UPI to throw away my money. The first time I try to defend my country's position through UPI, at that moment I would be digging UPI's grave," he told Editor & Publisher magazine.

That same year, Vazquez authorized the hiring of more than two dozen new reporters and photographers. Two of those reporters were expected to be stationed in Central America, probably in Nicaragua and Honduras.

UPI's Spanish-language wire now has more than 400 clients in Latin America and about 40 in the United States, mostly radio stations and a few newspapers in the predominantly Hispanic cities in New York, California, Florida, Illinois, and Texas.

The Latin American section of UPI has two wires. One goes to U.S. clients as well as those in Central America, Colombia, Venezuela, and the rest of the Caribbean. Its second wire goes to the South American media.

"The news is about the same for both wires," said Edwin Vidal, deputy Latin American editor. "We only have some minor differences. For example, a story on the Chicago election and how Hispanics voted may be of interest to our North American and Central American clients, but it would not go to the South Americans."

The two wires' main difference, however, is in the type of sports news they carry. The first wire carries news about baseball and basketball as well as soccer. Baseball, however, is not big in South America.

While the English-language wire's emphasis is on domestic U.S. news -- about 25 percent of the stories can be considered international -- the Spanish-language wire focuses on Latin America. About 50 percent of the news carried by the Latin American wire is written in Spanish, the rest is translated.

Yet, some of UPI's Spanish-language clients in the United States buy both the English-language and the Spanish-language wires. The latter, some media executives say, hardly carries U.S. news that could be of interest to their audiences. To provide readers and listeners with both Latin American, and local news, they are forced to subscribe to both.

Vidal said this is a common occurrence. "They want news that is aimed at them -- the United States. They also want a lot more sports," Vidal said.

The Latin American desk has at least one Spanish-speaking correspondent in each Latin American country. In its Washington, D.C. headquarters, there are 20 employees who edit and report. One covers the Organization of American States and a second specializes in economic news. UPI also employs a Spanish-speaking reporter in New York.

Associated Press (AP)

The Latin American service of AP started cable service to two newspapers in Cuba back in 1898. It was the first overseas operation for the 50-year-old AP. La Prensa Asociada (LPA), however, did not flourish until after World War II. Until then, only two editors worked at a desk that filed English and Spanish stories by radio transmission.

The Latin American service now employs 16 editors in its New York headquarters, all natives of Spanish-speaking countries. One reporter works out of Washington, D.C., and a Latin American correspondent covers the United Nations. AP also has bureaus in Latin American countries. LPA is a desk within the World Services department in New York and the only foreign-language operation at that headquarters.

AP's Spanish-language wire has more than 500 newspaper and broadcasting clients in the Americas. About 50 of those are in the United States.

About 200 stories, culled from 3,000 news items, are sent out by the Spanish-language wire every 24 hours. A special ATEX computer system is programmed to automatically change the daily weather conditions such as "cloudy" from English to Spanish. It also accents words at the push of a button.

The emphasis, of course, is on news from Latin America. According to Jose Abreu, AP editor for Latin American Services: "News that deserves 500 words on the AAA wire (AP's main domestic news wire) or on APPW English wires for international subscribers may get 50 words on LPA wires. But a brief from Washington about Argentina's plans to reschedule its debt would get an urgent slug on the LPA wire and be quickly followed up with phone calls for more copy."

Abreu added that lead paragraphs and angles of the story are often different. On an Atlantis space-shuttle flight, the Spanish-language AP focused on a Mexican astronaut and his studies on the effects of acupuncture on space sickness. The English-language wire for international subscribers, on the other hand, focused on the satellites launched from the shuttle.

LPA segments its news even further by channeling information into five different wires. One goes to Argentina, Paraguay, Uruguay, and any subscribers in Washington D.C., including embassies. A second serves Brazil alone, where it goes directly to media outlets there as well as being translated into Portuguese by the country's news agency. A third goes to Chile, Peru, Ecuador, and Bolivia, while a fourth circuit is tailored to Mexico, Central America, Panama, and the western and southwestern United States. Finally, the last wire goes to Puerto Rico, Colombia, Venezuela, and the Dominican Republic, and to U.S. subscribers in the Midwest, Southeast, and Northeast.

The most notable difference among these circuits is the sports. Caribbean subscribers want to read baseball news, while the rest are avid soccer fans. Bullfighting is also important in Peru, Ecuador, Mexico, and Colombia, but only of passing interest in other locales.

About one-third of the stories are originally filed in Spanish. The rest are translated from English, a task that is not at all simple.

"Trying to define which country speaks the purest Spanish always sparks a lively debate so the wire's compromise is an international Spanish," explained Abreu. "For example, a swimming pool is known as a 'pileta' in Argentina and several other countries and as an 'alberca' in Mexico and other areas. For simplicity's sake, LPA editors use the universal 'piscina.'"

V. English-Language Media

English-language press aimed at Hispanics has been around for a long, long time, carving for itself a niche in a growing market. Unlike the Spanish dailies, the English-language press rarely concerns itself with news south of the border, preferring to turn its attention to U.S. Hispanics and the future of that community.

The favored format is the magazine, with its slick presentation and ability to present information in a more leisurely and entertaining way. The magazine format is popular among affluent readers, the segment the English-language Hispanic press tries to attract.

Executives of the Hispanic magazines profiled here said they chose to present their products in English because they considered it the language of the future.

"Hispanics in this country go to schools and learn to read in English," said Harry Caicedo, editor of Vista magazine. "Most of the immigrants who come here want to learn English because they know that's what it takes to make it here. It is the language of business. But unlike other immigrants, they've developed a pride in their heritage and that generates an interest in the culture."

Hispanic Business

Jesus and Bonnie Chavarria founded Hispanic Business Inc. in January 1979. Less than four months later, the couple publshed a newsletter that focused on Hispanic-owned businesses. By 1982, Hispanic Business, "the magazine for growth companies and ladder-oriented professionals," had adopted a magazine format, published monthly.

Hispanic Business has always been published in English. It was a conscious choice on the part of the Chavarrias.

"English is the language of professional life and the English-speaking Hispanic is the most underserved segment of the community," said Jesus Chavarria.

Like other executives who run English-language media aimed at Hispanics, the Chavarrias believe that their targeted audience -- the upscale, well-educated professional -- prefers to speak English even though he or she may be bilingual.

Hispanic Business, as its name indicates, is a special-market magazine. It begins where Inc., Forbes, and other American business magazines leave off, according to Jesus Chavarria.

Its circulation, 100,000, is certified by Verified Audit Circulation. Though based in Santa Barbara, the magazine is printed in Columbia, Missouri. Its three largest readership markets are California, Texas, and Florida. The magazine also boasts a following in New York, New Jersey, and the Chicago area. There are no newsstand sales.

Hispanic Business readers are middle-and upper-middle-class men and women, according to a 1985 Scarborough Research Report. The median age is 41, with 79.8 percent of the subscriptions going to men. The average personal income is $45,500, with an average household income of $57,700. Eighty-three percent have some college education, and 19 percent have gone on to receive postgraduate degrees.

Thirty percent own their own business and the rest are executives, managers, or professionals (lawyers, doctors, engineers, architects, etc.)

Single copies sell for $2. A year's subscription costs $18. The magazine employs 19 full-time staff members: 13 in Santa Barbara, one in Chicago, and five in New York. Five employees work on the magazine's editorial content. About 80 percent of the magazine copy is either staff written or done by freelancers, according to Chavarria. The rest comes from press releases.

Although Hispanic Business is not a publication that editorializes, it does concentrate on what would be of benefit--or detriment--to Hispanics. For example, Hispanic Business has carried articles on the call for the abolishment of the Small Business Administration, and it invited Congressman Esteban Torres to write a column about it. The editors, however, did not take a stand.

The magazine has 10 standard "departments" every month: Direct Line, People, Art Garcia's Capital Gains, Foreign Trade, Business Notes, Career Intelligencer, Math-Based Careers, Media/Marketing, Books, and Research/Development. Direct Line is a column written by Publisher and Editor Jesus Chavarria. The others are short columns about a variety of topics: from choosing a financial planner to promotions of Hispanics in the business world to Brazilian export performance.

Like the rest of the magazine, these short articles are packed with useful information that readers can use readily. "That is why our readers read us," explained Chavarria.

In April 1985, Hispanic Business introduced a new lifestyle section to cover trends in travel, fashions, foods, and other consumer items. "Images," as the special consumer section is called, focuses on product performance evaluations "for busy executives and professionals who lack the time to research personal and office-related purchases." The inaugural section featured articles on vacationing in Mexico and the art of tire technology.

Every issue usually carries two such lifestyle pieces, lightly written, sometimes whimsical, but always informative. In the December 1985 issue, for instance, the article titled "A Feast Fit for Three Kings" gave several recipes for a traditional celebration of Three Kings Day (January 6), what the writer called "the equivalent of a United States Thanksgiving, Christmas, and New Year all rolled into one." The second such lifestyle piece was on a more serious note: rating the "1986 Business Cars of the Year." The winner: Ford's Taurus.

While these are the trimmings of Hispanic Business' monthly meal, the main course consists of at least six full-length feature articles on a variety of topics. Again, the emphasis is on presenting information that can be used. The March 1986 issue was typical. Its cover story concerned family financial planning. Related sidebars dealt with employee-benefit plans and a financial profile of a Hispanic family.

Inside was a feature on Mario Vazquez Rana, the Mexican news magnate who bought UPI. A second piece dealt with the addition of Hispanics to the National Minority Suppliers Development Council. Investing in thoroughbred horses and a booming New York real-estate market were the topics of the other two articles.

Theme issues are published throughout the year to mark developments in the Hispanic world. During 1986, the January issue profiled top Hispanic designers, such as Oscar de la Renta, Adolfo, and Carolina Herrera. Articles included "Carving a Niche in the High Flying Fashion Industry" as well as the standard lifestyle features on dressing for success and choosing cosmetics and accessories.

"Careers and Jobs" was the common thread of the February issue, while the April issue concentrated on the Hispanic contribution to U.S. agriculture. In May, Hispanic Business focused on the role of Hispanics in the U.S. defense industry.

In June, the magazine published the top 500 Hispanic-owned corporations in the mainland and Puerto Rico, along with profiles of industry leaders. There were accompanying articles on the top 10 auto dealers and top 10 banks, and profiles of five outstanding women executives.

The July/August 1986 double issue was devoted to travel, recreation, and conventions, while the High Tech market in the Hispanic world was the theme in September. The 50 fastest-growing Hispanic companies were profiled in November. The December issue closed with a look at the growing Hispanic market, with a breakdown of advertising expenditures by medium and market. It is one of the magazine's more popular issues.

Hispanic Business is profitable, Chavarria said. All of its advertisers are national accounts -- from the top three U.S. auto makers to beer and soft-drink companies to energy companies. Most ads run in English, but a few, such as an announcement for Lite Beer, used a Spanish slogan.

Chavarria expects a promising future: "1984 was the significant growth year for us. We have been growing at a 30- to 35-percent rate in revenues. We are fairly young and at this point we carry a fairly low debt."

Nuestro, Hispanic Review of Business

Back in the early 1970s, when Daniel Lopez founded a printing and graphics company, he dreamed of publishing an English-language magazine for Hispanics. He wanted to break the myth that "once you learn English, you lose your cultural ties," he said.

With the help of other Hispanic investors and minority companies, Lopez published the first monthly issue of Nuestro (Ours) magazine in March 1977. It was (and still is) intended for the upwardly mobile Hispanic, who, although fully bilingual and assimilated into mainstream America, was still interested in his culture, his people, and the U.S. Hispanic community at large. The magazine contained feature articles on business, profiles of Hispanic super achievers, and travel reports.

Hispanic Review of Business was an outgrowth of a special Nuestro issue. In the January/February 1979 Nuestro, the magazine published its first list of the 100 largest Hispanic-owned businesses. A year later, Nuestro Business Review became an insert in the magazine, and by the January/February 1982 issue a separate magazine with the title NBR's Hispanic Business Monthly was born. A year later, the new magazine's name was changed to Hispanic Review of Business, or HRB for short.

The overwhelming majority of both magazines' circulation is by mail. A single copy of Nuestro sells for $2.25, HRB for $2. Nuestro's circulation, according to Lopez, is 205,000, while HRB's is 125,000. Neither, however, is audited.

Lopez said that the typical Nuestro reader has a median income of $43,000, and HRB's is about $52,000. HRB readers tend to own their businesses or to work in a professional or managerial position. Both audiences are older than the Hispanic community at large. Nuestro readers' median age is 32 to HRB's 41. More than 85 percent vote, attend school-board meetings, and other community functions. They are what Lopez calls "solidly middle class" -- homeowners who drive two cars, consume brand-name products, and go on vacation.

"Both sets of readers tend to be better educated, more literate, more civic minded," Lopez said. "The real young are not reading these magazines."

The Nuestro reader, Lopez added, reads the magazine to satisfy an emotional need. "They read it because Nuestro speaks to Latinos as Americans. It is a magazine about us thinking of us as Americans, not as a separate entity."

HRB's audience, on the other hand, is motivated by something quite different: "self interest," he said. "They want to know how to make their businesses or careers better."

Nuestro has five monthly "departments" -- From the publisher; Regional Reports; Que Pasa (What's Happening); Lifestyles; and travel pieces. The favorite of readers is the "Que Pasa" section, with 70 percent reading that section before anything else, Lopez said.

"Que Pasa" is a collection of short items on U.S. Hispanics, written tightly and entertainingly. A March 1986 sampling: a national award for a thoroughbred managed by a Hispanic, an agreement to remedy the underrepresentation of Hispanics in the National Park Service, the first Hispanic Cultural Center in New England, and the departure of one of the teens who make up the Menudo singing group.

Like the "Que Pasa" section, the regional report contains snippets of news from around the country and Latin America. These tend to be newsier and more political. The "Accent" lifestyle pieces and travel stories, on the other hand, are longer and, as in the rest of the magazine, concentrated on Hispanic destinations and people, although not exclusively. The April 1986 travel section, for instance, was on Rome.

Nuestro runs about five to six full-length features every month. Occasionally, the staff also uses short stories, either about Hispanic life or Hispanic writers. Topics are varied -- from profiles of Hispanic stars to medical reports to sports reports. The focus, of course, is always on Hispanics.

In the April 1986 Nuestro, for example, there were stories about immigration reform, Nicaraguan art, the political battle for the Hispanic vote in Texas, a Hispanic-owned model agency, and the effects of President Reagan's budget on Hispanics.

Nuestro occasionally publishes special issues devoted almost entirely to one topic. Lopez said some have been quite successful. The all-time favorite was the first anniversary issue, April 1978, "The Latino Chronicles." "It showed there was a real thirst for the knowledge of who we are and where we came from," Lopez said.

Another Nuestro favorite was the June/July 1979 "The Latina Today." Through 12 articles, the magazine explored the past, present, and future of Hispanic women in the United States.

Nuestro, unlike its sister publication, does take editorial stands, both in the publisher's column and the rest of its pages. "The Nuestro philosophy is that we are against everything that is bad for Latinos. By the same token, everything that is of importance to Latinos we comment on," Lopez said.

HRB, although graphically similar to Nuestro, has a different audience and more specialized content. Like Nuestro, it has standard monthly sections, including a publisher's letter, business update, people, and travel. The reader favorite here is the "Business Update" section, followed closely by the "People" section. Both are collections of short news items -- the former concentrating on events and organizations, the latter on individuals.

Lopez said decisions for HRB's editorial content are made with the busy, information-hungry professional in mind. "We try to be specific about how we can help them develop their organizations or businesses," he added. In the January/February 1983 issue, for example, there were stories on franchising, the U.S. Hispanic Chamber, the funny (and embarrassing) translations into Spanish of some U.S. advertisements, and the issue of laying off senior employees for the sake of minorities. In addition, there was an article on basketball and the magazine's fifth-annual survey of the top 100 Hispanic businesses.

The New York-based magazines share a staff of 20 persons. Eleven of those are editorial employees. About half of the magazine is written by freelancers.

All of the advertising comes from national accounts and is published in English. Advertised goods and services vary -- from cigarettes to liquor to car manufacturers to the CIA.

"The magazines are self-sustaining," Lopez said. "But if you want to make money, magazines are not the way to go. No magazine can possibly make money in its first five years."

Vista

Vista, an English-language monthly insert in more than 20 newspapers across the country, is the latest addition to a growing list of magazine-style media aimed at Hispanics. But the idea of such an insert is not new. In the 1970s, there was a newspaper supplement aimed at blacks, but it lasted less than two years.

Harry Caicedo, Vista editor, had also attempted a similar publication for Latin American newspapers. When the Latin economy floundered, so did his Revista K (K Magazine). Caicedo and Vista publisher Arturo Villar got together in 1983 to develop the idea for a newspaper insert. The decision to publish in English was not a difficult one.

"The Hispanics we wanted to reach -- the young, educated, upscale -- are English dominant. We also looked at the combined circulation of the four Spanish-language dailies and saw that we would be limited to that if we published in Spanish," Caicedo said.

Caicedo and Villar drew together a group of investors from Texas, Florida, and New York to form Horizon-A U.S. Communications Co., run by an 11-member board. The company then commissioned a study by Strategy Research Corporation. The study confirmed the board's premise, and said that Hispanics in one area were indeed interested in what Hispanics in another area were doing.

In the spring of 1985, Caicedo and Villar published a prototype of Vista to show prospective newspaper customers. Within four months, Horizon had signed up 12 newspapers and had an initial circulation of 425,000. By August 1986, the number of newspapers using Vista had grown to 21 with a circulation of 802,300. Host newspapers are located in color front, has five departments every month: Voices, Vistascope, Letter, Spotlight, Newsnotes and Rootsearch. "Voices," as the name implies, is an opinion column open to essays written by readers. In past issues, community leaders and everyday people have written about "Spanglish," the growing awareness of the Hispanic market by Anglo advertisers, and Hispanics' role in American foreign policy.

"Vistascope" is a people column, with short, pithy notes and pictures. "Newsnotes," on the other hand, are announcements about upcoming events, contests, and programs of interest to Hispanics. "Newsnotes" always provides an address and, when needed, a phone number. On the same page with "Newsnotes," "Rootsearch" traces the history of Hispanic family names to help readers discover their roots. Finally, "Spotlight" focuses on Hispanics in interesting or high-placed jobs, telling the story of how they triumphed.

Vista carries five full-length feature stories in each issue, covering a gamut of topics and geographical locations. There are stories about fashion, sports, travel, entertainment, and the history of different Hispanic cities in the United States. In the August 3, 1986 edition, for instance, the cover story was "Hispanic Theater Olympics," about the Festival Latino at New York's Delacorte Theater that month. There was also a story about Hispanic cops earning laurels under the heading "Badge of

Hispanic Pride." Featured were policemen from Chicago, Tucson, Dallas, Washington, Los Angeles, New York, San Antonio, Houston, San Diego, and Fort Lauderdale.

Two other reports were about Santa Barbara celebrating its historic ties to Spain, and a profile of 18-year-old Texas runner Reuben Reina. The fifth piece was a one-page ode to mangos, a fragrant tropical fruit, complete with recipes.

In the six months from February to July 1986, Vista cover stories included a broad range of philosophies and topics: profiles of two Hispanic beauty queens; the historical allure of St. Augustine, Fla.; musicians crossing cultural barriers; a young California designer's swimwear creations; the problems and rewards of mixed marriages; and Hispanics living in small towns.

"Our readers are looking for things that say Hispanics are good and are making important contributions to society," Caicedo said. "The complaint we hear is that newspapers only publish the negative -- Hispanics on welfare rolls, on drugs, in crime. We want to provide an alternative, what the mainstream media doesn't do."

Vista does not editorialize. Said Caicedo: "We are non-political, non-ideological. We are not a cause magazine. Vista itself does not take a public stand on Hispanic issues, but we do provide a forum for different sides." One example is the July 1986 issue, in which New Mexico Gov. Tony Anaya wrote in favor of offering sanctuary to refugees -- and declared his state an official sanctuary -- while Edward L. Lujan, a Republican Party state chairman, wrote in opposition.

Vista's editorial office is located in Miami, but printing is done in San Antonio. The company also has advertising sales offices in New York and representatives in Chicago, Dallas, Los Angeles, and San Francisco. About 80 percent of the magazine is written by freelancers, Caicedo said. Vista employs 12 people, of whom six are on its editorial staff.

About 90 percent of Vista's advertising comes from national accounts, while the rest are large regional companies interested in reaching Hispanics in other parts of the country. Regional advertisers include Jackson Memorial Hospital in Miami; Flordia Power & Light; and Lone Star Beer in Texas. Vista's largest advertiser is Adolph Coors Co. Other frequent advertisers: AT&T Communications; Eastman Kodak; Ford; General Motors; and the U.S. Army.

In 1986 Vista was not yet profitable, Caicedo said. "We expected that. We didn't plan to turn around until the second year," he added.

VI. Conclusion

Whatever form they take, Hispanic news media in the United States perform an important and indispensable task. Written or broadcast in Spanish, they are preservers of the language. For many Latinos, particularly the elderly and the newer immigrants who do not speak or understand English well, these media are the primary source of information, providing a window into their new country. At the same time, they serve as a forum for some of the great Spanish-language writers and thinkers of our time.

Whether in English or Spanish, they have become a cultural vehicle, the keeper of customs and values. Thus, the Latino press boasts that readers benefit from a unique perspective -- news through the eyes and ears and words of somebody like themselves, a Hispanic. And Hispanic television, too, can boast of few American programs dubbed into Spanish. Instead, Hispanic TV prefers to import programs from Latin America, where the values more closely reflect those of U.S. Hispanics.

Moreover, Hispanic media fill a void left by their Anglo counterparts, which do not cover the barrios, the local softball league, the cocktail parties. Hispanics often complain that the English-language media cover their neighborhoods only when a crime occurs. And Latin America is rarely fodder for the nightly newscast -- unless there is a revolution or an earthquake.

U.S. Hispanic media are viewed as more personable and personal. In the eyes of their audiences, they are "our" newspapers or "our" stations. Hispanics do not hesitate to call a paper or station for help.

The fact that they are needed and wanted and, in many cases, beloved has kept many outlets afloat during difficult economic times. Most Spanish-language publications, like their English-language counterparts, fail before their first year -- not for lack of audience but as victims of undercapitalization. Some of the smaller publications survive by doing what some English-language community newspapers also do: writing stories on businesses if they buy ads, or exchanging the service of a writer or photographer for ad space.

Clearly, the growth of the Hispanic media is in the broadcast sector. Newspapers are popular, certainly, but they do not come close to the saturation level of radio or television. Reading, whether in English or Spanish, requires time and effort. Even the circulation of many large Spanish-language dailies in the major cities -- La Opinion, El Diario/La Prensa, Noticias del Mundo -- is less than one-tenth of the Hispanic population in their respective home cities. This, of course, is not a uniquely Spanish-language market phenomenon. The Anglo press is grappling, too, with the problem of circulation.

Television reaches more people in more areas than any medium has in the history of mankind. This holds true in the Latin sector, even though only one network, Univision, has dominated the airwaves. This domination will not last long, however. The debut of Telemundo in 1987, with stations in the top three U.S. Hispanic markets, is a significant development. There are now two forces jockeying for position in a lucrative market. What does this mean for Hispanic television in the United States?:

* More programs produced domestically by and for U.S. Hispanics and less programs imported from Latin America. This is already happening. Univision expanded its news division to produce weekend and late night news shows. It won't be long before it begins producing entertainment segments. The owners of Telemundo and the Reliance Capital Group LP have also publicly stated that the Hispanic audience can expect more locally produced programming from them.

* A growing interest among Anglo investors and large corporations, such as Hallmark and First Chicago Venture, who recognize the potential of the U.S. Hispanic market. There will be more money from big business for improvements, more extensive news coverage, and programming.

* Consolidation within the market. There will be fewer independent stations and more affiliated stations buying programming from a network. Without network affiliation and the corresponding access to domestically produced programming, the independents will find themselves at a disadvantage.

* The possibility of a third network. Foreign investors or a U.S. broadcast powerhouse may create such a network to tap the Hispanic market. Undoubtedly, the growth of U.S. television is within this virgin territory, and Anglo broadcast corporations are not oblivious to this.

Radio, on the other hand, probably has reached saturation levels in some cities such as Miami and Houston, with seven stations each. In other cities, such as Chicago (with three stations), Spanish-language radio still has not reached its full potential.

While most smaller publications are owned by Hispanics, minority-owned radio stations are few and far between. Two large chains -- Tichenor and

Lotus -- are slowly and quietly building a Spanish-language radio empire. They are controlled by Anglos. But there is a promising trend. Spanish Broadcasting System, a father-son Hispanic team, owns a station in New York and another in Los Angeles. They added an AM and FM in Miami to their holdings in 1986. In Dallas, the only two Spanish-language stations are also owned by a Hispanic.

Many executives, even those working for large companies, confide that money for improvements, projects, and experimentation is not available. But it is a complaint voiced by Anglo media executives as well, and the Spanish-language market has done well even without the capital.

Cost is also one reason many outlets' circulation or listenership is not audited. "We pay over six figures in terms of annual research expenditures," said general manager George Hyde, whose AM and FM stations in Miami subscribe to Arbitron and other research services. "Very few can afford to play in that kind of ballpark."

Radio-station executives question the rating services' methodology. They say Hispanic listeners are consistently undercounted. Press representatives also say circulation count does not accurately reflect their readership because the pass-along rate is much higher among Hispanics.

Though there is some basis for these explanations, the lack of any independent ratings or audit of circulation stymies the media's efforts to attract Anglo advertisers. While some newspapers and stations conduct their own in-house surveys and circulation audits, there always will be room for doubt until an independent firm does the count.

Hispanic media also suffer from an over-dependence on wire services. All services -- mainly EFE, AP, and UPI -- are either U.S. owned or foreign controlled. Thus, the news and issues of the U.S. Hispanic population is not of primary concern to these news sources; thus, the broadcast and print outlets must often do without the right perspective or the perfect angle in a story. Hispanic Link, a feature syndicate, is the closest thing to a U.S. Hispanic-controlled wire service but it syndicates columns, not spot-news stories.

Unfortunately, too, Hispanic media depend too much on press releases. Without the wherewithal to maintain a costly news staff, most outlets print or read press releases verbatim. Those who can afford the luxury of more personnel often rewrite the releases. But many simply cannot afford to chase the news or dig for exposes. For those that do -- whether the major dailies, the television newscasts, or the news/talk radio stations -- beating the Anglo competition on Latin stories is sweet reward. Univision's "Noticiero," for example, has consistently been one up on the other networks when it comes to day-to-day coverage from Latin America.

The lack of capital also has been a stumbling block for television stations. Few have the resources to produce more than a nightly newscast locally and, with luck, a variety show. Aside from its news show, for example, Univision's only regular self-produced program was the morning show, "Mundo Latino" (Latin World) until 1986. It added two new shows to its lineup in 1987. Certainly the talent -- and willingess -- is out there.

Even with these drawbacks, the fact remains: Hispanic media is big business -- and growing. Spanish-language radio stations in Miami, San Antonio, and other cities, for example, are among the biggest and most profitable within their markets. And such advertising networks as Caballero Spanish Media and NetSpan (now part of Reliance, as is John Blair) have been highly visible and accessible to businesses and corporations.

Hispanic media are increasingly attractive both to Anglo advertisers and investors. To wit: The shopping spree conducted by Reliance, Hallmark and First Chicago Venture, Tichenor, and Lotus. The lack of money executives complained about may soon be a thing of the past in many cases.

Particularly attractive to investors is the mostly untapped potential and the niche Hispanic media have carved for themselves. Their history, their contributions, and the needs they fill are much different than their Anglo counterparts. Indeed, their community flavor as well as their international news content is a definite draw and a big plus for their audience. Newspapers, as well as radio stations and television, are quite influential within their communities. They galvanize their publics and are vital in such public-service efforts as blood drives and fundraising.

Hispanic media will continue to be profitable. Despite some monetary setbacks in the past, the dailies have expanded their news coverage and circulation has grown. There also have been more entries into the radio and television market.

For many years, some Hispanic media have monopolized the market. Lack of competition always breeds complacency. Now, hungry and innovative newcomers will prod -- and in some cases are already doing so -- the older newspapers and radio and television stations into putting out a better product.

The future looks promising for Hispanic media, and executives of newspapers, television, and radio stations unanimously expressed that optimism in interviews. But just as there is room for improvement in the English-language market, there is also room in the Spanish-language field. The media will improve -- their audiences will demand it.

Outlets will have to put more local reporters on the street, in the courthouse, and around City Hall. And they will have to do so without losing that uniquely Hispanic flavor that has made them dear to their audiences. Some may change their formats. Newspapers, for instance, will be forced to be bold in their design and innovative in their use of graphics and photographs.

Radio stations, most of which now offer limited news, might try what some are already doing -- an expanded news block during morning and after-noon drives. And television must eventually wean itself from its dependence on Latin American-produced novelas, shows, and adventures.

In addition, there will be changes and shifts within the market:

* Increased segmentation for programming and from advertisers will be commonplace. There are many differences among U.S. Hispanics, and advertisers, realizing this, will target different groups in different ways.

* The big will get bigger, the smaller outlets will remain, but few will be in between. In television, Reliance has already said it wants to buy more stations and obtain more affiliates. Hallmark may do the same. Newspapers now privately owned might be acquired by a larger media corporation interested in reaching the Hispanic market, in much the same way that Gannett purchased El Diario/La Prensa and Knight Ridder publishes El Herald. Radio stations, too, may become part of national chains.

* More domestically produced programs in the broadcast sector are a certainty. Hallmark and First Chicago Venture have agreed to buy programming from Univision for two years after their puchase of the SICC stations is approved by the FCC. After that, Hallmark might set up its own production subsidiary.

* Instead of importing programming, U.S. Hispanic media will become exporters to Latin America. ECO, for instance, plans to sell its news product to subscribers.

* The creation of a Spanish-language news wire for, by, and of U.S. Hispanics would be a true coming of age for Hispanic media in a country that has the sixth-largest population of Spanish speakers in the world. (In addition to the feature syndicate Hispanic Link, an El Paso-based Latin American News Service was operating in late 1986, distributing radio news features and weekly news summaries on Latin American events.)

The future also means that Hispanic media will have to deal with challenges they have not yet encountered. Will their influence be limited because community and national leaders do not speak their language? It might, unless more translate editorials (as many newspapers already do), or find other ways to make their voices heard in the corridors of power.

Moreover, Hispanic media will face the assimilation of their audiences. But they will not disappear as other ethnic media have. While Hispanics will learn the new language and adopt certain customs in the generations to come, they are different from other ethnic groups that have migrated to the United States. Latin America is closer to the United States and the influx of Hispanics will continue, legally or illegally, as long as there is political and economic turmoil in Latin America. Finally, Hispanics are known for pride in their culture and interest in their homelands. These two factors will guarantee U.S. Hispanic media an audience for years to come.

The possibilities for change are many, the ideas for improvement plentiful. In the end, the winner will be the Hispanic media consumer.

HISPANIC MEDIA, USA

Section II

Directory of Print and Electronic
Hispanic News Media

The information in this section
was provided in part by
the Hispanic Media Services Department
of Burson-Marsteller

Burson·Marsteller

230 Park Avenue South
New York, NY 10003

About the Directory

This Directory lists selected Hispanic print, television, and radio outlets around the United States.

The Directory does not attempt to be comprehensive; it lists only those outlets which responded to a Media Institute questionnaire, and/or certain outlets listed in information provided by the Hispanic Media Services Department of the public-relations firm Burson-Marsteller in New York.

In July 1986, the editors sent questionnaires in both English and Spanish to selected print and electronic outlets. Only electronic outlets which devote at least one-half of their air time to Spanish-language broadcasting were surveyed. Reminders were sent to those not responding by early September. Outlets which did not respond to the questionnaire were not included in the directory.

The Hispanic Media Services Department of Burson-Marsteller provided us with information on certain print and electronic outlets; however, their information on electronic outlets was limited primarily to the top 20 markets.

The Media Institute welcomes your additions, changes, or corrections pertaining to the Directory. Please address your comments to Cynthia L. Bisset, The Media Institute, 3017 M St., N.W., Washington, DC 20007.

I. Print Media

EAST:

Title: AVANCE
Address: 1803 Manhattan Ave., Union City, NJ   07087
Phone No.: 201/865-1900
Publisher: Rene Avila
Editor: Rene Avila
Circulation: 25,000
Language: English
Frequency of Publication: Weekly
Distribution: not given

Regularly published sections: Editorial, Sports, Lifestyle/Arts

Type of news emphasized: International, National, State, Local

How majority of news is gathered: Staff Reporters

Best way to get information to outlets: Press Releases, Phone Calls,
                                          English, Spanish

Title: El Diario/La Prensa
Address: 143-155 Varick St., New York, NY   10013
Phone No.: 212/807-4600
Publisher: Carlos D. Ramirez
Editor: Manuel de Dios Unanue
Circulation: 65,000
Language: Spanish
Frequency of Publication: Daily (no Sat.)
Distribution: Statewide

Regularly published sections: Editorial, Business, Sports, Lifestyle/Arts

Type of news emphasized: International, State, Local

How majority of news is gathered: Staff Reporters, AP

Best way to get information to outlets: Press Releases, English, Spanish

137

Title: El Directorio Hispano
Address: 850 Lancaster Ave., Reading, PA 19607
Phone No.: 215/775-3101
Publisher: Aaron G. Lopez
Editor: Sara Lopez
Circulation: 9,000
Language: Bilingual
Frequency of Publication: Weekly
Distribution: Regional

Regularly published sections: Editorial, Sports, Lifestyle/Arts

Type of news emphasized: International, National, State, Local

How majority of news is gathered: Hispanic Link

Best way to get information to outlets: Press Releases, Phone Calls

Title: El Especial
Address: 501-45th St., Union City, NJ 07087
Phone No.: 201/864-8804
Publisher: not given
Editor: Juan Carlos Fernandez
Circulation: 85,000
Language: Spanish
Frequency of Publication: Bimonthly
Distribution: not given

Regularly published sections: not given

Type of news emphasized: not given

How majority of news is gathered: not given

Best way to get information to outlets: not given

Title: El Mundo
Address: 26 Bishop Richard Allen Dr., Cambridge, MA 02139
Phone No.: 617/876-4293
Publisher: Alberto Vasallo, Jr.
Editor: Jorge Mendoza
Circulation: 27,000
Language: Spanish
Frequency of Publication: Weekly
Distribution: Regional

Regularly published sections: not given

Type of news emphasized: not given

How majority of news is gathered: not given

Best way to get information to outlets: not given

Title: El Tiempo de N.Y.
Address: G.P.O. Box 1155, New York, NY 10116
Phone No.: 718/507-0832
Publisher: Ronald Hernandez
Editor: Elba R. Cayon
Circulation: 38,000 Weekly, 50,000 Special Editions
Language: Spanish
Frequency of Publication: Weekly
Distribution: N.Y., Miami, N.J., Puerto Rico, Dominican Republic

Regularly published sections: Editorial, Business, Sports, Lifestyle/Arts

Type of news emphasized: Local, Community

How majority of news is gathered: Staff Reporters, Correspondents

Best way to get information to outlets: Spanish

Title: **Impacto Latin News**
Address: 853 Broadway, Suite 811, New York, NY 10003
Phone No.: 212/505-0288
Publisher: Carlos G. Carrillo
Editor: Carlos Velasquez
Circulation: 72,000
Language: Bilingual
Frequency of Publication: Weekly
Distribution: not given

Regularly published sections: Editorial, Business, Sports, Lifestyle/Arts

Type of news emphasized: International, National, State, Local

How majority of news is gathered: UPI

Best way to get information to outlets: Press Releases, Phone Calls,
Spanish

Title: **La Actualidad**
Address: 4953 N. 5th St., Philadelphia, PA 19120
Phone No.: 215/324-3838
Publisher: Carlos Morales
Editor: Carlos Morales
Circulation: 20,000
Language: Spanish
Frequency of Publication: Weekly
Distribution: Local

Regularly published sections: not given

Type of news emphasized: not given

How majority of news is gathered: not given

Best way to get information to outlets: not given

Title: La Semana
Address: 161 Harbor St., Allston, MA 02134
Phone No.: 617/787-2626
Publisher: Peter Cuerca
Editor: Awilda Ramos
Circulation: 10,000
Language: Bilingual
Frequency of Publication: Weekly
Distribution: National

Regularly published sections: not given

Type of news emphasized: not given

How majority of news is gathered: not given

Best way to get information to outlets: not given

Title: La Tribuna de North Jersey
Address: P.O. Box 902, Newark, NJ 07101
Phone No.: 201/589-3742
Publisher: Gabriel Bidot
Editor: Gabriel Bidot
Circulation: 42,000
Language: Spanish
Frequency of Publication: Bimonthly
Distribution: Regional

Regularly published sections: not given

Type of news emphasized: not given

How majority of news is gathered: not given

Best way to get information to outlets: not given

Title: La Voz
Address: 948 Elizabeth Ave., Elizabeth, NJ 07201
Phone No.: 201/352-6654
Publisher: Abelardo Garcia Berry
Editor: Abelardo Garcia Berry
Circulation: 42,000 audited by The Chapman Agency
Language: Spanish
Frequency of Publication: not given
Distribution: Statewide

Regularly published sections: Editorial, Business, Sports, Lifestyle/Arts

Type of news emphasized: Local

How majority of news is gathered: Staff Reporters, Servicio Especial
                                   Selectivo

Best way to get information to outlets: Press Releases, Spanish

Title: La Voz de Colombia
Address: 69-07 Roosevelt Ave., Woodside, NY 11377
Phone No.: 718/803-0488, 803-9449
Publisher: Cesar Granados
Editor: Daniel Grandados Cohen
Circulation: 10,000
Language: Spanish
Frequency of Publication: Weekly
Distribution: Local

Regularly published sections: Editorial, Business, Sports, Lifestyle/Arts

Type of news emphasized: International, National, State, Local

How majority of news is gathered: Special Contributors from Colombia

Best way to get information to outlets: Phone Calls, English, Spanish

Title: La Voz Hispana
Address: 159 E. 116th St., New York, NY 10029
Phone No.: 212/348-8270
Publisher: not given
Editor: not given
Circulation: 60,800
Language: Spanish
Frequency of Publication: Weekly
Distribution: Regional

Regularly published sections: not given

Type of news emphasized: not given

How majority of news is gathered: not given

Best way to get information to outlets: not given

Title: Noticias Del Mundo
Address: 401 5th Ave., New York, NY 10016
Phone No.: 212/684-5656
Publisher: not given
Editor: Jose A. Cardinale
Circulation: 53,000
Language: Spanish
Frequency of Publication: Daily (no Sunday)
Distribution: National, Regional

Regularly published sections: not given

Type of news emphasized: not given

How majority of news is gathered: not given

Best way to get information to outlets: not given

Title: Nuevo Amanecer
Address: 1 Hanson Place, Brooklyn, NY 11243
Phone No.: 718/789-1500
Publisher: The Tablet Publishing Company
Editor: Eva Gillcrist, OP
Circulation: 11,000
Language: Spanish
Frequency of Publication: Monthly-1st Sat. of each month
Distribution: National

Regularly published sections: Editorial

Type of news emphasized: Latin American, Church, Local & Community

How majority of news is gathered: Staff Reporters, Reporters in Los
                                    Angeles & California, NC News Service,
                                    Noticias Aliadas de Lima

Best way to get information to outlets: Press Releases, Phone Calls,
                                            Spanish

Title: Nuevos Horizontes
Address: 484 Elmwood Ave., Providence, RI 02907
Phone No.: 401/941-3388
Publisher: Himas Salazar
Editor: Gioconda Salazar
Circulation: 25,000
Language: Spanish
Frequency of Publication: Weekly
Distribution: Regional

Regularly published sections: not given

Type of news emphasized: International, National, Local

How majority of news is gathered: not given

Best way to get information to outlets: not given

Title: Periodico Resumen
Address: 76-09 Roosevelt Ave., Queens, NY 11372
Phone No.: 718/899-8603
Publisher: Fernando F. Rojas
Editor: Fernando F. Rojas
Circulation: 14,000 audited by Spanish Media Auditing of N.Y.
Language: Spanish
Frequency of Publication: Weekly
Distribution: Regional

Regularly published sections: Editorial, Business, Sports, Lifestyle/Arts

Type of news emphasized: Local

How majority of news is gathered: Wires, Staff Reporters, Latin News
                                    Service

Best way to get information to outlets: Press Releases, Spanish

Title: Latin NewsLeader
Address: 100-05 Atlantic Ave., Richmond Hill, NY 11418
Phone No.: 718/849-9211
Publisher: Ms. Garie Negron
Editor: Ms. Garie Negron
Circulation: 20,000
Language: Bilingual
Frequency of Publication: Weekly
Distribution: Statewide

Regularly published sections: Editorial, Business, Sports, Lifestyle/Arts

Type of news emphasized: State, Local

How majority of news is gathered: Staff Reporters, Free Lance, Spanish
                                    Language Newspapers, Hispanic Link News
                                    Service

Best way to get information to outlets: Press Releases, English

Title: **Que Pasa**
Address: 115 Bedford St., Hartford, CT 06120
Phone No.: 203/522-1163, 522-1164
Publisher: Juan D. Brito
Editor: Juan Daniel Brito, Rebecca Delgado
Circulation: 10,000
Language: Bilingual
Frequency of Publication: Monthly
Distribution: Statewide

Regularly published sections: Editorial, Business, Sports, Lifestyle/Arts

Type of news emphasized: International, National, State, Local

How majority of news is gathered: Staff Reporters

Best way to get information to outlets: Phone Calls, English

Title: **The Brasilians**
Address: 28 W. 46th St., New York, NY 10036
Phone No.: 212/382-1631
Publisher: Jota Alves
Editor: Jota Alves
Circulation: 30,000
Language: Bilingual (Portuguese & English)
Frequency of Publication: Monthly
Distribution: International, National

Regularly published sections: Editorial, Business, Lifestyle/Arts

Type of news emphasized: International

How majority of news is gathered: Staff Reporters

Best way to get information to outlets: Press Releases, English

Title: USA Latino Magazine
Address: P.O. Box 213, Elizabeth, NJ 07207
Phone No.: 201/352-0734
Publisher: Antonio Truyol Rua
Editor: Antonio Truyol Rua
Circulation: 30,000
Language: Spanish
Frequency of Publication: not given
Distribution: National, Statewide

Regularly published sections: Editorial, Business, Sports, Lifestyle/Arts

Type of news emphasized: National

How majority of news is gathered: Staff Reporters

Best way to get information to outlets: Press Releases, Spanish

SOUTH:

Title: Diario las Americas
Address: 2900 N.W. 39th St., Miami, FL 33142
Phone No.: 305/633-3341
Publisher: Horacio Aguirre
Editor: Horacio Aguirre
Circulation: 66,850 by Sworn Publishers Statement
Language: Spanish, Editorials in Spanish & English
Frequency of Publication: 6 Days/Week
Distribution: National, Local

Regularly published sections: Editorial, Business, Sports, Lifestyle/Arts

Type of news emphasized: International, National, State, Local-- Strong
                          emphasis on news from all of the Americas.

How majority of news is gathered: Staff Reporters, UPI, EFE, AFP

Best way to get information to outlets: Press Releases, English

Title: El Heraldo de Broward
Address: 700 S.W. 27th Ave., Ft. Lauderdale, FL 33312
Phone No.: 305/792-7344, 794-7204
Publisher: Carmen Diaz Fabian
Editor: Carmen Diaz Fabian
Circulation: not given
Language: English
Frequency of Publication: Twice a Month
Distribution: Local

Regularly published sections: Editorial

Type of news emphasized: National, Local

IIow majority of news is gathered: n/a

Best way to get information to outlets: Press Releases, Phone Calls,
                                           Spanish

Title: El Latino Newspaper
Address: P.O. Box 43284, Washington, DC 20010
Phone No.: 202/232-0447
Publisher: Jose Sueiro
Editor: Jose Sueiro
Circulation: 12,000
Language: Spanish
Frequency of Publication: Weekly
Distribution: Regional, Local

Regularly published sections: Editorial, Business, Sports, Lifestyle/Arts

Type of news emphasized: International, National, State, Local

How majority of news is gathered: Staff Reporters, EFE, Hispanic Link,
                                  Compress

Best way to get information to outlets: Press Releases, Phone Calls,
                                           Spanish

Title: El Miami Herald
Address: No. 1 Herald Plaza, Miami, FL 33132-1693
Phone No.: 305/376-3531
Publisher: Richard G. Capen, Jr.
Editor: TBD
Circulation: 73,000 audited by ABC
Language: Spanish
Frequency of Publication: Daily & Sunday
Distribution: National

Regularly published sections: Editorial, Business, Sports, Lifestyle/Arts

Type of news emphasized: International, National, State, Local

How majority of news is gathered: UPI, AP

Best way to get information to outlets: Press Releases, English, Spanish

Title: El Pregonero
Address: 5001 Eastern Ave., Hyattsville, MD 20780
Phone No.: 301/853-4504
Publisher: Carroll Publishing Co.
Editor: Oscar Reyes
Circulation: 10,000
Language: Spanish
Frequency of Publication: Weekly
Distribution: Regional

Regularly published sections: Editorial, Sports

Type of news emphasized: International, Local

How majority of news is gathered: Wires, Staff Reporters, EFE

Best way to get information to outlets: Press Releases, Phone Calls,
                                          Spanish

Title: El Sol de Hialeah
Address: 436 Palm Ave., Hialeah, FL   33012
Phone No.: 305/887-8324
Publisher: not given
Editor: Esteban Yanis
Circulation: not given
Language: Spanish
Frequency of Publication: not given
Distribution: Local

Regularly published sections: Editorial, Business, Sports, Lifestyle/Arts

Type of news emphasized: International, Local

How majority of news is gathered: Staff Reporters

Best way to get information to outlets: Press Releases, Spanish

Title: Hispanic Link Weekly Report
Address: 1420 N St., N.W., Washington, DC   20005
Phone No.: 202/234-0280
Publisher: Hector Ericksen-Mendoza
Editor: Felix Perez
Circulation: 1,025
Language: English
Frequency of Publication: Weekly
Distribution: National

Regularly published sections: Column Service (3 columns weekly)

Type of news emphasized: not given

How majority of news is gathered: not given

Best way to get information to outlets: not given

Title: **Hispanic Review of Business**
Address: P.O. Box 75418, Washington, DC 20013
Phone No.: 202/547-8754
Publisher: not given
Editor: Betty South
Circulation: 135,000
Language: English
Frequency of Publication: 10 Times a Year
Distribution: National

Regularly published sections: not given

Type of news emphasized: not given

How majority of news is gathered: not given

Best way to get information to outlets: not given

Title: **La Gaceta**
Address: 3210 East 7th Avenue, Tampa, FL 33675
Phone No.: 813/248-3921
Publisher: Roland Manteiga
Editor: Roland Manteiga
Circulation: 18,000
Language: Trilingual
Frequency of Publication: Weekly
Distribution: not given

Regularly published sections: Editorial, Business, Sports, Lifestyle/Arts

Type of news emphasized: National, State, Local

How majority of news is gathered: not given

Best way to get information to outlets: not given

Title: La Nacion Newspaper
Address: 1393 SW 1st St., Miami, FL 33135
Phone No.: 305/649-9952
Publisher: Armando Garcia-Sifredo
Editor: Armando Garcia-Sifredo
Circulation: 12,000
Language: Spanish
Frequency of Publication: Weekly
Distribution: Local

Regularly published sections: Editorial, Sports, Lifestyles

Type of news emphasized: International, Local

How majority of news is gathered: n/a

Best way to get information to outlets: Press Releases, Spanish

Title: La Prensa
Address: 395 N. Orange Ave., Orlando, FL 32801
Phone No.: 305/425-9911/9912
Publisher: Manuel A. Toro
Editor: Misma persona arriba mencionada
Circulation: 10,000 Verified Estamos realizando el audit
Language: Spanish
Frequency of Publication: Weekly
Distribution: Local

Regularly published sections: Editorial, Business, Sports, Lifestyle/Arts

Type of news emphasized: International, Local

How majority of news is gathered: Wires, UPI

Best way to get information to outlets: Press Releases, Spanish

Title: La Semana
Address: 2483 John Young Parkway, Suite "K", Orlando, FL 32804
Phone No.: 305/297-0995
Publisher: Raul Delgado-Baguer
Editor: Raul Delgado-Baguer
Circulation: 10,500
Language: Spanish
Frequency of Publication: Weekly
Distribution: Regional

Regularly published sections: Editorial, Business, Sports, Lifestyle/Arts

Type of news emphasized: International, Local

How majority of news is gathered: Wires, Staff Reporters

Best way to get information to outlets: Press Releases, Spanish

Title: La Voz Catolica
Address: 9400 Biscayne Blvd., Miami Shores, FL 33138
Phone No.: 305/758-0543
Publisher: Catholic Archdiocese of Miami
Editor: Miss Araceli Cantero
Circulation: 25,400
Language: Spanish
Frequency of Publication: Biweekly
Distribution: Local, within archdiocese boundaries from Broward County to
the Keys

Regularly published sections: Editorial

Type of news emphasized: International, National, State, Local, Church
Related Only

How majority of news is gathered: Wires, Staff Reporters, National
Catholic News (NC)

Best way to get information to outlets: Spanish, Only if Religious Related

Title: Mundo Hispanico
Address: P.O. Box 13808, Station K, Atlanta, GA 30324
Phone No.: 404/881-0441
Publisher: Carola C. Reuben
Editor: Carola C. Reuben
Circulation: 10,400 audit to begin soon with verified audit circulation
Language: Bilingual
Frequency of Publication: Monthly
Distribution: Local

Regularly published sections: not given

Type of news emphasized: Local

How majority of news is gathered: Staff

Best way to get information to outlets: Not of Interest--Focus is Local
and Strictly Hispanic

Title: Prensa Hispana
Address: 8519 Piney Branch Rd., Silver Spring, MD 20901
Phone No.: 301/587-7217
Publisher: The Spanish Speaking Community of MD, Inc.
Editor: Emilio Perche Rivas
Circulation: approximately 3,000
Language: Spanish
Frequency of Publication: Monthly
Distribution: National

Regularly published sections: Editorial

Type of news emphasized: Local

How majority of news is gathered: News Bulletins, Meetings

Best way to get information to outlets: Press Releases, Phone Calls,
Spanish

154

Title: **Vista**
Address: 2355 Salzedo St., Suite 301, Coral Gables, FL 33134
Phone No.: 305/442-2462
Publisher: Arturo Villar
Editor: Harry Caicedo
Circulation: 920,200
Language: English
Frequency of Publication: Monthly
Distribution: National

Regularly published sections: General-interest newspaper supplement for Hispanic market

Type of news emphasized: not given

How majority of news is gathered: not given

Best way to get information to outlets: not given

MIDWEST:

Title: Dos Mundos Newspaper
Address: 824 Southwest Blvd., Kansas City, MO 64108
Phone No.: 816/221-4747
Publisher: Manuel Reyes
Editor: Clara Reyes
Circulation: 20,000
Language: Bilingual
Frequency of Publication: not given
Distribution: Local

Regularly published sections: Editorial, Lifestyle/Arts

Type of news emphasized: International, National, Local

How majority of news is gathered: Staff Reporter

Best way to get information to outlets: Press Releases, Phone Calls, English, Spanish

Title: El Heraldo
Address: 3740 W. 26th St., Chicago, IL 60623
Phone No.: 312/521-8300
Publisher: Joe Garcia
Editor: not given
Circulation: not given
Language: Spanish
Frequency of Publication: Weekly
Distribution: not given

Regularly published sections: not given

Type of news emphasized: not given

How majority of news is gathered: not given

Best way to get information to outlets: not given

Title: El Cometa
Address: 4744 S. Loomis Blvd., Chicago, IL 60602
Phone No.: 312/926-4381
Publisher: not given
Editor: Carlos Preciado
Circulation: 30,000
Language: Spanish
Frequency of Publication: Bimonthly
Distribution: not given

Regularly published sections: not given

Type of news emphasized: not given

How majority of news is gathered: not given

Best way to get information to outlets: not given

Title: El Heraldo de Chicago
Address: 3734 W. 26th St., 2nd Fl., Chicago, IL 60623
Phone No.: 312/521-8300
Publisher: Joe Gacia
Editor: Andres Bullon
Circulation: 30,000
Language: Spanish
Frequency of Publication: Weekly
Distribution: Local

Regularly published sections: not given

Type of news emphasized: not given

How majority of news is gathered: not given

Best way to get information to outlets: not given

Title: El Manana Daily News
Address: 2700 S. Harding, Chicago, IL 60623
Phone No.: 312/321-9137
Publisher: Gorki Teller
Editor: Humberto Perales
Circulation: 45,000
Language: Spanish
Frequency of Publication: Daily
Distribution: Local

Regularly published sections: Editorial, Business, Sports, Lifestyle/Arts

Type of news emphasized: International, National, State, Local

How majority of news is gathered: UPI, AP

Best way to get information to outlets: Press Releases, English, Spanish

Title: El Perico
Address: 1611 N. Mosley, Wichita, KS 67214
Phone No.: 316/263-1041
Publisher: Gerente
Editor: Alfonso Hernandez
Circulation: 3,000 audited by United Methodist Urban Ministry
Language: Bilingual
Frequency of Publication: Monthly
Distribution: National

Regularly published sections: not given

Type of news emphasized: National, State, Local

How majority of news is gathered: not given

Best way to get information to outlets: Press Releases, English, Spanish

Title: El Renacimiento
Address: 1132 N. Washington Ave., Lansing, MI 48906
Phone No.: 517/485-4389
Publisher: Jose A. Lopez
Editor: Jose A. Lopez
Circulation: 10,000
Language: Bilingual
Frequency of Publication: Monthly
Distribution: Statewide

Regularly published sections: Editorial, Sports, Lifestyle/Arts

Type of news emphasized: State

How majority of news is gathered: Staff Reporters

Best way to get information to outlets: Press Releases, English, Spanish

Title: **Estrella Magazine**
Address: 342 Massachusetts Ave., Suite 100, Indianapolis, IN 46204
Phone No.: 317/631-5882
Publisher: Estrella Magazine Inc.
Editor: David M.S. Hernandez
Circulation: 15,000
Language: Bilingual
Frequency of Publication: Monthly
Distribution: National

Regularly published sections: Editorial, Business, Sports, Lifestyle/Arts

Type of news emphasized: National, State, Local

How majority of news is gathered: n/a

Best way to get information to outlets: Phone Calls, English

Title: **La Raza Newspaper**
Address: 3909 N. Ashland Ave., Chicago, IL 60613
Phone No.: 312/525-9400
Publisher: Luis Heber Rossi
Editor: Jorge Vargas
Circulation: 40,000
Language: Spanish
Frequency of Publication: Weekly
Distribution: Regional

Regularly published sections: Editorial, Business, Sports, Lifestyle/Arts

Type of news emphasized: International, National, State, Local

How majority of news is gathered: Staff Reporters

Best way to get information to outlets: Press Releases, Spanish

Title: La Voz
Address: 308 SW 25, Oklahoma City, OK 73109
Phone No.: 405/632-8844
Publisher: The Hispanic Center
Editor: Joe Hutchison
Circulation: 5,000
Language: Bilingual
Frequency of Publication: Monthly
Distribution: Statewide

Regularly published sections: Editorial, Business

Type of news emphasized: National, Local

How majority of news is gathered: not given

Best way to get information to outlets: Press Releases, English

Title: La Voz
Address: 560 Hall South West, Grand Rapids, MI 49503
Phone No.: 616/452-4010
Publisher: not given
Editor: Jose Flores
Circulation: 20,500
Language: BiLingual
Frequency of Publication: Bi-Monthly
Distribution: not given

Regularly published sections: not given

Type of news emphasized: National, Local

How majority of news is gathered: not given

Best way to get information to outlets: not given

Title: Lawndale News
Address: (see West Town Publications)
Phone No.:
Publisher:
Editor:
Circulation:
Language:
Frequency of Publication:
Distribution:

Regularly published sections:

Type of news emphasized:

How majority of news is gathered:

Best way to get information to outlets:

Title: Logan Square Extra
Address: 3918 W. North Ave., Chicago, IL 60647
Phone No.: 312/252-3534
Publisher: Mila Tellez
Editor: Mary Montgomery
Circulation: 14,000
Language: Bilingual
Frequency of Publication: Weekly
Distribution: Local

Regularly published sections: Business

Type of news emphasized: Local

How majority of news is gathered: Staff Reporters

Best way to get information to outlets: Press Releases, Phone Calls,
                                         English, Spanish

Title: **Midwest Herald**
Address: (see West Town Publications)
Phone No.:
Publisher:
Editor:
Circulation:
Language:
Frequency of Publication:
Distribution:

Regularly published sections:

Type of news emphasized:

How majority of news is gathered:

Best way to get information to outlets:

Title: New West Herald
Address: (see West Town Publications)
Phone No.:
Publisher:
Editor:
Circulation:
Language:
Frequency of Publication:
Distribution:

Regularly published sections:

Type of news emphasized:

How majority of news is gathered:

Best way to get information to outlets:

Title: North Herald
Address: (see West Town Publications)
Phone No.:
Publisher:
Editor:
Circulation:
Language:
Frequency of Publication:
Distribution:

Regularly published sections:

Type of news emphasized:

How majority of news is gathered:

Best way to get information to outlets:

Title: Northwest Extra
Address: 3918 W. North Ave., Chicago, IL 60647
Phone No.: 312/252-3534
Publisher: Mila Tellez
Editor: Mary Montgomery
Circulation: 16,000 audited by VAC
Language: Bilingual
Frequency of Publication: Weekly
Distribution: Local

Regularly published sections: Business

Type of news emphasized: Local

How majority of news is gathered: Staff Reporters

Best way to get information to outlets: Press Releases, Phone Calls,
                                           English, Spanish

Title: **Northwest Herald**
Address: (see West Town Publications)
Phone No.:
Publisher:
Editor:
Circulation:
Language:
Frequency of Publication:
Distribution:

Regularly published sections:

Type of news emphasized:

How majority of news is gathered:

Best way to get information to outlets:

Title: **Tele Guia**
Address: P.O. Box 23133, Chicago, IL   60623
Phone No.: 312/788-8828
Publisher: Ezequiel Montes
Editor: Jose Suarez
Circulation: 20,000 Verified
Language: Spanish
Frequency of Publication: Weekly
Distribution: Local

Regularly published sections: Editorial, Sports, Lifestyle/Arts

Type of news emphasized: International, National, Local, Entertainment TV

How majority of news is gathered: n/a

Best way to get information to outlets: Press Releases, Spanish

Title: **West Side Times**
Address: (see West Town Publications)
Phone No.:
Publisher:
Editor:
Circulation:
Language:
Frequency of Publication:
Distribution:

Regularly published sections:

Type of news emphasized:

How majority of news is gathered:

Best way to get information to outlets:

Title: **West Town Publications**
Address: 2711 W. Dermak, Chicago, IL 60608
Phone No.: 312/247-8500
Publisher: not given
Editor: Antonio Zavala
Circulation: 55,000 (combined)
Language: Mainly English
Frequency of Publication: Weekly
Distribution: not given

Papers Published: N.W. Herald, Midwest Herald, Lawndale News, New West
Herald, West Side Times, North Herald

Regularly published sections: not given

Type of news emphasized: not given

How majority of news is gathered: not given

Best way to get information to outlets: not given

Title: Wiker Park/West Town Extra
Address: 3918 W. North Ave., Chicago, IL 60647
Phone No.: 312/252-3534
Publisher: Mila Tellez
Editor: Mary Montgomery
Circulation: 14,000 audited by VAC
Language: Bilingual
Frequency of Publication: Weekly
Distribution: not given

Regularly published sections: Business

Type of news emphasized: Local

How majority of news is gathered: Staff Reporters

Best way to get information to outlets: Press Releases, Phone Calls,
English, Spanish

TEXAS:

Title: El Arma
Address: 1612 Markley Lane, P.O. Box 2706, Laredo, TX 78044-2706
Phone No.: 512/722-7998
Publisher: Felix Garcia
Editor: Rafael Luque
Circulation: not given, audited by Pressmag
Language: Spanish
Frequency of Publication: Weekly
Distribution: National

Regularly published sections: Editorial

Type of news emphasized: International, National

How majority of news is gathered: Staff Reporters

Best way to get information to outlets: Press Releases, English

Title: **Correo**
Address: (see El Continental)
Phone No.:
Publisher:
Editor:
Circulation:
Language:
Frequency of Publication:
Distribution:

Regularly published sections:

Type of news emphasized:

How majority of news is gathered:

Best way to get information to outlets:

Title: **Del Rio News-Herald**
Address: 321 S. Main, Del Rio, TX   78840
Phone No.: 512/775-1551
Publisher: T.J. "Turk" Tergliaferq
Editor: Diana Gonzales
Circulation: 6391 Daily, 6881 Sunday Audited by ABC
Language: English
Frequency of Publication: Daily
Distribution: Local

Regularly published sections: Editorial, Business, Sports, Lifestyle/Arts

Type of news emphasized: International, National, State, Local

How majority of news is gathered: Staff Reporters, AP

Best way to get information to outlets: Press Releases, English

Title: El Bautista Mexicano (Religious publication)
Address: 511 North Akard, Suite 1043, Dallas, TX 75201-3355
Phone No.: 214/720-0550 (ext. 429)
Publisher: Baptist General Convention of Texas
Editor: Rev. Ruben V. Hernandez
Circulation: 2,500 audited by U.S. Postal Service
Language: Spanish
Frequency of Publication: Monthly
Distribution: National

Regularly published sections: Editorial

Type of news emphasized: State

How majority of news is gathered: Staff Reporters

Best way to get information to outlets: Press Releases, English, Spanish

Title: El Continental
Address: 2300 E. Yandell, P.O. Box 1950, El Paso, TX 79903
Phone No.: 915/532-6587
Publisher: El Continental News Co.
Editor: Alejandro Irigoyen Paez
Circulation: 40,000 (each)
Language: Spanish
Frequency of Publication: Daily
Distribution: Regional, Local

Regularly published sections: Editorial, Business, Sports, Lifestyle/Arts

Type of news emphasized: International, National, State, Local

How majority of news is gathered: Wires, Staff Reporters, API, OEM-MEXICO

Best way to get information to outlets: Press Releases, Spanish

Title: El Editor
Address: 2401 South 1st, Austin, TX
Phone No.: 512/447-2666
Publisher: Bidal Aguero
Editor: Bidal Aguero
Circulation: 10,000
Language: Bilingual
Frequency of Publication: not given
Distribution: Regional, Local

Regularly published sections: Editorial, Sports, Lifestyle/Arts

Type of news emphasized: State, Local

How majority of news is gathered: UPI

Best way to get information to outlets: Press Releases, English, Spanish

Title: El Editor
Address: P.O. Box 7797, Odessa, TX   79766
Phone No.: 915/337-7369
Publisher: Bidal Aguero
Editor: Manuel Orona
Circulation: not given
Language: Bilingual
Frequency of Publication: not given
Distribution: Regional

Regularly published sections: Editorial, Sports, Lifestyle/Arts

Type of news emphasized: State, Local

How majority of news is gathered: UPI

Best way to get information to outlets: Press Releases, English, Spanish

Title: El Editor
Address: 1211 Ave. O, mailing: P.O. Box 11250, Lubbock, TX 79408
Phone No.: 806/763-3841
Publisher: Bidal Aguero
Editor: Olga Riojas
Circulation: 15,000
Language: Bilingual
Frequency of Publication: Weekly
Distribution: Regional, Local

Regularly published sections: Editorial, Sports, Lifestyle/Arts

Type of news emphasized: State, Local

How majority of news is gathered: Staff Reporters, UPI

Best way to get information to outlets: Press Releases, English, Spanish

Title: El Editor-Permian Basin
Address: Rt. 12, Box 3220, P.O. Box 7797 Odessa, TX 79766
Phone No.: 915/337-7369
Publisher: Manuel J. Orona
Editor: not given
Circulation: 10,800
Language: Bilingual
Frequency of Publication: Weekly
Distribution: Regional, Local

Regularly published sections: Editorial, Business, Sports, Lifestyle/Arts

Type of news emphasized: International, National, State, Local

How majority of news is gathered: Staff Reporters, EFE

Best way to get information to outlets: Press Releases, Phone Calls, English, Spanish

170

Title: El Fronterizo
Address: (see El Continental)
Phone No.:
Publisher:
Editor:
Circulation:
Language:
Frequency of Publication:
Distribution:

Regularly published sections:

Type of news emphasized:

How majority of news is gathered:

Best way to get information to outlets:

Title: El Heraldo De Brownsville
Address: P.O. Box 351, Brownsville, TX 78520
Phone No.: 512/542-4301
Publisher: not given
Spanish Editor: Oscar J. De Castillo
Circulation: 2,200
Language: Spanish
Frequency of Publication: Daily (and Sunday)
Distribution: not given

Regularly published sections: not given

Type of news emphasized: not given

How majority of news is gathered: not given

Best way to get information to outlets: not given

Title: El Mexica
Address: P.O. Box 15201, Houston, TX 77020 / 601 Shotwell, Houston,
         TX 77020
Phone No.: 713/674-5501, 674-8022
Publisher: Mexica Publishing
Editor: Rogelio Noriega
Circulation: not given
Language: English
Frequency of Publication: Weekly
Distribution: Local

Regularly published sections: Sports, Lifestyle/Arts

Type of news emphasized: International, National, State, Local

How majority of news is gathered: Staff Reporters, Researchers

Best way to get information to outlets: Press Releases, Spanish

Title: El Mexicano
Address: (see El Continental)
Phone No.:
Publisher:
Editor:
Circulation:
Language:
Frequency of Publication:
Distribution:

Regularly published sections:

Type of news emphasized:

How majority of news is gathered:

Best way to get information to outlets:

Title: El Sol de Houston
Address: P.O. Box 3795, 3130 Navigation Blvd., Houston, TX 77003
Phone No.: 713/224-0616
Publisher: Rev. James L. Novarro
Editor: Rev. James L. Novarro
Circulation: 37,000 audited
Language: Bilingual
Frequency of Publication: Weekly
Distribution: National, Statewide, Regional, Local

Regularly published sections: Editorial, Business, Sports, Lifestyle/Arts

Type of news emphasized: International, National, State, Local

How majority of news is gathered: UPI

Best way to get information to outlets: Press Releases, Phone Calls, English, Spanish

Title: El Sol de Texas
Address: 4255 LBJ Freeway, Suite 105, Dallas, TX 75244
Phone No.: 214/386-9120
Publisher: not given
Editor: Enrique Gomez
Circulation: 44,500
Language: Spanish
Frequency of Publication: Weekly
Distribution: Local

Regularly published sections: Editorial, Sports

Type of news emphasized: International, Local

How majority of news is gathered: EFE, AP

Best way to get information to outlets: Press Releases, English, Spanish

Title: El Visitante Dominical
Address: P.O. Box 1136, San Antonio, TX 78294
Phone No.: 512/736-1916
Publisher: Fernando Pinon
Editor: Fernando Pinon
Circulation: 35,000
Language: Spanish
Frequency of Publication: Weekly
Distribution: National

Regularly published sections: not given

Type of news emphasized: not given

How majority of news is gathered: not given

Best way to get information to outlets: not given

Title: La Aurora
Address: 2639 Walnut Hill Lane, Suite 209, Dallas, TX 75229
Phone No.: 214/956-7100, 956-7187, 956-7188
Publisher: Jorge Arellano, Jose Palomo, Fernando Escobar
Editor: Fernando Escobar
Circulation: 25,000
Language: Spanish
Frequency of Publication: Weekly
Distribution: Regional

Regularly published sections: National, International, Lifestyle/Arts

Type of news emphasized: International, National, State, Local

How majority of news is gathered: Wires, Staff Reporters, EFE, UPI

Best way to get information to outlets: Press Releases, Spanish

Title: La Informacion Mundial
Address: 4010 Blue Bonnent Blvd., Houston, TX   77025
Phone No.:   713/661-9994
Publisher: Emilio Martinez Paula
Editor: Emilio Martinez Paula
Circulation: 47,000 audited by The Victoria Advocate
Language: Spanish
Frequency of Publication: not given
Distribution: National

Regularly published sections: Editorial, Business, Sports, Lifestyle/Arts

Type of news emphasized: International, Local

How majority of news is gathered: Staff Reporters, EFE, DPA

Best way to get information to outlets: Press Releases, Phone Calls,
                                          Spanish

Title: La Verdad
Address: 910 Francisca St., Corpus Christi, TX   78405
Phone No.:   512/882-7853
Publisher: Frank De La Paz
Editor: Santo De la Paz
Circulation: 45,000
Language: Bilingual
Frequency of Publication: Weekly
Distribution: Regional

Regularly published sections: not given

Type of news emphasized: not given

How majority of news is gathered: not given

Best way to get information to outlets: not given

Title: La Voz de Houston
Address: 7819 Easton, Houston, TX 77017
Phone No.: 713/644-7449
Publisher: Olga Ordonez
Editor: Maria Melero
Circulation: 40,000
Language: Spanish
Frequency of Publication: Weekly
Distribution: Regional

Regularly published sections: not given

Type of news emphasized: not given

How majority of news is gathered: not given

Best way to get information to outlets: not given

Title: La Voz del Campesino
Address: Rt. 2, Box 231-6, Pharr, TX 78577
Phone No.: 512/787-5984
Publisher: not given
Editor: Alfredo De Avila
Circulation: 30,000
Language: Spanish
Frequency of Publication: Quarterly
Distribution: Regional

Regularly published sections: Editorial

Type of news emphasized: International, National, State, Local, Issues
                          Affecting Mex-American Community

How majority of news is gathered: n/a

Best way to get information to outlets: Press Releases, Spanish

Title: Las Noticias De Fort Bend
Address: 1516 Ward, Rosenberg, TX   77471
Phone No.: 713/342-6509
Publisher: Joe R. Morales
Editor: Joe R. Morales
Circulation: 10,000
Language: Bilingual
Frequency of Publication: Weekly
Distribution: Regional

Regularly published sections: Editorial, Sports

Type of news emphasized: National, State, Local

How majority of news is gathered: n/a

Best way to get information to outlets: Press Releases, English, Spanish

Title: Southside Sun
Address: P.O. Box 2171, San Antonio, TX   78297
Phone No.: 512/225-7411
Publisher: Charles O. Patrick
Editor: Aurelio Ramirez
Circulation: 55,000
Language: Bilingual
Frequency of Publication: Weekly
Distribution: Local

Regularly published sections: not given

Type of news emphasized: not given

How majority of news is gathered: not given

Best way to get information to outlets: not given

Title: The Hispanic News
Address: 349 St. Cloud, San Antonio, TX   78201
Phone No.:   512/732-2534
Publisher: Dora Martinez
Editor: Elaine Hilario
Circulation: 81,000 by Post Office
Language: Bilingual
Frequency of Publication: Monthly
Distribution: Local

Regularly published sections: Editorial, Lifestyle/Arts

Type of news emphasized: State, Local

How majority of news is gathered: Staff Reporters

Best way to get information to outlets: Press Releases, Phone Calls,
                                          English, Spanish

Title: Westside Sun
Address: P.O. Box 2171, San Antonio, TX   78297
Phone No.:   512/225-7411
Publisher: Charles O. Patrick
Editor: Aurelio Ramirez
Circulation: 45,000
Language: Bilingual
Frequency of Publication: Weekly
Distribution: Local

Regularly published sections: not given

Type of news emphasized: not given

How majority of news is gathered: not given

Best way to get information to outlets: not given

WEST:

Title: **Ahora Spanish News**
Address: P.O. Box 3582, Reno, NV 89505
Phone No.: 702/323-6811
Publisher: Miguel A. Sepulveda
Editor: Miguel A. Sepulveda
Circulation: not given, audited by Verified Audit
Language: Bilingual
Frequency of Publication: Twice a Month--Going Weekly in 1987
Distribution: Statewide, Regional, Local

Regularly published sections: Editorial, Business, Sports, Lifestyle/Arts

Type of news emphasized: International, National, State, Local

How majority of news is gathered: n/a

Best way to get information to outlets: Press Releases, English, Spanish

Title: **El Hispano News**
Address: 900 Park Ave., S.W., Albuquerque, NM 87102
Phone No.: 505/243-6161
Publisher: A. B. Collado
Editor: A. B. Collado
Circulation: 12,000 audited by U.S. Post Office
Language: Spanish
Frequency of Publication: Weekly
Distribution: National, Statewide, Local

Regularly published sections: Editorial, Business, Sports, Lifestyle/Arts

Type of news emphasized: International, National, State, Local

How majority of news is gathered: Staff Reporters & Mail

Best way to get information to outlets: Press Releases, English, Spanish

Title: El Mundo
Address: 15 N. Mojave, Las Vegas, NV 89101
Phone No.: 702/384-1514, 385-5035
Publisher: Eddie Escobedo Sr.
Editor: Frank Corro
Circulation: 15,000
Language: Spanish
Frequency of Publication: Weekly
Distribution: Statewide

Regularly published sections: Editorial, Sports, Lifestyle/Arts

Type of news emphasized: International, National, State, Local

How majority of news is gathered: Staff Reporters

Best way to get information to outlets: Press Releases, Phone Calls,
                                          English, Spanish (prefer Spanish)

Title: El Sol
Address: 8686 N. Central Ave., Suite 206, Phoenix, AZ 85020
Phone No.: 602/870-1281
Publisher: Marcos Orona
Editor: Marcos Orona
Circulation: 15,000
Language: Spanish
Frequency of Publication: Weekly
Distribution: Regional

Regularly published sections: not given

Type of news emphasized: not given

How majority of news is gathered: not given

Best way to get information to outlets: not given

Title: La Voz de Colorado
Address: 812 Sante Fe Dr., P.O. Box 9650, Denver, CO 80209
Phone No.: 303/623-4814
Publisher: Wanda Padilla
Editor: James Padilla
Circulation: 12,500 by Colorado Press Association
Language: Bilingual
Frequency of Publication: Weekly
Distribution: Statewide

Regularly published sections: Editorial, Business, Sports, Lifestyle/Arts

Type of news emphasized: Local

How majority of news is gathered: Hispanic Link

Best way to get information to outlets: Press Releases, Phone Calls,
English, Spanish

Title: La Voz de Idaho
Address: P.O. Box 490, Caldwell, ID 83606
Phone No.: 208/454-1652
Publisher: Idaho Migrant Council
Editor: Meg Fereday
Circulation: 2,000
Language: Bilingual
Frequency of Publication: Monthly
Distribution: Statewide

Regularly published sections: Editorial

Type of news emphasized: State, Local

How majority of news is gathered: Editor, Hispanic Link, Vista Magazine,
other Hispanic publications

Best way to get information to outlets: Press Releases, Phone Calls,
English, Spanish

Title: Mundo Latino
Address: 840 West North Temple, Salt Lake City, UT 84116
Phone No.: 801/532-1611
Publisher: not given
Editor: Heber Rodriguez
Circulation: 7,500
Language: not given
Frequency of Publication: Weekly
Distribution: Regional

Regularly published sections: not given

Type of news emphasized: not given

How majority of news is gathered: not given

Best way to get information to outlets: not given

Title: Resource Center Bulletin
Address: Box 4506, Albuquerque, NM 87196
Phone No.: 505/266-5009
Publisher: The Resource Center
Editor: Tom Barry
Circulation: 5,000
Language: English
Frequency of Publication: Quarterly
Distribution: not given

Regularly published sections: n/a

Type of news emphasized: International

How majority of news is gathered: Staff Reporters

Best way to get information to outlets: Press Releases, English

Title: Revista Unidos
Address: 1517 E. Washington, Phoenix, AZ 85034
Phone No.: 602/269-7674
Publisher: not given
Editor: Luis M. Ortiz
Circulation: 6,000
Language: Bilingual
Frequency of Publication: Weekly
Distribution: Statewide

Regularly published sections: not given

Type of news emphasized: not given

How majority of news is gathered: not given

Best way to get information to outlets: not given

Title: The Hispanic News
Address: 2318 Second Ave., Seattle, WA 98121
Phone No.: 206/527-0750
Publisher: Pedro Cavazos
Editor: Pedro Cavazos
Circulation: 10,000
Language: Bilingual
Frequency of Publication: not given
Distribution: Statewide

Regularly published sections: Editorial, Business, Lifestyle/Arts

Type of news emphasized: State, Local

How majority of news is gathered: Staff Reporters

Best way to get information to outlets: Press Releases, English, Spanish

Title: The Taos News/ El Crepusculo
Address: P.O. Box U, Taos, NM 87571
Phone No.: 505/758-2241
Publisher: Robin Martin
Editor: Billie Blair
Circulation: 8,140 audited 3rd Quarter 1985 by ABC Audit
Language: Bilingual
Frequency of Publication: Weekly
Distribution: Local

Regularly published sections: Editorial, Business, Sports, Lifestyle/Arts

Type of news emphasized: Local

How majority of news is gathered: Staff Reporters

Best way to get information to outlets: Press Releases, Spanish

CALIFORNIA:

Title: Adelante! Publications
Address: 125 Imperial St., Oxnard, CA 93030
Phone No.: 805/485-7488
Publisher: not given
Editor: not given
Circulation: not given
Language: Bilingual
Frequency of Publication: Monthly
Distribution: Local

Regularly published sections: Editorial, Business, Sports, Lifestyle/Arts

Type of news emphasized: National, Local

How majority of news is gathered: Staff Reporters

Best way to get information to outlets: Press Releases, Phone Calls,
                                           English, Spanish

Title: Ahora Now Newspaper
Address: 134 E. San Ysidro Blvd., San Ysidro, CA 92073
Phone No.: 619/428-2277
Publisher: Bertha Alicia Gonzalez
Editor: Bertha Alicia Gonzalez
Circulation: 10,000
Language: Bilingual
Frequency of Publication: Weekly
Distribution: International

Regularly published sections: Editorial, Business, Sports, Lifestyle/Arts

Type of news emphasized: International, State, Local

How majority of news is gathered: Staff Reporters

Best way to get information to outlets: Press Releases, Phone Calls,
                                          English, Spanish

Title: Belvedere Citizen
Address: Northeast Newspapers, 5420 Figueroa St., Los Angeles, CA
90042
Phone No.: 213/259-6200
Publisher: Oran W. Asa
Editor: Roger Swanson
Circulation: 17,123
Language: Bilingual
Frequency of Publication: Weekly
Distribution: Local

Regularly published sections: Editorial, Sports, Lifestyle/Arts

Type of news emphasized: State, Local

How majority of news is gathered: Staff Reporters

Best way to get information to outlets: Press Releases, Phone Calls,
                                         English, Spanish

Title: City Terrace Comet
Address: (see Eastern Group)
Phone No.:
Publisher:
Editor:
Circulation:
Language:
Frequency of Publication:
Distribution:

Regularly published sections:

Type of news emphasized:

How majority of news is gathered:

Best way to get information to outlets:

Title: East L.A. Brooklyn/Belevedere Comet
Address: (see Eastern Group)
Phone No.:
Publisher:
Editor:
Circulation:
Language:
Frequency of Publication:
Distribution:

Regularly published sections:

Type of news emphasized:

How majority of news is gathered:

Best way to get information to outlets:

Title: **Eastern Group**
Address: 2912 E. Brooklyn Ave., Los Angeles, CA 90033
Phone No.: 213/263-5743
Publisher: Dolores Sanchez
Editor: Dolores Sanchez
Circulation: 50,000 (combined)
Language: Bilingual
Frequency of Publication: Weekly
Distribution: Local

Papers Published: Eastside Sun, Mexican American Sun, East L.A.
    Brooklyn/Belevedere Comet, Monteray Park Comet,
    City Terrace Comet, Wyvernwood Chronicle

Regularly published sections: not given

Type of news emphasized: not given

How majority of news is gathered: not given

Best way to get information to outlets: not given

Title: Eastside Journal
Address: 5420 N. Figueroa St., Los Angeles, CA 90041
Phone No.: 213/259-6200
Publisher: Oran W. Asa
Editor: Roger Swanson
Circulation: 17,000
Language: Bilingual
Frequency of Publication: Weekly
Distribution: Local

Regularly published sections: Editorial, Sports, Lifestyle/Arts

Type of news emphasized: State, Local

How majority of news is gathered: Staff Reporters

Best way to get information to outlets: Press Releases, Phone Calls,
                                        English, Spanish

Title: Eastside Sun
Address: (see Eastern Group)
Phone No.:
Publisher:
Editor:
Circulation:
Language:
Frequency of Publication:
Distribution:

Regularly published sections:

Type of news emphasized:

How majority of news is gathered:

Best way to get information to outlets:

Title: El Aguila
Address: P.O. Box 42116, Los Angeles, CA   90042
Phone No.:   213/266-1309
Publisher: Carlos Estrada
Editor: Ray Moshe
Circulation: 7,000
Language: Bilingual
Frequency of Publication: Weekly
Distribution: Local

Regularly published sections: Editorial, Business, Sports, Lifestyle/Arts

Type of news emphasized: International, National, State, Local

How majority of news is gathered: n/a

Best way to get information to outlets: Press Releases, English, Spanish

Title: El Bohemio News
Address: 3133 - 22nd St., San Francisco, CA 94110
Phone No.: 415/647-1924
Publisher: Fred Rosado
Editor: Fred Rosado
Circulation: 70,000 audited by Alonzo Printing Inc.
Language: Bilingual
Frequency of Publication: Weekly
Distribution: Regional

Regularly published sections: Editorial, Business, Sports, Lifestyle/Arts

Type of news emphasized: International, National, State, Local

How majority of news is gathered: Staff Reporters

Best way to get information to outlets: Press Releases, English, Spanish

Title: El Chicano Newspaper
Address: P.O. Box 827, Colton, CA 92324
Phone No.: 714/825-0964
Publisher: Gloria Macias Harrison
Editor: Gloria Macias Harrison
Circulation: 10,000
Language: Bilingual
Frequency of Publication: Weekly
Distribution: Regional

Regularly published sections: not given

Type of news emphasized: National, State, Local

How majority of news is gathered: Staff Reporters

Best way to get information to outlets: Press Releases, English, Spanish

Title: El Heraldo Catolico
Address: 5890 Newman Court, Sacramento, CA 95819
Phone No.: 916/452-3344
Publisher: Obispo Francis A. Quinn
Editor: Padre George Schuster
Circulation: 10,000
Language: Spanish
Frequency of Publication: Five Times per Year
Distribution: Regional

Regularly published sections: Editorial, Social-Religious

Type of news emphasized: Local

How majority of news is gathered: Staff Reporters

Best way to get information to outlets: Press Releases, Spanish

Title: El Mexicalo
Address: 931 Niles St., Bakersfield, CA 93305
Phone No.: 805/323-9334
Publisher: Esther H. Manzano
Editor: Tony Manzano Jr.
Circulation: not given
Language: Bilingual
Frequency of Publication: not given
Distribution: Local

Regularly published sections: Editorial, Business, Sports, Lifestyle/Arts

Type of news emphasized: Local

How majority of news is gathered: Staff Reporters

Best way to get information to outlets: Press Releases, English, Spanish

Title: El Mundo
Address: 630 - 20th St., Oakland, CA 94612
Phone No.: 415/763-1120
Publisher: Thomas L. Berkley
Editor: Abdon J. Ugarte
Circulation: 32,000 audited by Community papers verification service
Language: Bilingual
Frequency of Publication: Weekly
Distribution: Regional

Regularly published sections: Editorial, Business, Sports, Lifestyle/Arts

Type of news emphasized: International, National, State, Local

How majority of news is gathered: Staff Reporters, PSN, BCN

Best way to get information to outlets: Press Releases, Phone Calls,
                                           English, Spanish

Title: El Observador
Address: P.O. Box 1990, San Jose, CA 95109
Phone No.: 408/295-4272
Publisher: Maxine Goodman
Editor: Maxine Goodman
Circulation: 35,000
Language: Bilingual
Frequency of Publication: Weekly
Distribution: Local

Regularly published sections: not given

Type of news emphasized: not given

How majority of news is gathered: not given

Best way to get information to outlets: not given

Title: El Popular Spanish Newspaper
Address: 5512 S. Union Ave., Bakersfield, CA   93307
Phone No.: 805/398-1000, 398-1030
Publisher: Raul Camacho, Sr.
Editor: Raul Camacho, Sr.
Circulation: 25,000
Language: Spanish
Frequency of Publication: Weekly
Distribution: Local

Regularly published sections: Editorial, Sports, Lifestyle/Arts

Type of news emphasized: Local

How majority of news is gathered: not given

Best way to get information to outlets: Press Releases, Spanish

Title: El Sereno Star
Address: Northeast Newspapers, 5420 Figueroa St., Los Angles, CA   90042
Phone No.: 213/259-6200
Publisher: not given
Editor: Pepe Arciga
Circulation: 8,635
Language: not given
Frequency of Publication: Weekly
Distribution: not given

Regularly published sections: not given

Type of news emphasized: not given

How majority of news is gathered: not given

Best way to get information to outlets: English, Spanish

Title: El Sol
Address: P.O. Box 1610, Salinas, CA 93902-1610
Phone No.: 408/757-8118
Publisher: Oscar Parvol
Editor: Oscar Parvol
Circulation: not given
Language: English
Frequency of Publication: Weekly
Distribution: not given

Regularly published sections: Sports, Lifestyle/Arts

Type of news emphasized: Local

How majority of news is gathered: NEA

Best way to get information to outlets: Press Releases, Spanish

Title: El Tecolote
Address: P.O. Box 40037, San Francisco, CA 94140
Phone No.: 415/824-7878
Publisher: Juan Gonzales
Editor: Carlos Alcala
Circulation: 10,000
Language: Bilingual
Frequency of Publication: Monthly
Distribution: Local

Regularly published sections: Editorial, Lifestyle/Arts

Type of news emphasized: International, Local

How majority of news is gathered: Staff Reporters

Best way to get information to outlets: Press Releases, English, Spanish

Title: Hispanic Business
Address: 360 S. Hope Ave., Suite 100C, Santa Barbara, CA 93105
Phone No.: 805/682-5843
Publisher: Jesus Chavarria
Editor: John Coombes
Circulation: 60,000
Language: English
Frequency of Publication: Monthly
Distribution: National

Regularly published sections: not given

Type of news emphasized: not given

How majority of news is gathered: not given

Best way to get information to outlets: not given

Title: La Nacion
Address: 782 S. Valencia, Los Angeles, CA 90017
Phone No.: 213/484-2060
Publisher: not given
Editor: Ignacio Bermudez
Circulation: 12,600
Language: Spanish
Frequency of Publication: Bi-Weekly
Distribution: not given

Regularly published sections: not given

Type of news emphasized: not given

How majority of news is gathered: not given

Best way to get information to outlets: Press Releases, Spanish

Title: **La Nacion**
Address: 2250 Stewart, Suite #12, Stockton, CA 95205
Phone No.: 209/943-5143
Publisher: Porfirio Perez
Editor: Hilda Robles
Circulation: 10,000
Language: Bilingual
Frequency of Publication: Weekly
Distribution: Regional

Regularly published sections: Business, Sports, Lifestyle/Arts

Type of news emphasized: National, State

How majority of news is gathered: Staff Reporters

Best way to get information to outlets: Press Releases, Spanish

Title: **La Oferta Review**
Address: 3111 Alum Rock Ave., San Jose, CA 95133
Phone No.: 408/729-6397
Publisher: Frank & Mary Andrade
Editor: Ramiro Ascenico
Circulation: 40,000 Printer Certification
Language: Bilingual
Frequency of Publication: not given
Distribution: Local

Regularly published sections: Editorial, Business

Type of news emphasized: Local

How majority of news is gathered: Staff Reporters

Best way to get information to outlets: Press Releases, Phone Calls,
English, Spanish

Title: La Opinion
Address: 1436 South Main St., Los Angeles, CA 90015
Phone No.: 213/748-1191
Publisher: Ignacio E. Lozano, Jr.
Editor: Ignacio E. Lozano, Jr.
Circulation: 62,460 (D), 48,973 (S) -- 3/31/86 by ABC
Language: Spanish
Frequency of Publication: Daily & Sunday
Distribution: National

Regularly published sections: Editorial, Sports, Lifestyle/Arts

Type of news emphasized: International, National, State, Local

How majority of news is gathered: Staff Reporters, UPI, EFE, AP

Best way to get information to outlets: Press Releases, Spanish

Title: La Prensa de Los Angeles
Address: 1505 Gardena Ave., Glendale, CA 91204
Phone No.: 818/246-6968
Publisher: not given
Editor: Carlos G. Groppa
Circulation: 45,000
Language: Spanish
Frequency of Publication: Weekly
Distribution: Local

Regularly published sections: Editorial, Sports, Lifestyle/Arts

Type of news emphasized: International, National, State, Local

How majority of news is gathered: n/a

Best way to get information to outlets: Press Releases, Spanish

Title: La Prensa San Diego
Address: 1950 5th Ave., San Diego, CA 92101
Phone No.: 619/231-2873
Publisher: Daniel Munoz Sr.
Editor: Daniel H. Munoz Jr.
Circulation: 15,000 Print 45,000 Readership
Language: Bilingual
Frequency of Publication: Weekly
Distribution: National, Statewide, Regional, Local

Regularly published sections: Editorial, Business, Sports, Lifestyle/Arts

Type of news emphasized: National, State, Local

How majority of news is gathered: Staff Reporters, Correspondents,
                                   Free-Lance Columnists

Best way to get information to outlets: Press Releases, Phone Calls,
                                         English, Spanish

Title: La Republica
Address: 415 N. Abby St., Fresno, CA
Phone No.: 209/943-5243
Publisher: Porfirio Perez
Editor: Hilda Robles
Circulation: 10,000
Language: Bilingual
Frequency of Publication: Weekly
Distribution: Regional

Regularly published sections: Business, Sports, Lifestyle/Arts

Type of news emphasized: State

How majority of news is gathered: Staff Reporters

Best way to get information to outlets: Press Releases

Title: La Voz de Costa Rica
Address: P.O. Box 3166, 1824 Stuart Ave., W. Covina, CA 91722
Phone No.: 818/339-9322
Publisher: Jose R. Sanchez Sr.
Editor: Virginia de Sanchez
Circulation: 15,000
Language: Monthly
Frequency of Publication: Spanish
Distribution: National

Regularly published sections: Editorial, Business, Sports

Type of news emphasized: International, National, State

How majority of news is gathered: Staff Reporters

Best way to get information to outlets: Press Releases, Phone Calls

Title: La Voz Libre
Address: 3107 W. Beverly Blvd., Suite 1, Los Angeles, CA 90057
Phone No.: 213/388-4639, 388-2903
Publisher: Angel M. Prada
Editor: Angel M. Prada
Circulation: 37,000
Language: Spanish
Frequency of Publication: Weekly
Distribution: National

Regularly published sections: Editorial, Business, Sports, Lifestyle/Arts

Type of news emphasized: International

How majority of news is gathered: Staff Reporters, International Reporters

Best way to get information to outlets: Press Releases, Spanish

Title: La Voz Mestiza
Address: Cross Cultural Center, University of California, Irvine,
         Irvine, CA 92715
Phone No.: 714/856-7215, 856-7216
Publisher: Associated Students U.C. Irvine
Editor: not given
Circulation: 1,000
Language: Bilingual
Frequency of Publication: 3 Times per Academic Year
Distribution: Local

Regularly published sections: Editorial, Lifestyle/Arts

Type of news emphasized: Local

How majority of news is gathered: Staff Reporters

Best way to get information to outlets: Phone Calls, English

Title: Latin American Perspectives
Address: P.O. Box 5703, Riverside, CA 92517-5703
Phone No.: 714/787-5508
Publisher: Sage Publications, Inc.
Editor: Ronald H. Chilcote
Circulation: 1,800
Language: English
Frequency of Publication: Quarterly
Distribution: National

Regularly published sections: not given

Type of news emphasized: International

How majority of news is gathered: n/a

Best way to get information to outlets: Press Releases, Phone Calls,
                                          English, Spanish

Title: Lincoln Heights Bulletin News
Address: Northeast Newspapers, 5420 Figueroa St., Los Angeles, CA 90042
Phone No.: 213/259-6200
Publisher: not given
Editor: Fred Allen
Circulation: 8,747
Language: not given
Frequency of Publication: Weekly
Distribution: not given

Regularly published sections: not given

Type of news emphasized: not given

How majority of news is gathered: not given

Best way to get information to outlets: English, Spanish

Title: Mexican American Sun
Address: (see Eastern Group)
Phone No.:
Publisher:
Editor:
Circulation:
Language:
Frequency of Publication:
Distribution:

Regularly published sections:

Type of news emphasized:

How majority of news is gathered:

Best way to get information to outlets:

Title: **Monteray Park Comet**
Address: (see Eastern Group)
Phone No.:
Publisher:
Editor:
Circulation:
Language:
Frequency of Publication:
Distribution:

Regularly published sections:

Type of news emphasized:

How majority of news is gathered:

Best way to get information to outlets:

Title: **Neighborhood News**
Address: 1042 W. Santa Ana Blvd., Suite C, Santa Ana, CA   92703
Phone No.: 714/547-5521
Publisher: John Ochoa
Editor: John Ochoa
Circulation: 15,000
Language: English
Frequency of Publication: Weekly
Distribution: Local

Regularly published sections: Editorial, Sports, Lifestyle/Arts

Type of news emphasized: National, State, Local

How majority of news is gathered: Staff Reporters, Hispanic Link

Best way to get information to outlets: Press Releases, English

Title: Noticias Del Mundo
Address: 1301 W. 2nd St., Los Angeles, CA   90026
Phone No.:   213/482-9644
Publisher: Jose Valle
Editor: Jesus Hernandez
Circulation: 30,000
Language: Spanish
Frequency of Publication: Daily
Distribution: National

Regularly published sections: Editorial, Sports, Lifestyle/Arts

Type of news emphasized: International, National, State, Local

How majority of news is gathered: Staff Reporters, UPI, AP

Best way to get information to outlets: Press Releases, Spanish

Title: Semanario Azteca
Address: 323 N. Broadway, Santa Ana, CA   92701 or P.O. Box 207,
          Santa Ana, CA   92702
Phone No.:   714/972-9912
Publisher: Fernando Velo
Editor: Fernando Velo
Circulation: not given
Language: Spanish
Frequency of Publication: Weekly
Distribution: Regional

Regularly published sections: Editorial, Business, Sports, Lifestyle/Arts

Type of news emphasized: International, National, State, Local

How majority of news is gathered: n/a

Best way to get information to outlets: Press Releases, Spanish

Title: The Forum
Address: 1446 Front St., Suite 203, San Diego, CA   92101
Phone No.:   619/232-1010
Publisher: Mexican and American Foundation, Inc.
Editor: Ron Luis Valles
Circulation: 25,000 verified January 1987
Language: English
Frequency of Publication: Monthly
Distribution: National

Regularly published sections: Editorial, Business, Sports, Lifestyle/Arts

Type of news emphasized: International, National

How majority of news is gathered: Staff Reporters

Best way to get information to outlets: Press Releases, English

Title: Tiempo Latino
Address: 2595 Mission St., Suite 300, San Francisco, CA   94110
Phone No.:   415/821-3040
Publisher: Louis Alonso Munoz
Editor: Jose Bernardo Pacheco
Circulation: 30,000
Language: Spanish
Frequency of Publication: Weekly
Distribution: Regional

Regularly published sections: Editorial, Business, Sports, Lifestyle/Arts

Type of news emphasized: State, Local

How majority of news is gathered: Staff Reporters, Correspondents

Best way to get information to outlets: Press Releases, Spanish

Title: Unity/La Unidad
Address: P.O. Box 29293, Oakland, CA 94604
Phone No.: not given
Publisher: not given
Editor: not given
Circulation: not given
Language: Bilingual
Frequency of Publication: not given
Distribution: National

Regularly published sections: Editorial, Lifestyle/Arts

Type of news emphasized: National

How majority of news is gathered: Staff Reporters

Best way to get information to outlets: Press Releases, English, Spanish

Title: Ventura County Vida Newspaper
Address: P.O. Box 427, Oxnard, CA 93030
Phone No.: 805/983-3401
Publisher: Manuel M. Munoz
Editor: Carlos Olea
Circulation: 15,000
Language: Spanish
Frequency of Publication: Weekly
Distribution: National, Statewide, Regional, Local

Regularly published sections: Editorial, Business, Sports, Lifestyle/Arts

Type of news emphasized: Local

How majority of news is gathered: Staff Reporters

Best way to get information to outlets: Press Releases, Phone Calls

Title: Viente de Mayo (20 de Mayo)
Address: 1824 Sunset Blvd., Suite 202, Los Angeles, CA 90026
Phone No.: 213/483-8511
Publisher: Abel Perez
Editor: Abel Perez
Circulation: 25,000
Language: Spanish
Frequency of Publication: Weekly
Distribution: Regional

Regularly published sections: Editorial, Business, Sports, Lifestyle/Arts

Type of news emphasized: International, National, State, Local

How majority of news is gathered: Staff Reporters

Best way to get information to outlets: Press Releases, Spanish

Title: Voz Fronteriza
Address: U.C.S.D., Student Center, La Jolla, CA 92093
Phone No.: 619/534-4735
Publisher: Miguel Chavez & Bertha Ocoha
Editor: Salvador Reza
Circulation: 6,000-8,000
Language: Bilingual
Frequency of Publication: 9 times per year
Distribution: National, Statewide, Regional, Local

Regularly published sections: Editorial

Type of news emphasized: International, National, State, Local

How majority of news is gathered: Staff Reporters

Best way to get information to outlets: Press Releases, Phone Calls,
                                          English, Spanish

Title: Wyvernwood Chronicle
Address: (see Eastern Group)
Phone No.:
Publisher:
Editor:
Circulation:
Language:
Frequency of Publication:
Distribution:

Regularly published sections:

Type of news emphasized:

How majority of news is gathered:

Best way to get information to outlets:

II. Electronic Media

TELEVISION

EAST:

Station: WNJU-TV (CH. 47)
Address: 39 Industrial Ave., Teterboro, NJ 07608
Phone No.: 212/233-6240, 201/288-5550
Assignment Editor: Miguel Angel Torres
News Director: Hector Aguilar

Station: WXTV-TV (UNIVISION, CH. 41)
Address: 24 Meadowland Parkway, Secaucus, NJ 07094
Phone No.: 201/348-4141 (office)
Assignment Editor: Jaime Leal, Jeannette Mayorca
News Director: Conrado Roldan

SOUTH:

Station: UNIVISION
Address: 2322 NW 7th St., Miami, FL 33125
Phone No.: 305-642-7990

5420 Melrose Ave., Los Angeles, CA 90038
213/466-3434

460 W. 42nd St., 4th Floor, New York, NY 10036
212/502-1300

444 N. Capitol St., N.W., Suite 601 G, Washington, DC 20001
202/783-7155

Assignment Editor: Yolanda Zugasti (6:30 p.m. news)
News Director: TBD

Station: Hispanic American Broadcasting Corporation (HBC)
Address: 2475 West 8th Court, Hialeah, FL 33010
Phone No.: 305/884-8200
Assignment Editor: Robert Lenz
News Director: Gustavo Gudoy
   *Note: To date, broadcast newscasts to following stations in Telemundo
          network: KVEA-TV, WNJU-TV, & WSCV-TV

Station: WLTV-TV (UNIVISION, CH. 23)
Address: 2103 Coral Way, Suite 400, Miami, FL 33145
Phone No.: 305/856-2323 (office)
Assignment Editor: Barbara Gutierrez (6:00 news)
                   Elizabeth Hernandez (10:00 news)
News Director: Gustavo Pupo

Station: WSCV-TV (CH. 51)
Address: 4035 N. 29th Ave., Hollywood, FL 33020
Phone No.: 305/920-9400
Assignment Editor: Sonyha Rodriquez
News Director: Roberto Rodriguez

Station: W14AA Ch. 14 UNIVISION
Address: 4801 Massachusetts Ave., N.W., Washington, DC 20016
Phone No.: not given
Assignment Editor: not given
News Director: not given
President: Antonio Guernica

MIDWEST:

Station: WCIU-TV (CH. 60)
Address: 552 N. Broadway, Chicago, IL 60604
Phone No.: 312/750-5800
Assignment Editor: Don Aquirre
News Director: Don Aquirre

Station: WSNS-TV (UNIVISION, CH. 44)
Address: 430 W. Grant Place, Chicago, IL 60614
Phone No.: 312/929-1200
Assignment Editor: Yvonne Cueva
News Director: Ed Villareal

TEXAS:

Station: KINT-TV (UNIVISION, CH. 26)
Address: 5426 N. Mesa, El Paso, TX 79912
Phone No.: 915/581-1126
Assignment Editor: Javier Sanchez
News Director: Javier Sanchez

Station: KORO-TV (UNIVISION, CH. 28)
Address: 102 N. Mesquite, Corpus Christi, TX 78401
Phone No.: 512/883-2823
Assignment Editor: n/a
News Director: Roberto Perez

Station: KWEX-TV (UNIVISION, CH. 41)
Address: 411 E. Durango, San Antonio, TX 78204
Phone No.: 512/227-4141
Assignment Editor: Mike Ramirez
News Director: Jesus Javier

Station: K12TV (UNIVISION, CH. 12)
Address: 2308 S. 77th Sunshine Strip, Harlingen, TX 78550
Phone No.: 512/425-1202
Assignment Editor: not given
News Director: not given

Station: K45AK-TV
Address: Rosenberg, TX
Phone No.: 713/261-4545
Assignment Editor: not given
News Director: not given

Station: Television Hispana de Houston
Address: Houston, TX
Phone No.: 713/645-3738
Assignment Editor: not given
News Director: not given

Station: SATV (CH. 17)
Address: Rogers Cable Systems, 609 Augusta, San Antonio, TX 78215
Phone No.: 512/225-2323
Assignment Editor: Ovidio Rodriquez
News Director: Rolando Romero

Station: UNIVISION-TV DFW
Address: 6015 Commerce Dr., Suite 440, Irving, TX 75062
Phone No.: 214/751-0090
Assignment Editor: not given
News Director: Jim Pratt

WEST (South & North):

Station: KGSW-TV (CH. 14)
Address: 2017 San Mateo, NE, Albuquerque, NM 87110
Phone No.: 505/265-6626
Assignment Editor: not given
News Director: not given

Station: KTVW-TV (UNIVISION, CH. 33)
Address: 3019 E. Southern Ave., Phoenix, AZ 85040
Phone No.: 602/243-3333
Assignment Editor: n/a
News Director: Juan Antonio Garces

Station: K48AM-TV (UNIVISION, CH. 48)
Address: Albuquerque, NM
Phone No.: 505/243-5511
Assignment Editor: not given
News Director: not given
Contact: Dr. Grace Olivares (505/292-6833)

CALIFORNIA:

Station: KCBA-TV (UNIVISION, CH. 35)
Address: P.O. Box 3560, Salinas, CA 93912 (mailing)
Phone No.: 408/422-3500
Assignment Editor: n/a
News Director: Daniel Jarque

Station: KCSO-TV (UNIVISION, CH. 19)
Address: 2842 Iowa Ave., Modesto, CA 95351
Phone No.: 209/578-1900
Assignment Editor: n/a
News Director: Fidel Soto

Station: KDTV-TV (UNIVISION, CH. 14)
Address: 2200 Plou Ave., San Francisco, CA 94124
Phone No.: 415/641-1400
Assignment Editor: Guillermo Alcaine
News Director: Osvaldo Villazon

Station: KFTV-TV (UNIVISION, CH. 21)
Address: 3239 West Ashlan, Fresno, CA 93711 (mailing)
Phone No.: 209/222-2121
Assignment Editor: n/a
News Director: Jeff Gonzalez

Station: KMEX-TV (UNIVISION, CH. 34)
Address: 5420 Melrose Ave., Los Angeles, CA 90038
Phone No.: 213/466-3434
Assignment Editor: Jaime Garcia
News Director: Pete Moraga

Station: KSCI-TV (CH. 18)
Address: 1954 Cotner Ave., Los Angeles, CA 90025
        280 I St., San Bernardino, CA 92410
Phone No.: 213/479-8081 (LA); 714/824-7560 (S.B.)
Assignment Editor: Bill Welch
News Director: Jose Luis Logreyera

Station: KVEA-TV (CH. 52)
Address: 1139 Grand Central Ave., Glendale, CA 91201
Phone No.: 818/502-1000
Assignment Editor: Mabel Solares
News Director: Enrique Gratas

Station: XETV-TV (CH. 6)
Address: 8253 Ronson Rd., San Diego, CA 92111
Phone No.: 619/279-6666
Assignment Editor: not given
News Director: n/a

Station: XEWT-TV
Address: San Ysidro, CA
Phone No.: not given
Assignment Editor: not given
News Director: not given

RADIO

EAST:

Station: WADO-AM
Address: 277 Paterson Plank Rd., Carlstadt, NJ 07072
Phone No.: 201/343-1280
News Director: Frank Saldana

Station: WJIT-AM (Sonido Suave)
Address: 655 Madison Ave., New York, NY 10021
Phone No.: 212/935-5170
News Director: Mike Torres

Station: WKDM-AM (Radio Musical 1380)
Address: Paterson Plank Rd., Carlstadt, NJ 07072
Phone No.: 212/594-1380
News Director: Alipio Coco

Station: WLVH
Address: 18 Asylum St., Hartford, CT 06114
Phone No.: 203/549-1175
News Director: Pedro Biaggi

Station: WSKQ-AM
Address: 1500 Broadway, New York, NY 10036
Phone No.: 212/398-3820
News Director: Jose Enrique Girona

Station: WTEL-AM
Address: 1349 Cheltenham Ave., Philadelphia, PA 19126
Phone No.: 215/276-0500
News Director: n/a

SOUTH:

Station: Radio Marti
Address: Stuart Sweet, Executive Director, Pres. Advisory Board on
         Broadcasting to Cuba, 2100 6th St., N.W., Washington, DC 20547
Phone No.:
News Director:

Station: WAMA
Address: 5203 N. Armenia Ave., Tampa, FL 33601
Phone No.: 813/875-0086
News Director: Gabriel Castillo

Station: WAQI-AM (Radio Mambi)
Address: 8000 SW 67 Ave., Miami, FL 33143
Phone No.: 305/445-4020
News Director: Jorge Boulbakis

Station: WCMQ-AM/FM
Address: 1411 Coral Way, Miami, FL 33145
Phone No.: 305/854-1830
News Director: Eugenio Bueno

Station: WOCN-AM
Address: 1779 West Flagler St., Miami, FL 33135
Phone No.: 305/649-1450
News Director: Oscar Ibarra

Station: WQBA-AM/FM
Address: 2828 Coral Way, Miami, FL 33145
Phone No.: 305/447-1140, 447-9108 or 441-2140
News Director: Tomas Regaldo (AM)

Station: WRHC-AM
Address: 330 SW 27th Ave., 2nd Fl., Miami, FL 33135
Phone No.: 305/642-9742, 541-3300
News Director: Daniel Mocate/Nirso Pimentel/Armando Garcia Sifredo

Station: WSUA-AM (Radio Suave)
Address: 2100 Coral Way, Miami, FL 33145
Phone No.: 305/285-1260
News Director: Jose Valdes

Station: WTYM
Address: 228 Bullard Parkway, Temple Terrace, FL 33617
Phone No.: 813/989-9896
News Director: Mario Quevedo

MIDWEST:

Station: KBNO-AM
Address: 4785 Tejon St., Denver, CO 80211
Phone No.: 303/455-0275
News Director: Ana Gonzalez

Station: KUVO-AM
Address: P.O. Box 11111, Denver, CO 80211
Phone No.: 303/534-5880
News Director: not given

Station: WCEV-AM
Address: 5356 W. Belmont Ave., Chicago, IL 60641
Phone No.: 312/282-8787
News Director: Armando Perez

Station: WCRW-AM
Address: 2856 N. Pine Grove Ave., Chicago, IL 60614
Phone No.: 312/327-6860
News Director: Raul Cardona

Station: WCYC-FM
Address: 2801 S. Ridgeway, Chicago, IL 60623
Phone No.: 312/762-2400
News Director: not given

Station: WEDC-AM
Address: 5475 Milwaukee Avenue, Chicago, IL 60630
Phone No.: 312/631-0700
News Director: Carmen Castro

Station: WIND-AM (La Tremenda)
Address: 625 N. Michigan, Chicago, IL 60611
Phone No.: 312/751-5560
News Director: Antonio Navas

Station: WLCO-FM
Address: 1859 W. McPherson, Clyde, OH 43410
Phone No.: 419/547-8792
News Director: Eddie Cruz

Station: WOJO-FM
Address: 2425 Main St., Evanston, IL 60202
Phone No.: 312/273-4010
News Director: Luis De Gonzales

Station: WSBC-AM
Address: 4949 W. Belmont Ave., Chicago, IL 60641
Phone No.: 312/777-1700
News Director: Jose Chapa

Station: WTAQ-AM (Radio Fiesta)
Address: 9355 West Joliet Rd., La Grange, IL 60525
Phone No.: 312/352-1300
News Director: Arturo Montemayor

Station: WVVX-FM
Address: 210 Skokie Valley Rd., Suite 12, Highland Park, IL 60035
Phone No.: 312/831-5250
News Director: n/a

TEXAS:

Station: KALY-AM
Address: 4180 N. Mesa, El Paso, TX 79902
Phone No.: 915/532-2019
News Director: Jorge Chrisman

Station: KAMA-AM
Address: 4150 Pinnacle, Suite 120, El Paso, TX 79902
Phone No.: 915/544-7600
News Director: Jose Luis Torre

Station: KCCT-AM
Address: P.O. Box 5278, Corpus Christi, TX 78405
Phone No.: 512/289-0999
News Director: Leopoldo Luna

Station: KCOR-AM
Address: 1115 W. Martin, San Antonio, TX 78207
Phone No.: 512/225-2751
News Director: Ramiro Cordoba

Station: KEDA-AM
Address: 510 S. Flores, San Antonio, TX 78204
Phone No.: 512/226-5254
News Director: Pedro Fernandez

Station: KESS-FM
Address: 661 Seminary South, Ft. Worth, TX 76115
Phone No.: 817/429-1037
News Director: Berta Obregon

Station: KEYH-AM
Address: P.O. Box 907, Sugarlane, TX 77487
Phone No.: 713/277-2559
News Director: Teresa Aliaga

Station: KFHM-AM
Address: 501 W. Quincy St., San Antonio, TX 78212
Phone No.: 512/224-1166
News Director: Carlos Garcia

Station: KFRD-AM
Address: 1501 Radio Lane, Rosenberg, TX 77471
Phone No.: 713/342-6601
News Director: Mario Campos

Station: KGBT-AM
Address: P.O. Box 711, Harlingen, TX 78550
Phone No.: 512/423-3910
News Director: Martin Carrillo

Station: KIRT-AM
Address: 608 S. Ten, McAllen, TX 78501
Phone No.: 512/686-1580
News Director: Joe Morales

Station: KITM-FM
Address: 109 East Expressway 83, Mission, TX 78572
Phone No.: 512/581-2151
News Director: Ben Valdez

Station: KIWW-FM
Address: 5621 S. Expressway 83, Harlingen, TX 78552
Phone No.: 512/423-3211
News Director: Francisco Velasco

Station: KLAT-AM
Address: 1415 N. Loop West, Suite 400, Houston, TX 77008
Phone No.: 713/868-4344
News Director: Mariano Garcia

Station: KLVL-AM
Address: 111 North Ennis St., Houston, TX 77003
Phone No.: 713/225-3207
News Director: Pedro Gomez

Station: KNON-FM
Address: Dept. 139, P.O. Box 14119, Dallas, TX 75214
Phone No.: 214/823-7490
News Director: n/a

Station: KQXX-FM
Address: 608 S. Ten, McAllen, TX 78501
Phone No.: 512/686-2111
News Director: Tony Cavazos

Station: KSSA-AM
Address: 100 N. Central Expressway, Suite 101, Dallas, TX 75201
Phone No.: 214/939-0822
News Director: Sal Valdez

Station: KUNO-AM
Address: 1301 Horne Rd., Corpus Christi, TX 78416
Phone No.: 512/851-1414
News Director: Ms. Billie Baker

Station: KXET-AM (Radio Exitos)
Address: 1130 E. Durango Blvd., San Antonio, TX 78210
Phone No.: 512/533-0095
News Director: Javier Roman

Station: KXKX-FM
Address: 2501 Palmer Highway, #270, Texas City, TX 77590
Phone No.: 713/484-8210
News Director: Elizabeth Paraviceni

Station: KXTO-AM
Address: P.O. Box 1151, Odem, TX 78370
Phone No.: 512/368-2555
News Director: Margarita C. Benavives

Station: KXYZ-AM
Address: 2700 East Pasadena Freeway, Pasadena, TX 77506
Phone No.: 713/472-2500
News Director: Rolando Becerra

Station: KYST-AM
Address: 8181 N. Stadium Dr., Houston, TX 77054
Phone No.: 713/791-9292
News Director: John Hernandez

Station: Radio Centro
Address: 10670 N. Central Expressway, Suite 401, Dallas, TX 75231
Phone No.: 214/363-3922
News Director: not given
Contact: Carlos Aguirre

Station: Spanish Information Service, Texas State Network
Address: 7901 Carpenter Freeway, Dallas, TX 75247
Phone No.: 214/688-1133
News Director: Jose Madrigal

Station: United Broadcast Sales
Address: P.O. Box 3567, El Paso, TX 79903
Phone No.: 915/533-9300
News Director: not given

Station: Grupo La Super Estacion, El Paso Network
Address: 1000 1/2 East Yandell, El Paso, TX 79902
Phone No.: 915/533-9300
News Director: Brigido Hernandez

WEST:

Station: KABQ-AM
Address: 1309 Yale S.E., Albuquerque, NM 87106
Phone No.: 505/243-1744
News Director: Amparo Garcia

Station: KLTN-AM
Address: 9100 North 2nd, Albuquerque, NM 87114
Phone No.: 505/898-5586
News Director: Alberto Albila

Station: KXKS-AM
Address: 1923 San Matteo NE, Albuquerque, NM 87110
Phone No.: 505/265-8331
News Director: Miguel Delgado

Station: KNNN-FM
Address: 4548 West Osborn Rd., Phoenix, AZ 85031
Phone No.: 602/269-5666
News Director: not given

Station: KPHX-AM
Address: 1975 S. Central Ave., Phoenix, AZ 85004
Phone No.: 602/257-1351
News Director: Rene Boeta

Station: KQTL-AM
Address: P.O. Box 1511, Tucson, AZ 85702
Phone No.: 602/628-1200
News Director: not given

Station: KVVA-AM (Radio Viva)
Address: 1641 East Osborn, Suite 8, Phoenix, AZ   85016
Phone No.: 602/266-2005
News Director: Marcos Garcia Ayala

Station: KXEW-AM/KXMG-FM
Address: 889 West El Puente Lane, Tucson, AZ   85713
Phone No.: 602/623-6429
News Director: Joy Tucker

CALIFORNIA:

Station: KALI-AM (Radio Variedades)
Address: 5723 Melrose Ave., Hollywood, CA   90038
Phone No.: 213/466-6161
News Director: Alberto Aguilar

Station: KAZA-AM
Address: P.O. Box 1290, San Jose, CA   95108
Phone No.: 408/984-1290
News Director: Jose Luis Lopez

Station: KBFA-FM
Address: 2207 Shattuck Ave., Berkley, CA   94704
Phone No.: 415/848-6767
News Director: not given

Station: KBRG-FM
Address: 39111 Paseo Parkway, Suite 121, Fremont, CA   94538
Phone No.: 415/491-1049
News Director: Paul Maltez

Station: KCAL AM-FM
Address: P.O. Box 390, Redlands, CA   92373
Phone No.: 714/793-2757
News Director: Jim Ness

Station: KCTY-AM/KRAY-FM
Address: P.O. Box 1939, Salinas, CA   93902
Phone No.: 408/449-2421
News Director: Jose Valenzuela

Station: KCVR-AM
Address: P.O. Box 600, Lodi, CA   95240
Phone No.: 209/368-0628
News Director: Jose Ortiz

Station: KGST-AM
Address: P.O. Box 11868, Fresno, CA   93775
Phone No.: 209/266-9901
News Director: Diego Mendizabal

Station: KIQI-AM
Address: 2601 Mission St., San Francisco, CA 94110
Phone No.: 415/648-8800
News Director: Mario Barahona

Station: KLOC-AM
Address: P.O. Box 542, Modesto, CA 95353
Phone No.: 209/521-5562
News Director: Dennis Crasquilla

Station: KLOQ-AM
Address: 708 West Main, Merced, CA 95340
Phone No.: 209/722-1580
News Director: Juan Rodriquez

Station: KLVE-FM/KTNQ-AM
Address: 5724 Hollywood Blvd., Hollywood, CA 90028
Phone No.: 213/465-3171
News Director: Jaime Jarrin

Station: KMPO-AM
Address: 701 H. Street, Modesto, CA 95352
Phone No.: 209/523-2636
News Director: n/a

Station: KNSE Radio
Address: 8729 E. 9th St., Cucamonga, CA 91730
Phone No.: 714/981-8893
News Director: Humberto Hernandez

Station: KOFY-AM
Address: 1818 Gilbreth Rd., Burlingame, CA 94010
Phone No.: 415/692-2433
News Director: Jorge Guevara

Station: KOXR-Radio
Address: 418 W. Third St., Oxnard, CA 93030
Phone No.: 805/487-0444
News Director: Santiago Lopez

Station: KMAX-FM
Address: 3844 East Foothill Blvd., Pasadena, CA 91107
Phone No.: 213/681-2486
News Director: William Angulo

Station: KNTA-AM (KANTA)
Address: 1241 Franklin Mall, Santa Clara, CA 95050
Phone No.: 408/244-1430
News Director: Jose Armedaris

Station: KRCX-AM (Radio Capital)
Address: P.O. Box 111D, Roseville, CA 95661
Phone No.: 916/791-4111
News Director: Armando Botello

Station: KSJV-FM
Address: P.O. Box 12682, Fresno, CA 93778
Phone No.: 209/486-5174
News Director: Samuel Orozco

Station: KSKQ-AM
Address: 5700 Sunset Blvd. at Wilton, Los Angeles, CA 90028
Phone No.: 213/466-3001
News Director: Antonio Gonzales

Station: KTNQ-AM/KLVE-FM
Address: 5724 Hollywood Blvd., Hollywood, CA 90028
Phone No.: 213/465-3171
News Director: Jaime Jarrin

Station: KUBO-AM
Address: 161 Main Street, Salinas, CA 93901
Phone No.: 408/757-8039
News Director: n/a

Station: KWAC
Address: 5200 Standard St., Bakersfield, CA 93308
Phone No.: 805/327-9711
News Director: Ramon Garza

Station: KWKW-AM
Address: 800 Sierra Madre Villa, Pasadena, CA 91107
Phone No.: 818/351-9343
News Director: Luis A. Bravo

Station: KXES-AM
Address: 7 Midtown Lane, Salinas, CA 93901
Phone No.: 408/757-1910
News Director: Humberto Herrera

Station: KXEX-AM
Address: 2247 W. Church Ave., Fresno, CA 93706
Phone No.: 209/233-8803
News Director: Rene Canto

Station: XEMO-AM
Address: 3648 Main St., Chulavista, CA 92020
Phone No.: 619/466-9366
News Director: Julio Rodriquez

Station: Radio Espanol
Address: 9520 Washington Blvd., Culver City, CA 90232
Phone No.: 213/204-5000
News Director: not given

Station: XPRS-AM
Address: P.O. Box 1250, Hollywood, CA 90028 (mailing)
Phone No.: 213/466-8462
News Director: n/a

III. Hispanic Media Organizations

ASOCIACION DE PERIODISTAS Y
LOCUTORES INTERAMERICANOS (APLI)
   President: Guillermo Bauta
   3147 W. Logan Blvd., Suite 8
   Chicago, IL 60647
   312/235-9800

ASSOCIATION OF HISPANIC ARTS
   Executive Director: Jane Delgado
   200 East 87th Street, 2nd Floor
   New York, NY 10028
   212/369-7054

ASSOCIATION OF LATIN AMERICANS
IN COMMUNICATIONS, INC.
   President: Dalia Diaz St. Marie
   P.O. Box 785
   Natick, MA 01760
   617/653-8089

CALIFORNIA ASSOCIATION OF LATINOS
IN BROADCASTING (CALIB)
   President: Fernando del Rio
   c/o KHJ-TV
   5515 Melrose Avenue
   Hollywood, CA 90038
   213/467-5459

CALIFORNIA CHICANO NEWS MEDIA
ASSOCIATION (CCNMA-LOS ANGELES)
   Executive Director: Suzanna Manriquez
   School of Journalism
   University of Southern California
   Los Angeles, CA 90089-1695
   213/743-7158

CCNMA-FRESNO
   Contact: Thomas Uribes
   P.O. Box 1234
   Fresno, CA 93777
   1-800-828-8118

CCNMA-SACRAMENTO
   Contact: Mike Castro
   c/o The Sacramento Bee
   P.O. Box 15779
   Sacramento, CA 95852
   916/321-1060

CCNMA-SAN DIEGO
   Staff Director: Henry Fuentes
   Journalism Department
   San Diego State University
   San Diego, CA 92182
   619/265-6212

CENTRAL TEXAS ASSOCIATION OF
HISPANIC JOURNALISTS
   President: Mario Villafuerte
   Box 9057
   Austin, TX 78766
   512/445-3685

CONCERNED MEDIA PROFESSIONALS
   President: Ernest Gurule
   P.O. Box 44034
   Tucson, AZ 85733
   602/628-9262

CONNECTICUT HISPANIC MEDIA
ASSOCIATION (CHMA)
   President: Joseph Rodriguez
   56 Congress Street, Suite 202
   Hartford, CT 06114
   203/724-2001

CORPUS CHRISTI ASSN. OF
HISPANIC JOURNALISTS
   President: Juan Cardenas
   6717 Everhart Street, Apt. 245
   Corpus Christi, TX 78413
   512/884-2011 ext. 312

EL PASO ASSOCIATION OF
HISPANIC JOURNALISTS
   Contact: Ray Chavez
   9616 Bellis Street
   El Paso, TX 79925
   915/598-3197

FLORIDA ASSOCIATION OF
HISPANIC JOURNALISTS
   President: Evelyn Hernandez
   P.O. Box 531369
   Miami Shores, FL 33153-1369
   305/895-4983

HISPANIC ACADEMY OF MEDIA ARTS
AND SCIENCES (HAMAS)
   National Chairman: Phil Reyna
   5451 Laurel Canyon Blvd., #100
   North Hollywood, CA 91607
   818/954-3568

HAMAS-NEW YORK
    President: Ray Blanco
    c/o WCBS-TV
    524 West 57th Street
    New York, NY 10019
    212/975-6344

HISPANIC NEWS MEDIA ASSOCIATION
OF WASHINGTON, DC (HNMA)
    President: Charles Ericksen
    1420 N Street, N.W.
    Washington, DC 20005
    202/234-0280

HISPANIC PUBLIC AFFAIRS ASSOCIATION
    President: Armando Rendon
    P.O. Box 5488
    Washington, DC 20016
    202/244-7000

HISPANIC PUBLIC RELATIONS ASSOCIATION
    President: John Echeveste
    5400 E. Olympic Blvd.
    Los Angeles, CA 90022
    213/721-1655

HISPANICS IN COMMUNICATIONS
    Chairman: Jackie DaCosta
    P.O. Box 4937
    New York, NY 10185-0041

HISPANICS IN TELEVISION (HIT)
    President: Yolanda Custer
    Alumni Hall, Box 4348
    University of Illinois at Chicago
    Chicago, IL 60608
    312/687-6930

LATINO PROFESSIONALS IN COMMUNICATION
    Contact: Juana Montgomery
    P.O. Box 7334
    Oakland, CA 94601
    415/532-1829 ext. 530

MICHIGAN HISPANIC MEDIA ASSOCIATION
    Contact: Jose Lopez
    P.O. Box 17112
    Lansing, MI 48901
    517/485-4389

NATIONAL ASSOCIATION OF HISPANIC
JOURNALISTS (NAHJ)
    Executive Director: Frank Newton
    National Press Bldg., Suite 634
    529 14th Street, N.W.
    Washington, DC   20045
    202/783-6228

NATIONAL ASSOCIATION OF HISPANIC
PUBLICATIONS
    Admin. Coordinator: Pauline Marquez
    P.O. Box 54307
    Los Angeles, CA   90054
    213/222-1349

NATIONAL FEDERATION OF HISPANICS
IN COMMUNICATIONS
    Contact: Charles Rivera
    P.O. Box 2106
    Fairfax, VA   22031
    703/978-2872

NETWORK OF HISPANIC COMMUNICATORS
    President: Yolette Garcia
    P.O. Box 22313
    Dallas, TX   75222
    214/871-1390

NEW MEXICO MINORITY MEDIA ASSOCIATION
    President: Paula Maes
    P.O. Box 1351
    Albuquerque, NM   87103
    505/243-4411

PENNSYLVANIA HISPANICS IN THE MEDIA
    Contact: Elisabeth Perez-Luna
    P.O. Box 1685
    Philadelphia, PA   19105
    215/893-0203

PROFESSIONAL ORGANIZATION OF MEXICAN
AMERICANS IN COMMUNICATIONS (POMAC)
    President: Bert Salazar
    503 1/2 Prospect Street
    El Paso, TX   79902
    915/534-7109

RIO GRANDE ASSOCIATION OF HISPANIC
JOURNALISTS
    Contact: Rick Diaz
    c/o KRGV-TV
    900 E. Expressway
    Weslaco, TX   78596
    512/968-5178

SAN ANTONIO ASSOCIATION OF HISPANIC JOURNALISTS
  Contact: Javier Rodriguez
  P.O. Box 161
  San Antonio, TX 78291
  512/271-2700